Pr

Other McGraw-Hill Books of Interest

To order or to receive additional information on these or any other McGraw-Hill titles, please call 1-800-822-8158 in the United States. In other countries, contact your local McGraw-Hill representative.

KEY = WM16XXA

InfoMaker 5
Professional Reference

**A Guide to Developing
Client/Server Applications**

Jane Roseen

McGraw-Hill

New York San Francisco Washington, D.C. Auckland Bogotá
Caracas Lisbon London Madrid Mexico City Milan
Montreal New Delhi San Juan Singapore
Sydney Tokyo Toronto

Library of Congress Cataloging-in-Publication Data

Roseen, Jane.
    InfoMaker 5 Professional Reference : a guide to developing client/server applications /
Jane Roseen.
        p.   cm.
    Includes index.
    ISBN 0-07-053999-5
    1. Client/server computing.   2. InfoMaker.   3. Application
software—Development.   I. Title.
    QA76.9.C55R67   1997
    005.75'8—dc21

                                                            97-1554
                                                            CIP

McGraw-Hill

*A Division of The **McGraw·Hill** Companies*

1 2 3 4 5 6 7 8 9 0   FGR/FGR   9 0 2 1 0 9 8 7

ISBN 0-07-053999-5

*The sponsoring editor for this book was John Wyzalek, the editing supervisor was
Bernard Onken, and the production supervisor was Clare Stanley. It was set in
Century Schoolbook by Estelita F. Green of McGraw-Hill's Professional Book
Group composition unit.*

Printed and bound by Quebecor / Fairfield.

McGraw-Hill books are available at special quantity discounts to use as premiums
and sales promotions, or for use in corporate training programs. For more information, please write to the Director of Special Sales, McGraw-Hill, 11 West 19th
Street, New York, NY 10011. Or contact your local bookstore.

This book is printed on recycled, acid-free paper containing
a minimum of 50% recycled, de-inked fiber.

To my husband Randy: Without his support and encouragement, this book would not have been possible.

Contents

Chapter 14. Building Graphs

Preface

InfoMaker is Powersoft's reporting and data manipulation tool. InfoMaker has a point-and-click GUI interface that makes building forms and reports a simple exercise. And if special circumstances dictate that more customization is needed, PowerBuilder developers can add special functionality to forms, which can then be integrated into the InfoMaker environment. *InfoMaker 5 Professional Reference: A Guide to Developing Client/Server Applications* is designed as a handy reference and tutorial you'll refer to often. This book will help you learn the InfoMaker environment quickly and easily. And best of all, when you've finished reading this book, you'll have an application you can customize and use in your daily work.

The Purpose of This Book

This book is a practical guide introducing you to the InfoMaker development environment. We go into detail about what InfoMaker is and how to install it, with a brief discussion of special words used throughout the book to help non-technical people understand the environment. The book discusses ways to optimize and customize InfoMaker and some of the naming conventions and planning ideas to use that will make ongoing development and maintenance easier. This book covers in detail each of the painters available in InfoMaker in the logical sequence in which they are accessed when building an application. Chapters throughout the book build blocks which are used in the InfoCenter application. This application is completed and distributed near the end of the book. By the time you finish this book, you will understand exactly how to optimize your productivity with InfoMaker.

Who Should Read This Book

This is a book for anyone who wants to use InfoMaker to gain control of her or his data. It doesn't matter if you're new to InfoMaker or an experienced PowerBuilder developer, you will find yourself referring to this book often.

Before reading this book, you should be completely comfortable in the Windows environment and should understand what terms such as *click and drag* mean. Although it would be helpful to have a working knowledge of relational database theory, there is a short introduction to the subject included with the book.

Developers new to InfoMaker

This book focuses on the beginning to intermediate-level computer user who has a basic familiarity with InfoMaker. This book works in conjunction with the InfoMaker product manuals. It is tailored to assist beginning InfoMaker users get up to speed quickly and understand how and why the product works as it does. Intermediate users will find that the book contains helpful suggestions, tips, and detailed examples on how best to optimize InfoMaker's many features, resulting in increased productivity. The book builds an application in a step-by-step manner, and when finished, you have a complete working application that can be modified to fit your needs and can be used in your day-to-day work.

PowerBuilder developers

This book is beneficial not only to InfoMaker users, but also to PowerBuilder developers who must support InfoMaker applications. The book contains descriptions and examples of form styles, functions, and libraries of objects which can be used between the two environments. With this book, you'll become familiar with the InfoMaker environment to help support InfoMaker users in your organization, and you will learn how to customize the environment to help them do their jobs more efficiently. InfoMaker eases your workload because it enables end users to build their own reporting objects, freeing you for the more difficult tasks in your organization.

How This Book Is Organized

This book is organized into a logical sequence of events that must be followed when you build an InfoMaker application. You'll learn the steps necessary to build the forms and reports you need to take control of your data.

In Chap. 1 you'll learn InfoMaker basics such as what InfoMaker is and how to install and customize the environment. There is a section covering InfoMaker and other computing terminology you'll need to understand before becoming proficient with this tool. You will learn how to use and customize the toolbars and access options on the property sheets in this chapter. When you finish this chapter, you will have a more thorough understanding of the basics of InfoMaker.

In Chap. 2 you'll read about each of the painters in InfoMaker. You'll learn what each painter does and when it should be used. By the time you finish this chapter, you'll know which tool to choose when you want to build an InfoMaker object.

Chapter 3 talks about setting preferences using InfoMaker initialization files. Although most of these attributes are set automatically from painters in

InfoMaker, it's a good idea to be aware of the initialization files and what they do if any problems or needs for additional customization arise. You'll also be introduced to how InfoMaker stores extended attributes for each of the objects.

Chapter 4 explains the standards and guidelines which can be used to build an InfoMaker application. These guidelines include a brief discussion of why to implement standards and suggested naming conventions for forms, reports, and other InfoMaker objects. By the time you finish this chapter, you will understand how to make your InfoMaker applications easier to build, enforce consistency, and make them more maintainable.

Chapter 5 defines how to plan an InfoMaker project. You will learn the phases that all computer applications go through and what you can do to ensure that your projects are completed successfully.

Chapter 6 is an overview of the Environment painter. This chapter explains what a library is and how to maintain one. You will learn how to access a form or query library and how these libraries can help you build forms and reports more quickly. How to manipulate and access objects in the Environment painter is also covered. By the time you finish this chapter, you will be completely comfortable creating libraries and manipulating objects in the Environment painter.

In Chap. 7 you'll learn how to work with databases in the InfoMaker environment. You will learn the basics of databases, tables, columns, keys, indexes, and views. You will learn what each of these items is, how to access and manipulate them, and how best to use them in InfoMaker. At the end of this chapter is a demonstration of how to create a database and validate data.

Chapter 8 talks about working with actual data in a database. You will learn how to retrieve, change, sort, filter, and import data. You will discover the Data Manipulation painter and learn how to access data quickly without having to build a form or report. By the end of this chapter, you will be able to import and enter data into a database and manipulate the data to fit your needs.

Chapter 9 explains the data sources available in InfoMaker. You will learn what a data source is and why they are important in building InfoMaker objects. You will learn about the data sources that can be used in each of the InfoMaker objects. You will learn how to access and become proficient in their use. By the time you finish reading this chapter, you will be able to define the data you will use in each of the data source types.

Chapter 10 discusses each of the different form styles available in the Form painter. You will learn in what circumstances it is best to use a particular form style and how to create it. At the end of this chapter, you will be comfortable with each of the form styles and be able to create a basic form which can be modified further.

Chapter 11 talks about enhancing forms. You will learn how to modify form attributes, add controls, and validate data on a form. You will learn how to save forms to Web pages and save data to other formats for further data manipulation, such as spreadsheets. By the time you finish reading this chapter, you will be able to create a completely customized form to enter, extract, and export data to and from your database.

Chapter 12 illustrates how to create and access reports. This chapter goes into detail about each of the report types available in the Report painter. You will learn when and how to use a particular report style to present data in the format you want. When you finish reading this chapter, you will be familiar with each of the report types and be able to create a basic report.

Chapter 13 explains the many different methods used to enhance reports. Topics discussed are how to store data in a report, retrieving data for fastest performance, and setting up retrieval criteria. There is also an explanation of the edit styles available and how to use them. You will learn how to save reports and send them as e-mail text. By the end of this chapter, you will be able to create a completely customized report to present data effectively.

In Chap. 14 we discuss in detail how to build graphs. There is a discussion of each of the parts of a graph. You will learn about each of the different graphs available in InfoMaker and the types of data they are best used to present. By the time you finish reading this chapter, you will be a proficient graph builder.

In Chap. 15 you will learn about the data pipeline. You will understand what a pipeline is and how to define one to transfer data in the InfoMaker environment. You will learn how to set up the source and destination databases of a pipeline. By the end of this chapter, you will be able to transfer data between tables in a database or between two different databases.

In Chap. 16 you will learn how to create and distribute a complete working application. This chapter illustrates the advantages to using applications and how to build one. You will learn in detail how to distribute applications using the new InstallBuilder. By the end of this chapter, you will be able to share applications you've built with others.

Chapter 17 talks about InfoMaker and the PowerBuilder connection. This chapter explains how and why these two products are so closely integrated and how the interoperability between the two environments enhances the power of both InfoMaker and PowerBuilder. By the end of this chapter, PowerBuilder developers will be able to enhance the InfoMaker environment.

How to Use This Book

The chapters in this book are organized into the same sequence of events that would be used to build an application. In those chapters that can build a particular piece of an application, there is a short tutorial at the end of the chapter demonstrating some of the techniques used to create the object. If you need assistance with a particular InfoMaker tool, you can quickly turn to that chapter and find the information you need.

Why Read This Book?

In reading this book you will learn how OLE 2.0 gives InfoMaker users the ability to build much more powerful applications. You'll discover how to save forms and reports to HTML format to take advantage of the Internet. Additionally, you'll learn how to send a report as an e-mail message which others can then continue to modify. You'll learn how to create and distribute an application. You'll find the chapter on using InfoMaker and PowerBuilder together will optimize your investment in both environments. You'll enjoy the discussion on standards and guidelines because standards are so important in any development project, and this gives beginners a thumbnail sketch of where to begin. You'll learn to work with databases after reading the database design primer.

How You Can Further Explore InfoMaker after Finishing the Book

Appendix A includes a complete discussion of where you can go to get help after reading this book, including CompuServe, the Internet, Powersoft service providers, and so on.

About the Example Application

Throughout this book you will build an application called *InfoCenter*. This application is a contact manager which, when completed, you can use in your day-to-day work. We'll be creating an SQL Anywhere database to contain the information for our application. InfoCenter allows you to enter business contacts, tasks, and scheduling information, and it includes reports needed for mailing labels, employee, and contact lists. You will learn how to export data to other systems and create form letters to send to clients. You will learn how to distribute this application so others can use it.

All the files necessary to run this application are available at http://www.rrv. net/roseen.

InfoMaker 5.0 Overview

If you've used a previous version of InfoMaker, you'll be pleasantly surprised with the new functionality Powersoft added in 5.0. The entire interface is redesigned to include the Windows 95 look and feel. First, pop-up menus are completely redesigned. In InfoMaker 4.0, the pop-up menu contained a list of options for setting borders, colors, fonts, etc. Now in 5.0, the pop-up menu has an option called Properties which, when clicked, brings up a property sheet with tabs for setting object properties. Depending on the type of object selected, text or column, the property sheet is modified to take into account the different properties available for an object. Additionally, the toolbars are redesigned to include drop-down toolbars. For instance, several of the buttons on the Report painter bar have arrows next to the button. Click on the button, and a drop-down toolbar displays showing additional options for placing objects on the report, selecting colors, aligning objects, and so on. You can also create your own custom toolbars. It's possible to have up to four PowerBars and eight different PainterBars in each painter available at one time.

Powersoft also added OLE 2.0 support in reports. InfoMaker reports can be included in OLE 2.0–compatible products, such as Word and Excel. Conversely,

OLE 2.0 objects can be embedded in InfoMaker reports. This functionality presents a great deal of flexibility in designing powerful reports.

Another must-have tool Powersoft has added to InfoMaker is the ability to send reports as mail text. This allows even non-InfoMaker users to access reports. Also new in 5.0 is the ability to save report data as an HTML file, which can then be used on a Web page.

InfoMaker includes DataExpress, which is a wizard to walk you through the steps of filling out problem reports which can be faxed or sent via e-mail to Powersoft. DataExpress makes it easy to report problems to Powersoft, and it gives the technicians the information they need to solve problems quickly.

Jane Roseen

1

Getting Started

What You Will Learn

In this chapter you will learn how InfoMaker builds powerful applications that help you get your work done faster. You will learn how to install InfoMaker and customize it to fit your needs. You will find out how easy it is to navigate within the InfoMaker environment. You will also become familiar with some of the terms you will need to know to understand both InfoMaker and discussions carried on throughout this book. Examples of how to use and customize the toolbars and how to change the way screens appear are included in this chapter. When you reach the end of this chapter, you will be armed with the information you need to start becoming productive with InfoMaker today.

About InfoMaker

InfoMaker is a product developed by Powersoft Corp., which is a subsidiary of Sybase. Powersoft developed InfoMaker to work in conjunction with its flagship development product, PowerBuilder, or as a stand-alone data maintenance and reporting tool. Using InfoMaker, nonprogrammers can build applications that contain powerful forms, reports, and graphs which are all accessible from an easy-to-use menu or toolbar. InfoMaker includes all the data manipulation tools needed to build completely functional database maintenance screens, with insert, update, and delete options, and the tools to maneuver within a database. And InfoMaker's Data Pipeline tool provides the capability to move data within a single database or between two different databases. Many products promise this type of functionality without programming, but no tool delivers on this promise more completely. Powersoft has made building a sophisticated application as easy as pointing and clicking. These capabilities allow users to create some applications on their own, which relieves the Information Systems (IS) department to focus on other, more pressing tasks in the corporation.

Powersoft released the 5.0 version of InfoMaker in June 1996. InfoMaker has a point-and-click graphical-user interface (GUI) available for both the Windows and Macintosh environments. Bundled with InfoMaker is a single-user version of SQL Anywhere, Watcom's desktop database. SQL Anywhere has the capability to connect to about 30 desktop and server-based databases.

Words You Should Know

As you begin work in InfoMaker, there are several terms and some basic knowledge you should know to understand InfoMaker more completely. These terms are also used throughout this book. This book assumes you are familiar with the Windows actions of clicking, double-clicking, dragging, etc. If you are not, please refer to your Windows manual or another Windows book before proceeding further. Your understanding of these terms will greatly enhance your knowledge of InfoMaker and prepare you to start building powerful applications quickly.

Data

You will see the word *data* used throughout this book. Data refers to information. Information can be someone's address, name, social security number, or hair color. Data is any information you want to track.

Database

Data is contained in a *database*. A database is a mechanism to contain all the data, or information, you want to track. For instance, one database may contain product information, and another database may contain employee information, such as payroll. Refer to Fig. 1.1.

Table

A database is composed of many tables. A *table* is a group of logical information contained in one place. So, for instance, within a database, you may have one table that contains all the personal information about someone, and another table may contain all the information related to that person's purchases from your company. Refer to Fig. 1.1.

Fields and columns

A *field,* also called a *column,* is one piece of information within a table. A person's name is a column, and so is his or her social security number. Refer to Fig. 1.1.

SQL

Structured Query Language is a programming language used in most databases today to retrieve information. InfoMaker contains tools that build SQL

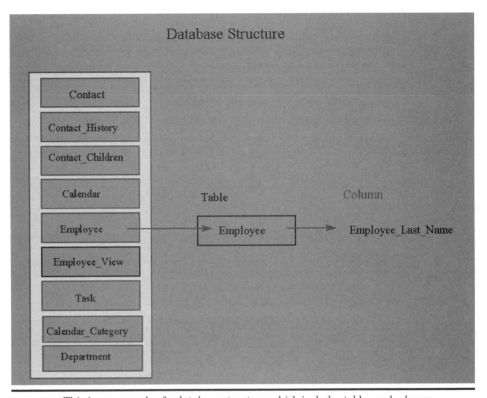

Figure 1.1   This is an example of a database structure which includes tables and columns.

statements by using a point-and-click interface. Knowledge of SQL is not required to work with InfoMaker.

Data source

Data source is a term used in InfoMaker to denote how a particular form or report retrieves information and displays it. A data source can be a SQL Select statement or a Stored Procedure. It is simply a way to tell InfoMaker what method is being used to retrieve information.

Another instance of a data source occurs when you are copying a form or report to another program, such as an Excel spreadsheet. In this case, the InfoMaker form is also referred to as a data source.

Repository

The *Repository* is where InfoMaker stores all the information related to a data item, such as display formats and edit styles. The Powersoft Repository is a set of system tables maintained by the Database painter in InfoMaker or in PowerBuilder. When placing columns on a form or report, InfoMaker pulls data from the Repository. By using the Repository, information does not have to be reentered in each form or report. It is saved automatically when you are building a table in the Table painter. However, the values set in the Repository can be overridden with changes made in the Report or Form painter applying only to the current report or form. The advantage of letting the Repository do all the work, rather than defining extended attributes for each report or form individually, is that it saves time and enforces consistency. The attributes have to be specified only once in the database.

Primary key

In order to be updated using a SQL Anywhere database management system (DBMS), a table must be assigned a primary key. A *primary key* is a unique identifier to a row of information contained in a table. So, for instance, to uniquely identify a customer in a table, the unique identification might be SMIT-1234.

Foreign key

A *foreign key* is a key that uniquely identifies a row of information in which the primary key is located in another table. So, for instance, if we were to assign a customer named Smith to one of our employees named Jones, we would have a column in the table to relate the customer to the employee.

Index

An *index* is created to improve access speed when one is retrieving information from a table. Indexes are automatically created for primary keys; but if there are specific columns in the table which are used for frequent searches, it is advantageous to create an index on the column.

Executable

An *executable* file is a file that contains all the information necessary to run a particular program. For instance, an executable is invoked when Word is started. An executable can also contain all the InfoMaker objects in an application which can be run outside the InfoMaker environment and distributed to others.

Application

An *application* consists of all the InfoMaker objects which are needed to enter information into and extract information from a database. This collection of forms, reports, and so on is commonly referred to as an application.

Library

A *library* contains all the objects for an application. You can access only one library at a time in InfoMaker.

Presentation style

The *presentation style* refers to the type of form or report style used in a particular instance of a form or report. Forms and reports each have different types of presentation styles.

Attribute

An *attribute* refers to how an object appears. For instance, an attribute can be a form color or a text item font size. Attributes are saved in the Powersoft repository and are invoked whenever a form or report is created. Attributes can be overridden in individual objects.

Pibble

InfoMaker creates a `.pbl` file, pronounced "pibble." This pibble contains all the forms, reports, and other items created in an InfoMaker application.

Object

Simply put, an *object* in InfoMaker is anything. A form, report, data pipeline, and other items created in InfoMaker are referred to as objects. Additionally, a text item on a form, such as customer name, is considered an object. A customer's address on a report is an object. Radio buttons, pictures, etc. are all objects.

Pop-up menus

Pop-up menus are used throughout InfoMaker to access many features in each of the painters and even within the main workspace. An example of a pop-up menu is shown in Fig. 1.2. Pop-up menus are accessed by right-clicking the mouse on an object. Pop-up menus contain options that allow the user to change colors, fonts, and a multitude of other attributes.

Toolbars

A *toolbar* is a group of buttons on the InfoMaker workspace and in each of the InfoMaker painters. A toolbar is a fast way to access tools in InfoMaker.

Properties...	
Cut	Ctrl+X
Copy	Ctrl+C
Clear	Del
Bring to Front	
Send to Back	

Figure 1.2 This is an example of a pop-up menu, accessed by right-clicking on an object.

PowerBar and PowerPanel toolbars. The PowerBar and the PowerPanel are toolbars used to access painters and other tools in InfoMaker. The difference between the PowerBar and the PowerPanel is that the PowerBar (see Fig. 1.3) is a long row of buttons placed at the top, bottom, or sides of the InfoMaker work area. In contrast, the PowerPanel (see Fig. 1.4) is a separate window containing a list of all the painters available in InfoMaker, and it can be moved anywhere on the workspace. The PowerPanel is always accessible from the File menu. The use of either the PowerBar or the PowerPanel is entirely up to you.

PainterBar. The PainterBar toolbars change depending on the painter currently in use. Each PainterBar has buttons for opening tools used in the current painter. So, for instance, there is one set of buttons to access tools for building a form, and a different set of tools is available to build a report. Figures 1.5 and 1.6 show the

Figure 1.3 This is the default PowerBar installed with InfoMaker.

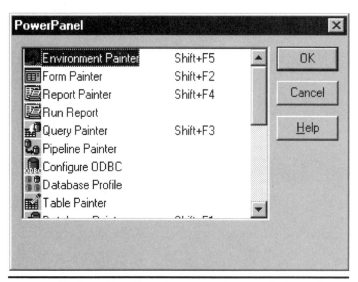

Figure 1.4 The PowerPanel is used to access painters and other tools in InfoMaker. It is accessible from any File menu in InfoMaker.

Figure 1.5 This is the PainterBar available in the Form painter

Figure 1.6 This is the PainterBar available in the Report painter.

Form and Report painter bars, respectively. They illustrate the similarities and the differences between the tools available in each of the painters.

Drop-down toolbars. InfoMaker includes drop-down toolbars. These special toolbars are accessed from both the PowerBar and the PainterBars. The Object drop-down toolbar in Fig. 1.7 is in the Form painter. Clicking on the arrow next to the Object button in the Form painter bar shows additional options available to choose from on the drop-down toolbar.

StyleBar. The StyleBar (see Fig. 1.8) can be found in the Form and Report painters and is used to change fonts and font size, add bold and italic, and select other options with a click of a button. When text objects are modified, the text area on the far left of the StyleBar is enabled, allowing object text changes.

Property sheets

A *property sheet* is a special tabbed window where object attributes, or options, are set for each object on a form, report, or other object. Figure 1.9 shows an example of a property sheet. For more information about property sheets, see the section "Using Property Sheets" later in this chapter.

Figure 1.7 An example of a drop-down toolbar available from the Form painter.

Figure 1.8 The StyleBar, available in the Form and Report painters, has options to set font types.

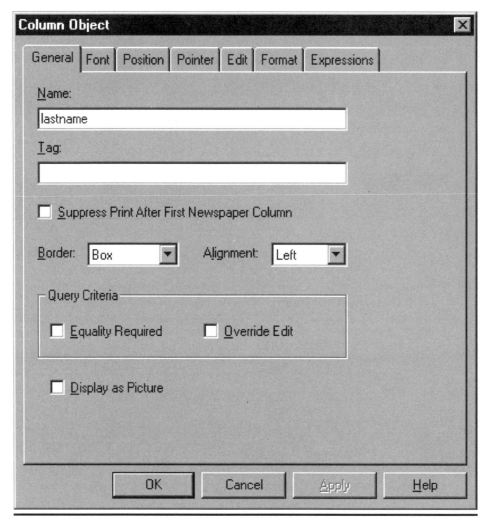

Figure 1.9 This is a property sheet for a column object placed on a report.

Installing InfoMaker

Before you install InfoMaker, determine how InfoMaker will be used within the organization. If reporting capability or the ability to move data from one database to another is all that is needed, InfoMaker includes separate modules that can be installed to use less room on a computer's hard drive.

If you are upgrading from InfoMaker 4.0 to InfoMaker 5.0, you do not have a lot to worry about. InfoMaker 5.0 automatically opens any reports, forms, etc. that were built in 4.0. However, there is one caveat. Once you open an object in 5.0, you cannot open it again in 4.0. It is highly recommended that you backup your 4.0 versions before converting them.

The InfoMaker package includes two CD-ROMs. One CD is used to install InfoMaker, and the other contains the Online Books. InfoMaker needs at least a 486SX with 12 Mbytes of memory to run. Powersoft recommends 16 Mbytes of memory. InfoMaker for Windows will run on Windows 3.1/95/NT. A complete installation of InfoMaker requires about 24-Mbyte hard drive space, but this can be less depending on the modules installed.

To install InfoMaker, do the following:

1. Insert the InfoMaker CD-ROM into the drive. InfoMaker setup starts automatically.

2. The first screen displayed prompts to either install or uninstall products. To install InfoMaker, make sure the Install Product radio button is selected, and click the Next button.

3. The next screen is where the InfoMaker version is chosen to install. This option depends on the operating system running on the target computer (see Fig. 1.10). There are three choices available: 16-bit, 32-bit short names, and 32-bit long names. If InfoMaker will run on Windows 3.1, choose the 16-bit version. If InfoMaker will run on Windows 95/NT, you can

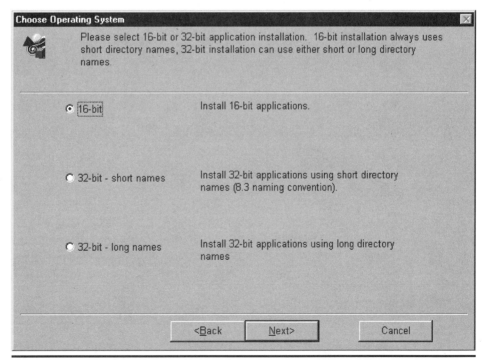

Figure 1.10 The Choose Operating System dialog box that displays during the InfoMaker installation prompts for the Windows version InfoMaker will run on a 16-bit version for Windows 3.1 or 32-bit versions for Windows 95/NT.

choose any of the three different versions. The difference between the 32-bit short and long names is that the 32-bit short names version maintains the 8.3 file-naming conventions, whereas the 32-bit long names version allows long file-naming conventions. Choose the appropriate version, and click on the Next button.

4. The next screen displayed has a choice of three different setup options: Typical, Compact, or a Custom installation. The Compact option installs InfoMaker as a reporting tool only. As such, only the Report, Query, and Environment painters are installed. The Typical option installs four additional painters to work with data: the Database, Table, Form, and Data Pipeline painters. And finally, the Custom option allows you to choose specific painters and other optional components to install. Choose the setup option, and click on the Next button.

5. The next screen displays the product that will be installed (in this case InfoMaker and the Deployment Kit). To install, click on the Next button.

6. The Products Available screen displayed next shows InfoMaker and the Deployment Kit, as shown in Fig. 1.11. To share forms and reports among many people, be sure to install the Deployment Kit. The Deploy-ment Kit is explained in detail in Chap. 16, Creating and Distributing a Complete Application.

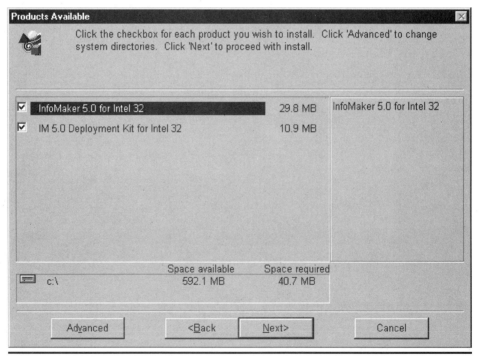

Figure 1.11 The Products Available dialog box allows you to install both InfoMaker and the Deployment Kit.

7. When the Advanced button is chosen on the Products Available dialog box, the Advanced Windows Directory Support dialog box displays, as shown in Fig. 1.12. There are three options: Prompt only when an update fails, Skip all updates to system directories, and Write all updates to the alternate directories below.

The Prompt only when an update fails option tells InfoMaker to pause the install process and confirm the file update only those times when it is unable to update a system file during the installation.

The Skip all updates to system directories option tells InfoMaker not to update system files during the installation. When the installation process is finished, you will have to modify these files manually, if necessary.

When the Write all updates to the alternate directories below option is selected, the three directory boxes are enabled and it is possible to modify the locations of where to install the system files.

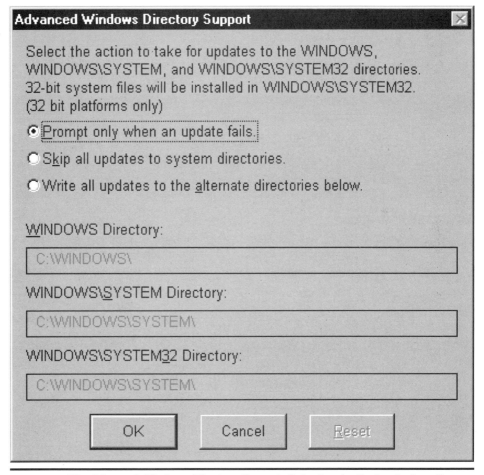

Figure 1.12 The Advanced Windows Directory Support dialog box is displayed when the Advanced... button is selected from the Products Available dialog box. In most cases the default setting of Prompt only when update fails is acceptable.

In most cases you can accept the default, Prompt only when an update fails. In those cases where InfoMaker is being reinstalled or InfoMaker is installed in a different directory, you may choose to skip updates or write the file updates elsewhere.

When you have finished, choose Next.

8. The Update Duplicate Files screen displays, as shown in Fig. 1.13. This window prompts for how the installation should handle any duplicate files it finds that currently reside on the hard drive compared to what it wants to install. There are five options. The first, Prompt for each, tells setup to confirm a file overwrite. The option Overwrite all tells setup not to confirm—just to go ahead and copy everything. The Overwrite none option says if a file already resides on the hard drive, do not rewrite it. Leave the file as it is. The Rename existing option tells setup to rename any files on the system before copying the new ones. The files will have different file extensions. The Alternate directory option tells setup that if there are files already on the system, load the new files in a different directory that you specify.

For most sessions, accept the default of Prompt for each and click Next.

9. The final screen in setup asks one more time if you are sure that you want to install InfoMaker. Clicking Exit and Next leaves the setup program.

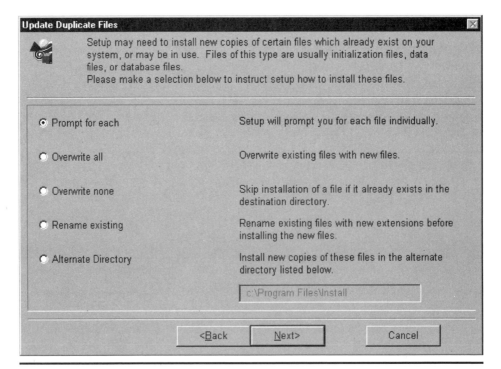

Figure 1.13 The Update Duplicate Files dialog box prompts for how the installation should handle duplicate files.

Choosing the Install Now button starts the actual file transfer. In a few moments the process is finished, and InfoMaker is installed.

10. Reboot the machine before running InfoMaker. Otherwise InfoMaker will not be able to find the initialization files it needs and will not load.

Upgrading to SQL Anywhere

InfoMaker can be installed in its own subdirectory or in a subdirectory of a previous version of InfoMaker, which overlays all the files. However, the installation does not automatically upgrade Watcom SQL, the previous version of the database management system (DBMS) to Sybase SQL Anywhere. SQL Anywhere 5.0 does run databases created with the earlier versions of Watcom SQL, but to use the new features available in the 5.0 version, the database installation utility must be run.

If InfoMaker runs in Windows 3.1, use the DBUPGRDW utility. For Windows 95/NT, use the DBUPGRD utility.

To upgrade a specific database built in a previous version of Watcom do the following:

In Windows 3.1

1. Choose File | Run from the Program Manager menu.

2. Enter the command

```
dbupgradw -c "dbf-mytestdb.db;uid-dba;pwd-sql"
```

In Windows 95/NT

1. Choose Run from the Start menu.

2. Enter the command

```
dbupgrad -c "dbf-mytestdb.db;uid-dba;pwd-sql"
```

The person who runs this utility must have database authorization to do so.

When the upgrade utility runs, it opens a DOS window. It drops system views, creates new views, creates a compatibility view, creates constraints and new stored procedures, and notifies you when the upgrade is complete.

Setting up the Online Books

Powersoft's enhanced Online Books make it easy to find specific information (see Fig. 1.14). There are plenty of graphics available to facilitate your understanding of the product. The User Guide provides much more detailed information than it did in 4.0; there are plenty of step-by-step instructions and lots of references telling you where to get more information if you need it. If you are in the InfoMaker Help system and need more information, you can click on a CD-ROM icon in the subject, and you are quickly transported to the appropriate item in the Online Books.

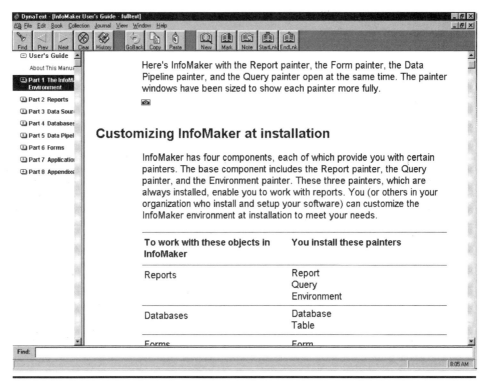

Figure 1.14   The User's Guide in InfoMaker's Online Books.

To install the InfoMaker Online Books, do the following:

1. Place the Online Books CD in the drive.

2. Run `setup.exe` from the CD drive.

3. The setup interface is the same as was used for the InfoMaker installation. Just follow the instructions.

Using Property Sheets

Property sheets are new to Windows 95. InfoMaker is now Windows 95 logo-compliant, which means that the product now includes the new GUI design principles. Property sheets are included in this category. A *property sheet* is a special tabbed window where object attributes, or options, are set for each object on a form, report, or other object.

To access a text object property sheet, do the following:

1. Click on a text label. See Fig. 1.15 for an example of a text label being selected on a report. Object selection is denoted by the small blocks at each corner of the text object.

2. Right-click on the text object. A pop-up menu displays.

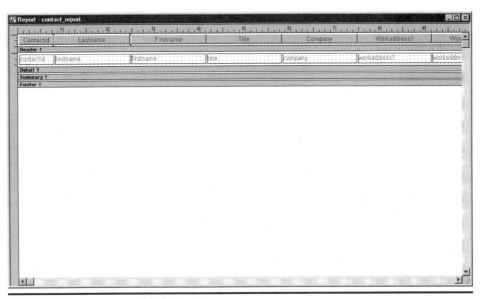

Figure 1.15 Selecting a text label object in a report.

3. Choose Properties… and the Text Properties property sheet displays, as shown in Fig. 1.16.

The Text Object property sheet contains options to set such attributes as the text label, font, and position of the label on the form or report; to set a different pointer to appear when the mouse passes over the object; or to define calculations to set background colors and other options when there is a specific type of data in the column. The options available on the property sheet are described in detail in Chap. 11, Enhancing Forms.

Now let's take a look at the Column Object property sheet. You will find that accessing a column object property sheet is really no different from accessing a text column property sheet.

To access the Column Object property sheet, do the following:

1. Select a column on a form or report, as shown in Fig. 1.17.

2. Right-click on the column.

3. Click on the Properties… option from the pop-up menu. The Column Object property sheet displays, as shown in Fig. 1.18. One thing you should notice right away is that the Column Object property sheet is different from the Text Object property sheet. The Column Object property sheet has tabs called *Edit* and *Format,* in addition to the others that were available on the Text Object property sheet. These additional tabs include options to change edit masks and styles, add passwords to the column, and set display formats. Again, we go over the options in greater detail in Chap. 11, Enhancing Forms, and Chap. 13, Enhancing Reports.

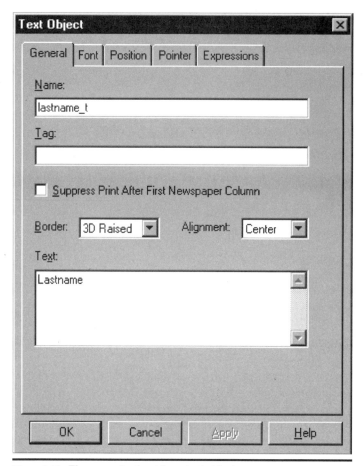

Figure 1.16   The property sheet for a text object.

File Editor

InfoMaker's File Editor is a simple text editor used to modify text, initialization, and other types of files without leaving the InfoMaker environment. It
works much as Windows' Notepad.

To access the File Editor from InfoMaker, do one of the following:

Select the File Editor item from the PowerPanel.

or

Press the SHIFT + F6 key combination.

or

Customize the PowerBar and add the editor icon for access from there.

For instructions on customizing the toolbar, see the "Customizing the Toolbars"
section later in this chapter.

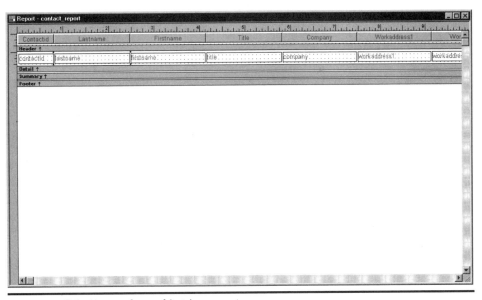

Figure 1.17 Selecting a column object in a report.

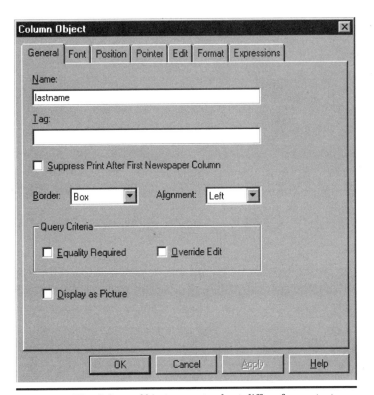

Figure 1.18 The Column Object property sheet differs from a text object property sheet in that display formats and edit masks are set for a column.

Importing and exporting text in the
File Editor

The Import and Export options bring in and send out files to and from the File Editor. Importing and exporting are invaluable when you want to merge the contents of two or more files.

To import a file, do the following:

1. Start File Editor by using one of the methods described previously. The usual File Open dialog box displays.

2. Select the file into which you want to import text, and choose the Open button.

3. Move the cursor to the location in the file to import the text.

4. Choose the File | Import... option from the File Editor menu.

5. Select the file that contains the text to import into the first file, and choose the Open button.

6. Choose File | Save As... from the menu.

7. Name the file. The title at the top of the window will change to the name given.

8. Choose the Save button.

To export a file, do the following:

1. Start the File Editor.

2. Open the file from which you want to export text.

3. Choose File | Export from the Editor menu.

4. Choose the file to which you want to export the current file, and click on OK.

5. Choose the file to which you want to export the text in the File Export box, and click on OK. InfoMaker then exports the text to the specified file.

Commenting and uncommenting text

The Comment and Uncomment options are used mainly when the File Editor is accessed from the Data Administration painter. These options direct InfoMaker to ignore specific lines of code in a SQL statement. This subject is covered in greater detail in Chap. 8, Working with Data in InfoMaker.

Moving to specific lines of a file

The File Editor has the capability to move to a specific line in a large file. This functionality makes the viewing of specific areas of a file much faster.

To view a specific line in a file, do the following:

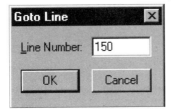

Figure 1.19 The Goto Line box in the File Editor accepts a line number and moves the cursor to the specified line.

1. Choose Search | Go To Line... from the File Editor menu, or press the CTRL + SHIFT + G key combination. InfoMaker brings up the Go To Line box, as shown in Fig. 1.19.

2. Enter an integer and press Return. The File Editor moves to the line specified. This is a quick and easy way to maneuver in large files.

Changing fonts in the File Editor

The property sheet in the File Editor has two tabs, General and Font. Note that in a text file the only attribute which can be changed on the General tab is the tab stop. All the other options are disabled. However, in the Data Administration painter, it is possible to activate auto-indenting, specify the type of warnings you want to see, etc. We cover this in detail in Chap. 8. To change the fonts in a file, access the property sheet for the File Editor by choosing Design | Options from the menu. For now, we can see the available options on the Font tab. This is where the default font size, type, and color are changed.

For more information about other options in the File Editor, see the InfoMaker documentation.

Customizing the Toolbars

Powersoft has included the capability to customize toolbars, allowing you to work the way you want to. A button can be added, removed, or moved to a different location within a toolbar. In addition, the location of the toolbar can be moved around on the screen.

Choosing a toolbar

First, you can choose to work with the PowerBar, the PowerPanel, or both. Move the mouse cursor to the PowerBar and right-click. The toolbar pop-up menu displays, as shown in Fig. 1.20. The first item on the menu is PowerBar1. If there is a check mark next to it, this means the PowerBar is active. Any cus-

Figure 1.20 The pop-up menu for the PowerBar has several options to set the PowerBar to the way you work.

tom toolbars defined in InfoMaker will also display here. The one with a check mark next to it is the active toolbar. To choose a different toolbar, click on the one you want.

Setting the location of the toolbar

From the toolbar pop-up menu, the five options—Left, Top, Right, Bottom, and Floating—refer to the placement of the PowerBar on InfoMaker's workspace. A check mark next to the item means this is where the PowerBar is located.

Showing Text and PowerTips on toolbars

At the bottom of the PowerBar pop-up menu are two other options: Show Text and Show PowerTips. Show Text displays text on the buttons. If this option is off, only icons display. I recommend you keep Show Text on until you become familiar with each icon's meaning. Another option available here is Show PowerTips. Setting PowerTips displays a message when the mouse cursor passes over the buttons on the PowerBar. A yellow message line describes the button's purpose. See Fig. 1.21 for a demonstration of the Show Text and Show PowerTips options.

Changing options on a toolbar

Toolbars are completely customizable. When the Customize... menu item on the toolbar pop-up menu is selected, the Customize window appears. This window has options which modify the PowerBar or create a new toolbar. To modify a PainterBar, open the painter and then choose Customize... from the toolbar pop-up menu. The PainterBar radio button is then enabled.

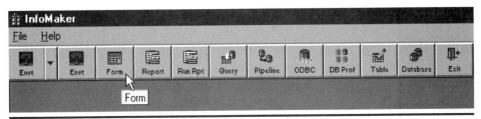

Figure 1.21 The PowerBar with the Show Text and Show PowerTips options turned on.

Adding a button

If there is a specific action not available on a toolbar, InfoMaker has the functionality to add it. To add a button, do the following:

1. In the area marked Select palette, choose the PowerBar.

2. In the Selected palette area, scroll down until you see the icon you want to place on the toolbar.

3. Then in the Current toolbar area, scroll until there is a blank area. The screen should look similar to Fig. 1.22.

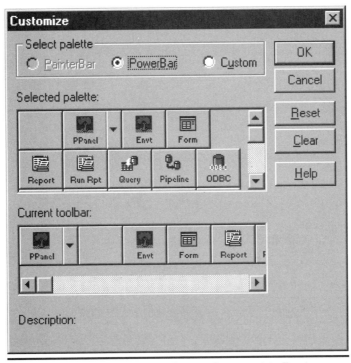

Figure 1.22 Selecting a button to place on the current toolbar is as easy as dragging and dropping on the toolbar.

4. Now, using the mouse, click on a button in the Selected palette area and drag it down until it is over a blank button in the Current toolbar area. When it is over the area, release the mouse and the button is now on the PowerBar.

5. Click OK to accept the changes.

Resetting a toolbar to default

If at any time you decide you do not like the changes you have made, you can access the Customize window and click Reset. This will reset the button to InfoMaker's default setup. Any customized buttons or other buttons that you have added to the toolbar are removed.

Removing a button from a toolbar

To remove a button from a toolbar, drag it from the Current toolbar back to the Selected palette area. Each button is removed individually.

Clearing a toolbar

If you created a completely new toolbar and later decide to do something totally different, choosing Clear on the Customize dialog box removes all buttons from a toolbar.

Moving buttons on a toolbar

You can also move a button from one area of a toolbar to another. Simply click on it with the mouse, and drag it to the new position.

Adding custom buttons to a toolbar

In addition to the predefined buttons InfoMaker includes, it is possible to define buttons to perform customized routines. These buttons can open other applications, such as Windows' Paint, or can run specific reports and queries.
    To add a custom button to a toolbar, do the following:

1. Select the Custom button in the Select palette area. In the Selected palette area, a different selection of toolbar buttons is accessible.

2. Select one of the icons, and drag it onto the PowerBar from wherever you would like. The Toolbar Item Command window displays.

3. Click on Browse... and select the application you wish to run from the button.

4. Enter the item and MicroHelp text. Fig. 1.23 shows an example of defining a button to run Windows Paint.

5. Then click on OK, and click OK again in the Customize window. The PowerBar now shows the icon you added. Click on it, and the application starts.

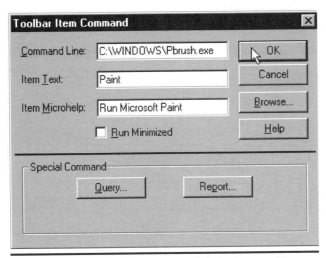

Figure 1.23 The Toolbar Item Command dialog box specifies the command to start a program, the text for the icon, and the MicroHelp to display.

Running a report or query from the toolbar

It is possible to run a report or query that you have previously defined in either the Report or Query painter from a toolbar.

To define a toolbar button to run a report, do the following:

1. Right-click in the toolbar area to open the toolbar pop-up menu.

2. Select Customize... from the toolbar pop-up menu.

3. Select Custom in the Select palette area of the Customize dialog box.

4. Choose an icon for the report or query from the Selected palette area, and drag it to the desired location on the Current toolbar area.

5. Choose Report... or Query... from the Toolbar Item Command dialog box.

6. The Select Report or Select Query dialog box displays. All the reports or queries defined in the current library display.

7. To change the library or to search for a specific item in a report, choose the Browse... button. The Browse Reports or Browse Queries dialog box displays, as shown in Fig. 1.24.

8. To select a report or query, double-click on it in the Select Report or Select Query dialog box. The command to start the report is entered automatically in the Command Line text area of the Toolbar Item Command dialog box, as shown in Fig. 1.25. Enter the Item and MicroHelp text.

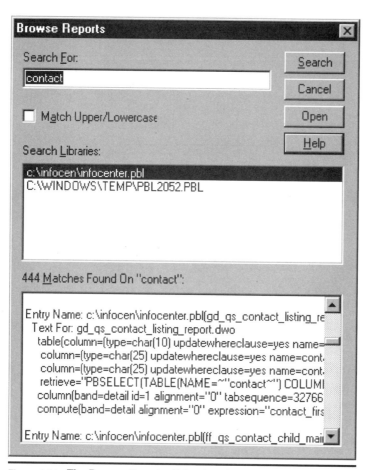

Figure 1.24 The Browse Reports dialog box is accessible from the Select Report dialog box to search for specific items within a report.

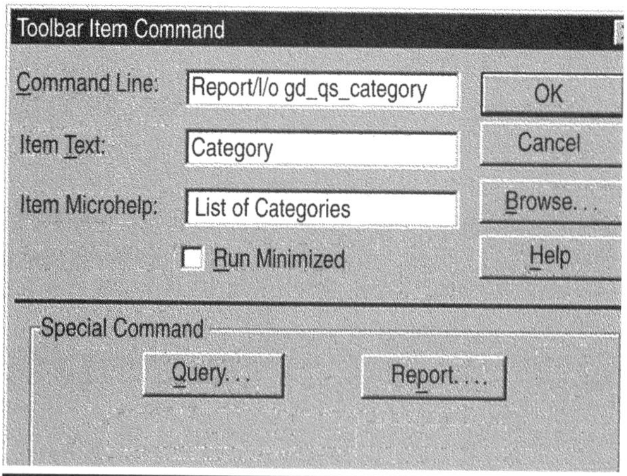

Figure 1.25 This is an example of a toolbar definition to run a report from a button.

Summary

You now have a basic familiarity with InfoMaker's environment. You know how to access the different painters and change object attributes. You successfully installed InfoMaker on your system and customized the environment to work according to your preferences. You should also know in what instances each of the toolbars is used and how to customize them. In the next chapter we discuss what you can accomplish by using each of the different painters.

2

The InfoMaker
Painters

What You Will Learn

In this chapter you will learn the purpose of each of the painters in InfoMaker and in what situations you would want to use them. You will find that all the painters work together to create a complete application quickly and easily. We will discuss at a high-level view what can be built in each painter and some of the functionalities available. By the end of this chapter you will know the types of activities that can be accomplished, what each painter does, and how to access them.

About the Painters

InfoMaker consists of several graphical painters to assist in building forms, reports, and other objects. These painters are sophisticated enough to build even the most complex reports and forms without any programming on your part. Let us take a look at each of the painters now.

Environment painter

The Environment painter is used to manage the many forms, reports, queries, and pipelines in a pibble file. Remember from Chap. 1 that a library is simply a collection of objects. The Environment painter works with one library at a time. Think of the Environment painter as InfoMaker's File Manager or Explorer. The Environment painter's main function is to manage all the objects in a library. Within the Environment painter, tools are available to move or copy objects from one library to another and to delete objects from the library. It opens existing libraries and creates new libraries. The Environment painter

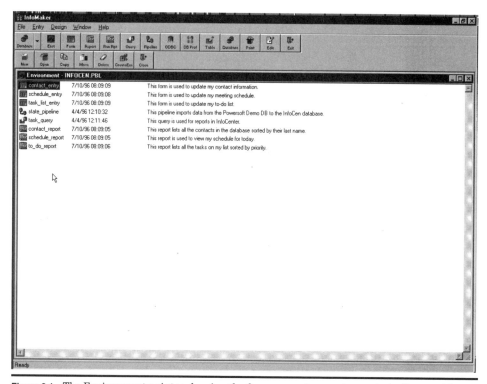

Figure 2.1   The Environment painter showing the forms, reports, queries, and pipelines residing in a library.

displays only forms, reports, queries, and pipelines. Other objects, such as tables, are only viewed from the Database painter. Figure 2.1 shows an open library in the Environment painter.

To access the Environment painter, do one of the following:

From the InfoMaker PowerBar, select the Environment painter button.

or

Press the key combination SHIFT + F5.

or

Select the Environment painter item from the PowerPanel.

Query library.   A Query library is a set of predefined data selection statements that is housed on a network for common access by all InfoMaker users. All InfoMaker users can access these libraries and create forms and reports much more quickly based on these queries. Having a Query library is a convenient way to make carefully developed and well-tested queries a part of forms and reports. Then when you create a new report, form, or pipeline, and Query is specified as the data source, InfoMaker includes the queries from the Query library in the list of available queries. The queries can be created in either PowerBuilder or InfoMaker.

The Environment painter is used to identify a Query library. Query libraries are covered in greater detail in Chap. 6, The Environment painter and in Chapter 17, InfoMaker and the PowerBuilder Connection.

Style library. Style libraries contain form styles created by PowerBuilder developers. These form styles are used to contain standardized forms used throughout an organization. The custom forms can enforce standards for company logos or standard operations which are used consistently throughout an organization. We will discuss Style libraries in more depth in Chap. 6, The Environment Painter, and in Chap. 17, InfoMaker and the PowerBuilder Connection.

Creating executables. It is in the Environment painter that an executable is created from objects in a library. The executable gathers all the forms and reports in a library and combines them into one file for easy distribution. InfoMaker automatically creates menus and toolbars to access these objects, freeing developers and end users from coding. Creating executables is covered in greater detail in Chap. 16, Creating and Distributing a Complete Application.

Form painter

The Form painter is used to create forms to add, delete, and update data in a database. The Form painter also has tools to view data and move the cursor to specific display pages, such as the first or last page, or anywhere in between.

Although the Data Manipulation painter has the same type of functionalities as the Form painter (meaning there are tools to view, add, change, and delete data and maneuver around the database), the presentation styles in the Data Manipulation painter cannot be modified. This makes viewing and updating information difficult. In contrast, the Form painter includes features such as validation and the ability to view one row at a time. The Form painter also has features to preview and print a form. Figure 2.2 shows an example of a form built with the Form painter.

To access the Form painter, do one of the following:

Select the Form painter button on the PowerBar.

or

Press the key combination SHIFT + F2.

or

Choose the Form painter item from the PowerPanel.

Presentation styles. A form style refers to how the form appears. There are several different form styles. When you are creating a new form, there are four types of forms to choose from: free-form, grid, master/detail one-to-many, or a master/detail many-to-one. The presentation styles are covered in depth in Chap. 10, Building Forms. Additionally, PowerBuilder developers can create

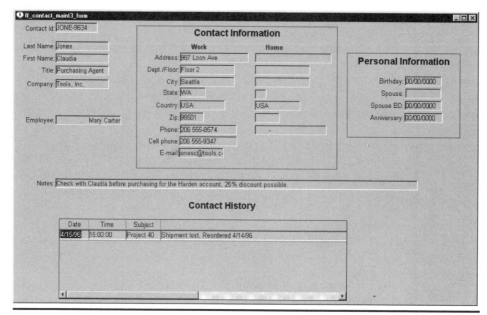

Figure 2.2 This is an example of a free-form master/detail one-to-many form built with the Form painter.

custom forms and add them to a style library for InfoMaker users to access. We will discuss how PowerBuilder developers can create these forms in Chap. 17, InfoMaker and the PowerBuilder Connection.

Form data sources.   Forms retrieve information by using SQL Select statements. The methods used to contain these SQL statements are called *data sources*. A variety of data sources are available to build a form. A data source called Quick Select is used for simple selection criteria and sorting. SQL Select is used for more advanced selections. Finally, Query is used to access a predefined SQL query created in InfoMaker's Query painter. Data sources are discussed in depth in Chap. 9, Data Sources.

Web access.   A new feature in forms added in version 5.0 is that when a form is running, it can be saved as an HTML file for easy loading to an Internet browser, such as Netscape's Navigator. This file can then be loaded and run on a Web page, which makes Web page creation much easier. Only forms using either the free-form or grid presentation style can be loaded to a Web page. Figure 2.3 shows an example of a form saved to an HTML document.

Report painter

The Report painter builds reports and graphs. Data cannot be updated from a report. The report is used merely to retrieve and display data. Figure 2.4 shows an example of a report built in the Report painter.

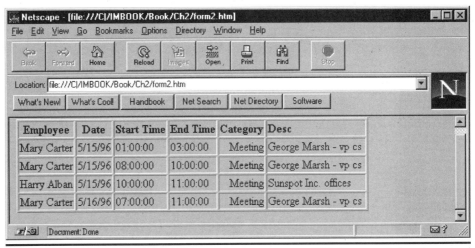

Figure 2.3 This is an example of an InfoMaker form saved in HTML format and placed on a Web page.

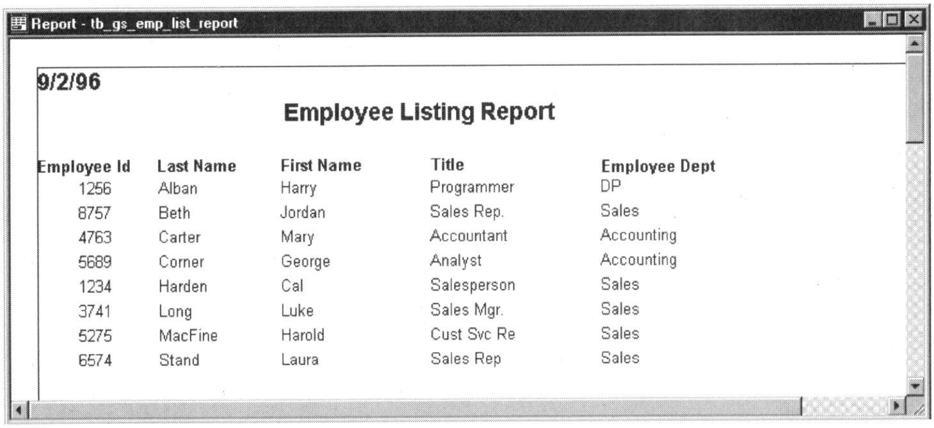

Figure 2.4 This is an example of an InfoMaker report using the Tabular presentation style.

To access the Report painter, do one of the following:

Select the Report painter button on the PowerBar.

or

Press the key combination SHIFT + F4.

or

Select the Report painter item from the PowerPanel.

Report data sources.   Reports contain the data sources Quick Select, SQL Select, and Query exactly as the forms do, but also include the External and Stored

Procedure data sources. The External data source is used to specify data that comes from a source other than a database, such as from a tab-delimited file like a .txt or .dbf file. A Stored Procedure data source is used to specify data coming from a stored procedure created in the database. Stored procedures can only be accessed in a report if the database to which the report is connected supports stored procedures. We cover data sources in depth in Chap. 9

Report presentation styles.   There are several presentation styles for reports, including composite, cross-tab, free-form, graphs, grid, groups, and label, plus two new presentation styles in version 5.0, Ole 2.0 and RichText, as shown in Fig. 2.5.

Report graphs.   Graphs are either embedded in reports or built as stand-alone by using the Report painter. InfoMaker has several different types of graphs available including area, bar, column, line, pie, and 3D graphs. Figure 2.6 shows some of the graphs available and the options that can be set.

Reports and the Web.   One of the formats in which you can choose to save a report is the HTML Table format. If this format is used, the saved file can be opened in a browser such as Netscape. Once the file is in HTML Table format, the file can be enhanced.

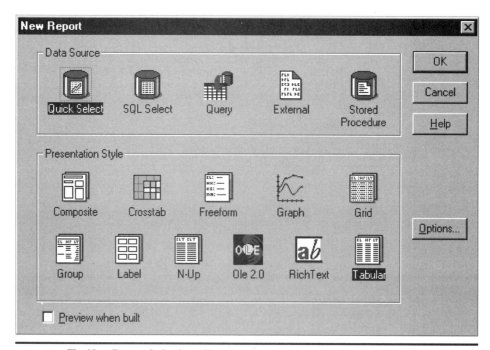

Figure 2.5 The New Report dialog box allows you to select the data source and the presentation styles, including the two new presentation styles in 5.0, Ole 2.0 and RichText.

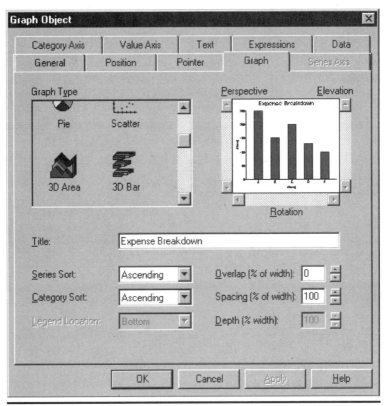

Figure 2.6 The Graph Object displays some of the properties available in InfoMaker.

Mailing reports. Powersoft has added the ability to send a report as a mail message using a MAPI-compliant mail server such as Microsoft's Exchange. The procedure is very easy. Simply preview a report and select Send from the File menu. Fill out to whom you want to send the report, and InfoMaker mails the report, which includes both the actual report with the data and the design. This allows the recipient to redesign the actual report if necessary.

Database painter

The Database painter is used to access and administer databases. In a database, tables (which hold the data), views (which provide limited access to data from larger tables), indexes, and primary and foreign keys are created and modified. The extended attributes for columns in a table can be defined and modified.

Some painters can be accessed only from the Database painter. These are the Data Manipulation painter, the View painter, and the Database Administration painter. Also within the Database painter, the Table painter and the Data Pipeline painter are available. But these two painters can also be accessed from

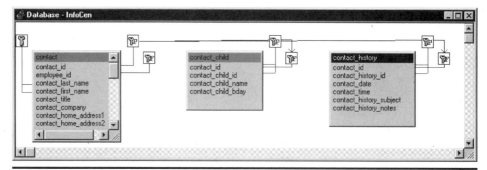

Figure 2.7 This is an example of the Database painter showing the primary and foreign keys and indexes for specified tables in the InfoCenter application.

the InfoMaker environment and worked in independently. Figure 2.7 shows an example of several tables open in the Database painter.

To access the Database painter, do one of the following:

Select the Database painter button from the PowerBar.

or

Press the key combination SHIFT + F1.

or

Select the Database painter item from the PowerPanel.

Data Manipulation painter.   The Data Manipulation painter is used to retrieve, change, add, and update data in any database. Of course, you must have security access to the database, and you must have the correct drivers needed to connect to the database installed on your machine before any change can be made to the database. Figure 2.8 shows an example of a table open in the Data Manipulation painter.

Database Administration painter.   The Database Administration painter controls access to the database and executes SQL commands directly. Figure 2.9 shows

Contact Id	Employee Id	Last Name	First Name	Title	Company	Home Address	Home Address	City	St
JONE-963-	Mary Carter	Jones	Claudia	Purchasing Agent	Tools, Inc.				
HARD-458-	George Comer	Harden	Paul	Owner	Snowcat & Assoc.				
ANDE-897:		Anderson	Randall	Marketing Rep	Widgets R Us	4376 Oak Lane		Summerville	NH
SMIT-1234	Cal Harden	Smith	John	CEO	Acme Bldg	1234 Main St.	Apt 3B	Warden	UT
MART-5728	Luke Long	Martin	Joe	VP Mfg	Bits, Inc.				
SOMM-568	Jordan Beth	Sommers	Lloyd	President	Deskwrite Consol.				
HALL-2414	Jordan Beth	Hall	Mike	Gen Mgr	Wallpage, Inc.	98 Coon Hollow		Grand Park	IA

Figure 2.8 A table in the Data Manipulation painter can be viewed in a grid, table, or free-form format.

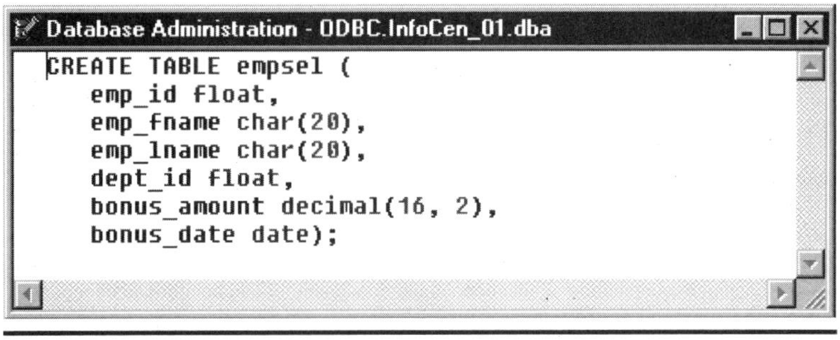

```
Database Administration - ODBC.InfoCen_01.dba        _ □ ×
CREATE TABLE empsel (
    emp_id float,
    emp_fname char(20),
    emp_lname char(20),
    dept_id float,
    bonus_amount decimal(16, 2),
    bonus_date date);
```

Figure 2.9 Advanced users will appreciate the Database Administration painter. SQL statements can be created directly instead of using a graphical interface.

an example of the Database Administration painter with a command to create a table.

View painter.   The View painter is used to create views. A view is used to limit access to data. For instance, an Employee table containing information such as an employee's birthdate, social security number, and salary may not be open for public knowledge, but other employees in a corporation may need to know such things as name, hire date, etc. Creating a view, we can specify which columns are accessible to everyone and which are available only to personnel in the human resources department. A view is handled in much the same way as a regular database table.

Creating and deleting databases.   A SQL Anywhere database accessed from within the Database painter can be created or deleted. However, when working in another DBMS, you cannot create or delete a database. This is an administrative task which only the database administrator with the correct security can do for you.

Table painter

In the Table painter, tables are created and opened. Once a table is open, all the columns in the table are available for viewing or modification, including the attributes, such as column width and data type. For instance, if a column is named *id,* the label can be set so that when you are building a report or form, the heading is *Customer number.* Edit masks, validation rules, initial, and default values are also set here.

InfoMaker employs a single-user version of the SQL Anywhere database. The Table painter can connect to SQL Anywhere databases or to any other accessible database. Additionally, the Table painter adds data to tables quickly by importing data from text files. Or data can be entered directly, although it is more time-consuming than if a form is used. Figure 2.10 shows an example of a table opened in the Table painter.

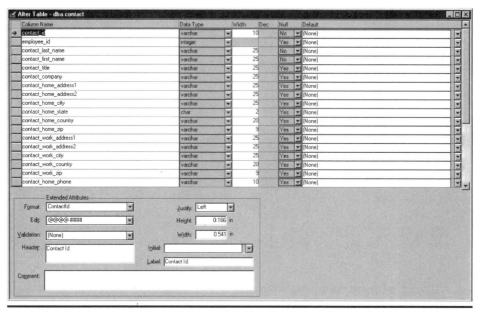

Figure 2.10 This is an example of a table as viewed in the Table painter. Columns, including extended attributes, are modified here.

To access the Table painter, do one of the following:

Select the Table button on the PowerBar.

or

Choose the Table painter item in the PowerPanel.

or

Select the Table painter button in the Database painterbar.

or

Select Object | New | Table from the Database painter menu.

Data Pipeline painter

Another tool in the InfoMaker arsenal is the Data Pipeline painter. Data pipelines are used to copy data from one or more source data tables to a new or existing table. Once a pipeline is defined, it can be saved and reused repeatedly to transfer data. Figure 2.11 shows an example of a data pipeline.

To access the Data Pipeline painter, do one of the following:

Select the Data Pipeline painter button on the PowerBar.

or

Choose the Data Pipeline painter option in the PowerPanel.

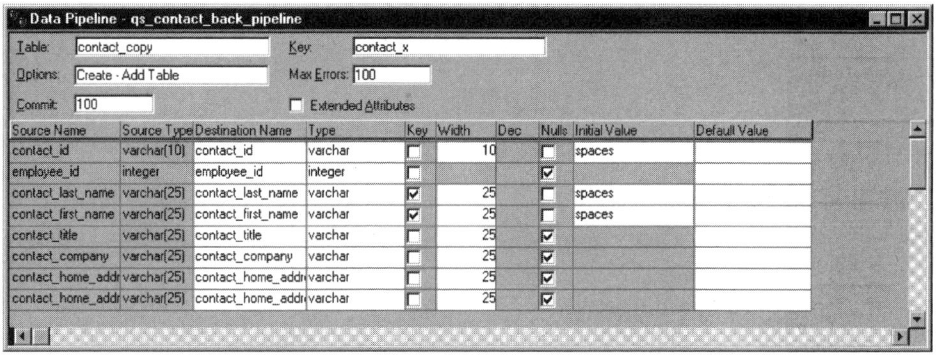

Figure 2.11   This is an example of a Data Pipeline definition.

or

Choose the Data Pipeline painter button on the Database painterbar.

or

Select Object | Data Pipeline from the Database painter menu.

Query painter

Reports, forms, and data pipelines use data from a database. Each time a report, form, or data pipeline is created, after selection of a data source in the New Report, New Form, or New Data Pipeline dialog box, the data requirements are specified. When finished, InfoMaker creates a SQL SELECT statement.

A query is a SQL SELECT statement with a name. Queries are defined in the Query painter, named, and saved. Then anytime a new report, form, or data pipeline is created, data requirements are specified by using a query as the data source.

Queries save time because all the data requirements are specified just once. For example, the columns, which rows to retrieve, and the sorting order are specified in a query. Whenever a report, form, or pipeline is created using that data, simply specify the query as the data source. Figure 2.12 shows an example of a Query data source.

To access the Query painter, do one of the following:

Select the Query painter button from the PowerBar.

or

Press the key combination SHIFT + F3.

or

Select the Query painter item from the PowerPanel.

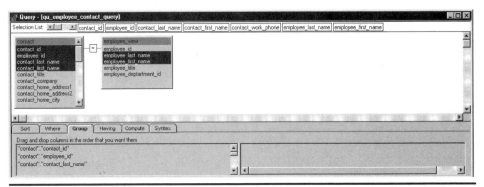

Figure 2.12 This is an example of the Query painter. It works exactly as the Select painter.

Select painter

The Select painter is invoked automatically whenever a SQL Select statement is created or is changed. It cannot be accessed from the PowerBar or the PowerPanel. In the Select painter, there are graphical tools to select tables and columns, specify sort and selection criteria, set up retrieval criteria, and so on. Once you are an accomplished user on the Select painter, you will be able to also create queries and views with minimal effort. The Select painter is discussed in detail in Chap. 9, Data Sources. Figure 2.13 shows an example of the Select painter.

Summary

The InfoMaker painters all work together to help you build a cohesive set of tools to access and manipulate data in myriad ways. Each painter has a distinct use and uses a common interface, which makes learning them much easier and faster. In the next chapter, we discuss how you can customize the InfoMaker environment to suit your needs.

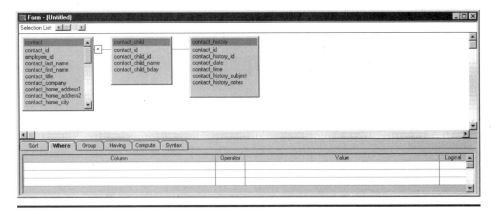

Figure 2.13 The Select painter is used throughout InfoMaker to create SQL Select statements.

3

Setting Preferences

What You Will Learn

Chapter 3 covers setting preferences by using initialization files. Each of the sections in the initialization file are outlined, with descriptions of the types of information they contain. And you will learn how InfoMaker stores extended attributes. By the end of this chapter, you will be able to customize the complete InfoMaker environment to your needs.

Setting Preferences

Preferences are settings specified in an initialization file which direct InfoMaker to look and act in a certain way—the way you prefer. For the most part, the initialization file is modified automatically when changes are made in the InfoMaker environment, without your even knowing about it. Although the occasion where you will need to modify the initialization file directly is rare, it is still a good idea to be aware of the file and know what each of the different sections does to help pinpoint any problems that may arise.

About `im.ini`

Each time InfoMaker starts, InfoMaker first looks at an initialization file called `im.ini` in the InfoMaker folder (or in whichever folder InfoMaker was installed). The initialization file on your system contains settings to set up the InfoMaker environment. The `im.ini` file is a text file containing many sections and variables for setting the environment. Some of these variables remember how the toolbar was last set, for instance, with text or without, and where Help files are located, settings for building forms, etc. The `im.ini` file can be viewed and modified by using any text editor, including InfoMaker's File Editor. Figure 3.1 shows an example of an initialization file.

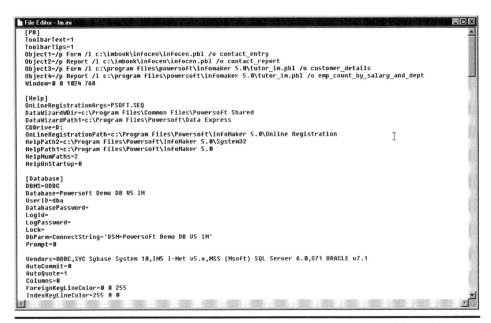

Figure 3.1 This is an example of an initialization file with several sections and variables visible.

The default im.ini file that comes with InfoMaker contains several sections: PB, Help, Database, DataWindow, Window, SQL Painter, and Application, among others. The order of the sections and the variables within each section can vary. However, each variable relating to a specific section of the im.ini file must be in that section. Each of these different sections contains variables that can be set to make InfoMaker work the way you specify. Some of the variables shown in Fig. 3.1 have no value listed next to them, for instance, Database Password =. This means InfoMaker is using the default setting in this instance.

Normally, the im.ini file will never have to be modified directly. Whenever settings are changed in InfoMaker, the initialization file is automatically updated. So, for example, to show text on the toolbar, select that option from the toolbar pop-up window and InfoMaker makes the changes to im.ini behind the scenes (see Fig. 3.2).

Each InfoMaker user usually has his or her own im.ini file on his or her local computer, even if the user is working on a copy of InfoMaker that resides on a network. This is because each user will have a different set of preferences. Make sure you have a backup copy of im.ini and keep it in a safe place. InfoMaker will not start without it.

Locating the Initialization File

If for some reason you find that the initialization file is not in your InfoMaker folder, you can tell InfoMaker where to find it. To find the initialization file,

Figure 3.2 Modifying toolbar preferences. Changes to the im.ini file are automatically saved.

when InfoMaker starts, it first looks for the path in the Registry or in the [InfoMaker] section of the win.ini file. If InfoMaker cannot find it, InfoMaker uses the im.ini file in the folder where InfoMaker is installed. And if the im.ini file is not on the system, InfoMaker will not start. The System Options in InfoMaker must be set with the correct path name if InfoMaker cannot find the initialization file.

To set the location of the initialization file, do the following:

1. Select the Tool drop-down toolbar on the InfoMaker PowerBar, or open the PowerPanel.

2. Choose System Options, as shown in Fig. 3.3.

3. In the System Options dialog box, choose the General tab, as shown in Fig. 3.4.

4. Enter the path where the initialization file is located.

5. Click OK.

InfoMaker saves the path name in the Windows 95 registry or the Windows 3.1 win.ini file. As mentioned previously in the "About im.ini" section, the im.ini file consists of several sections, containing variables for each section. We now take a look at what each section contains.

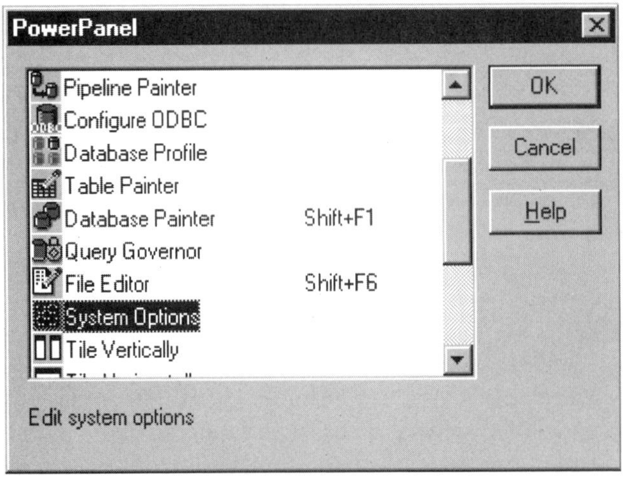

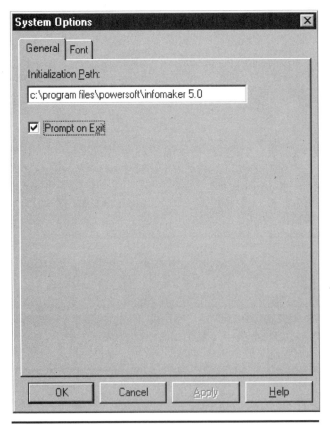

Figure 3.3 Choosing System Options from the PowerPanel.

Figure 3.4 Specifying the path name of the InfoMaker initialization file in the System Options property sheet.

PB section

The PB section of the InfoMaker initialization file contains variables that affect the InfoMaker environment itself. In this section are variables setting toolbar preferences, fonts for the Environment painter, MicroHelp, the Database Administration painter, and File Editor settings. There are also variables to set InfoMaker to run full-screen and in a specific resolution. Some of these options are set by using the System Options property sheet from the PowerPanel, and others are set by accessing the Design | Options menu in the Database Administration painter.

Help section

The Help section of the im.ini file contains variables to set the Help environment in InfoMaker. These variables specify where the Help files for InfoMaker reside and where the Online Books are located on CD-ROM. Other variables direct InfoMaker to the files needed when registering on-line and running Data Express to report problems to Powersoft.

Database section

The Database section of the InfoMaker initialization file contains variables that affect the current database and the Database painter environment. The Database section contains variables that set the current database, set transaction processing preferences, and hold information for all the accessible databases.

DataWindow section

The DataWindow section contains variables that set options for reporting. Many of these are set in the Query Governor, discussed later in this chapter. Variables in this section determine whether cross products are allowed, set SQL preferences, etc. Additionally, there are many variables for setting colors, borders, and text for each of the different report styles.

Window section

The Window section of the im.ini file contains variables that determine whether controls display 3D, and which data source is the default, and sets grid options. Additionally, there are many variables for setting colors, borders, and text for each of the different form styles.

SQL Painter section

The SQL Painter section contains variables that set options in the Select and Query painters. Comments, labels, or data types displayed in the SQL painter and colors of the different items in the two painters are controlled from this section.

DBMS_Profiles section

The DBMS_Profiles section contains variables that affect the currently active database. The DBMS_Profiles section is followed by additional sections for each database profile defined in InfoMaker. So, for instance, after the DBMS_Profiles section, there is a section called Profile Powersoft Demo DB V5 IM. This is because the Powersoft demo database is set up automatically when InfoMaker is installed. The DBMS_Profiles section details what database is current and what other profiles are defined. Each of the individual database profiles contains variables or connection information to the database, such as connect strings, if necessary, and user ids.

Application section

The Application section contains variables affecting the current library and the library entries that display in the Environment painter. Variables affecting which default library to connect to each time InfoMaker is started, the working directory, whether to display comments and dates, and toolbar settings are found in this section.

Query Governor

The Query Governor is used to set options relating to how to retrieve data from the database and to change data selection and retrieval settings to optimize performance. Changing settings in the Query Governor automatically updates the im.ini file's Data Window section. The Query Governor accepts changes at any time. However, keep in mind that if you are in the Select painter when you change any options, you will have to exit the Select painter and reenter it for the changes to take effect. The Query Governor is accessed from the Environment painter.

When a data source is chosen, InfoMaker does not restrict access to tables or views in the database. This must be accomplished by the database administrator. To access the Query Governor, select Query Governor from the PowerPanel, as shown in Fig. 3.5, or press CTRL + SHIFT + N.

The Query Governor contains choices to set data selection and retrieval options. See Fig. 3.6 for a look at the Query Governor.

Specifying the maximum number of tables in a join

To set the maximum number of tables that can be combined in a join, check the Specify maximum number of tables in a join box on the Query Governor dialog box, and specify the number of tables in the spin control. If this box is marked and has a value entered, this means there is a maximum number of tables that can be specified in a SQL Select statement. The higher the number, the fewer the restrictions on the data selections available, but also the longer the times to retrieve data.

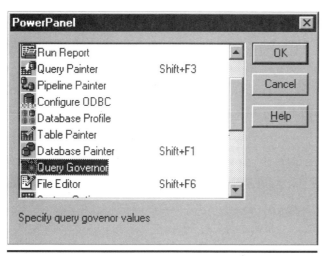

Figure 3.5 Accessing the Query Governor from the Power-Panel.

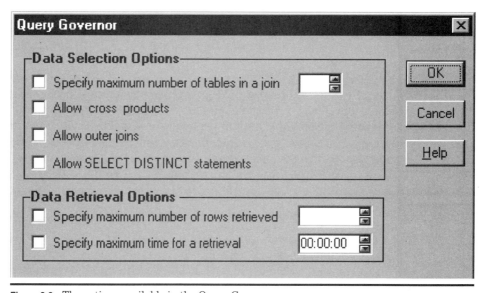

Figure 3.6 The options available in the Query Governor.

Allowing cross products

To allow cross products when data is selected from the database, select the Allow cross products box on the Query Governor dialog box. When the Allow cross products box is checked, for every row in a table that matches a row in another joined table, both rows will be retrieved.

Allowing outer joins

To allow outer joins when data is selected from the database, check the Allow outer joins box on the Query Governor dialog box. Outer joins occur when all rows in a table are retrieved, regardless of whether there is a matching row in another table.

Allow SELECT DISTINCT statements

Allowing SELECT DISTINCT SQL statements means duplicate rows are restricted when data is retrieved from the database. Normally when a SELECT statement is issued, all rows meeting the selection criteria are retrieved, but using the DISTINCT clause limits the rows returned. Unfortunately, retrieval times are usually much longer when DISTINCT is specified.

Specifying the maximum number of rows retrieved

To set the maximum number of rows to retrieve, check the Specify maximum number of rows retrieved on the Query Governor dialog box. If this option is checked, the greatest number of rows that can be retrieved using a SELECT statement is specified. Limiting the number of rows means shorter retrieval times, resulting in better system response.

Specifying the maximum time for retrieval

To set the maximum time for the database to retrieve data, check the Specify maximum time for retrieval box on the Query Governor dialog box. If this option is checked, the maximum time the database will try to retrieve rows from the database is set. Once the time specified is reached, InfoMaker will time out. Setting a time here results in better performance with shorter retrieval times. The maximum retrieval time is specified in hours, minutes, and seconds.

The Repository

The Powersoft Repository is a set of system tables maintained by the Database painter in InfoMaker or in PowerBuilder, which contain information about database tables and columns.

By using the Database painter, information is put into the Powersoft Repository. Column attributes such as text label and display formats are saved in the repository. Then each time the column is used throughout an application, these attributes are not redefined. They are carried over automatically. Of course, attributes can be overridden at any time when you are building a form or report. The changes will only apply to the current report. The advantage of letting the repository do all the work, rather than defining extended attributes for each report or form individually, is that it saves time and enforces consistency. The attributes have to be specified only once in the database. If there is no information for the database tables and columns being used or if you do not want to use the default settings held in the repository, you can change them in each report. The changes made in the report do not change what is held in the repository.

The Powersoft Repository is a collection of five system tables that InfoMaker maintains automatically. These are the PBCatCol, the PBCatEdt, the PBCatFmt, the PBCatTbl, and the PBCatVld tables. Each of these tables contains a distinct set of data related to columns and their extended attributes. It is not necessary to modify these files. Just be aware that they exist and know where they are located.

The PBCatCol system table contains information for columns, such as the column name and heading, and labels for forms and reports.

The PBCatEdt system table contains edit style names and definitions.

The PBCatFmt system table contains display format names and definitions.

The PBCatTbl system table contains information about tables, such as names, fonts, and comments.

The PBCatVld system table contains validation rule names and definitions.

You can open system tables in the Database painter just as you would any other table. To do so, when viewing the Select Table dialog box, you check the Show System Tables option, as shown in Fig. 3.7.

Figure 3.8 shows an example of the PBCatCol system table being viewed in the Data Manipulation painter.

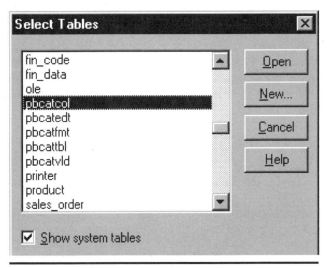

Figure 3.7 Displaying the System Tables from the Select Table dialog box in the Database painter.

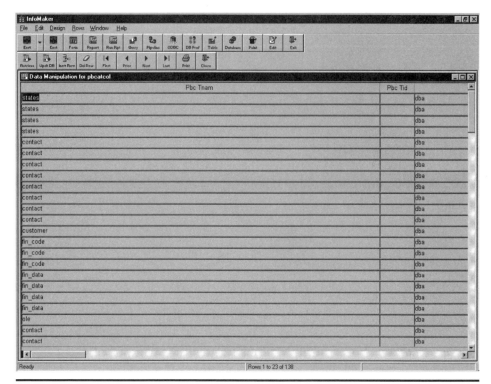

Figure 3.8 An example of the PBCatCol system table displayed in the Data Manipulation painter.

Summary

You now know where the initialization file for InfoMaker is located and its purpose. We also covered how InfoMaker stores extended attributes in the repository. We discussed the Query Governor and the settings available to improve performance. You should now feel comfortable in modifying InfoMaker to work the way you want.

Standards and
Guidelines

What You Will Learn

Chapter 4 explains the standards and guidelines that can be used to build an InfoMaker application. These guidelines include a brief discussion of why to implement standards and the need for consistent design. Suggested naming conventions for forms, reports, and other InfoMaker objects are discussed. Additionally, interface standards regarding control usage on forms, error messages, and other items to keep in mind when developing an application are covered in this chapter.

Why Use Standards?

When you are developing InfoMaker objects that will be shared among many people, or even if you are working solo, there are many reasons for deciding to use standards and guidelines. Standards and guidelines promote consistency and order, especially on projects that involve many components. Following consistent guidelines not only helps you remember what you did 6 months ago, but also helps anyone else working with an application to understand what you built.

Consistency

It is important that applications be consistent in appearance and construction so that users know what to expect. Application use, maintenance, and enhancements are more efficient when consistent standards are followed.

Beginners need consistency. Experienced users demand easy-to-use applications. New employees are always brought on board and must learn how to use the applications. If an interface is too complicated to understand, then users think the system is too complicated. If it is easy to use, people will quickly adopt the system and become productive.

Design consistencies are integral to an application because they reduce the requirements for learning by allowing skills learned in one situation to be transferred to another similar situation.

Consistency has certain benefits. It

- Helps in moving from one application to another with ease and speed
- Facilitates the learning process
- Minimizes training requirements
- Increases overall productivity
- Minimizes user confusion and the time that it takes a new user to become confident
- Provides users with a sense of stability, thereby increasing their confidence and the reliability of the applications

Maintainability

You will find you can create applications quickly when following standards such as naming conventions and interface guidelines. If all objects are named in the same way when you create a new application, you will not have to struggle with problems such as, "Now what should I name this form?" Naming a form is very straightforward when naming conventions are in place. And when it comes time to make changes to an existing application, you will be able to find the objects you want quickly. And last, if someone else has to change an application you created, he or she can modify the system much faster because you took the time to put those standards and guidelines in place. Standards and guidelines are not just something that is nice to have in place; they are a necessity.

By establishing naming conventions, you are helping not only yourself, but also anyone who has to maintain the systems you build. And when following the rules of implementing a good interface, you make it easy for users to learn how to use the application. It is also easier for them to remember how to use the application. Naming conventions and interface guidelines are two of the most important things you can use to help yourself and whoever has to work with the application.

Naming Conventions

Naming conventions are a set of rules to follow when you name InfoMaker objects such as forms, reports, queries, and pipelines. A sound naming convention will substantially improve the longevity of an application by making it easier to support and modify.

Naming forms, reports, pipelines, and queries

Any valid InfoMaker name must begin with a letter. There can be up to 40 characters in the name, but spaces are not allowed. A name can include any combination of letters, numbers, and special characters, such as a dash -, underscore _, dollar sign $, number sign #, and percent sign %.

If a name consists of multiple words, such as *order number,* join them with either a hyphen or an underscore. For example, *Order-Number* and *order_number* are both valid. My personal preference is the underscore method (order_number), and this is what I use throughout the book. But feel free to use your own convention.

This is the naming convention I use to name my InfoMaker objects:

```
{style}_{source}_<object name>_{object type}
```

Names consist of one required segment (object name) and three optional segments (style, source, and object type).

Style segment.   The {style} segment is optional. Remember that forms and reports are the only objects with a presentation style. The style for an object is the presentation style that was used to build the object. Table 4.1 lists the style segments for each of the form and report presentation styles and some examples of object names.

Source segment.   The *source segment* refers to the data source. Since queries do not have a data source, this applies only when naming a form, report, or data pipeline. The source for an object is the data source from which the object is populated. Table 4.2 lists the source segments for each of the data sources.

TABLE 4.1   Style Segments for Each of the Presentation Styles

Presentation style	Style segment	Example
Freeform	ff_	ff_order_entry
Grid	gd_	gd_emp_contact
Master/Detail One-To-Many	om_	om_customer_to_orders
Master/Detail Many-To-One	mo_	mo_sales_to_salesperson
Composite	cm_	cm_invoice
Crosstab	cr_	cr_tax_by_week
Graph	gr_	gr_line_sales
Group	gp_	gp_inventory_report
Label	la_	la_customer_mailing_list
N-up	n[umber of cols]_	n3_salesregion
Ole 2.0	ol_	ol_excel_orders
RichText	rt_	rt_sales_letter
Tabular	tb_	tb_customer_report

TABLE 4.2   Source Segment Names for Each of the Data Sources

Source	Source segment	Example
Quick Select	qs_	qs_customers
SQL Select	sql_	sql_customers_and_orders
Query	qu_	qu_employee_payroll
External	ex_	ex_dbf_orders
Stored Procedure	sp_	sp_inventory_update

The object name and type.   The object name is any descriptive legal name. And finally, the object type segment refers to the type of object, whether it be a form, report, query, or pipeline.

Naming objects in this manner makes it much easier to tell exactly what the object does and if it is what you want. If we put these prefixes together, we will end up with object names such as ff_qs_order_entry_form, meaning this is a free-form form derived from a Quick Select data source for order entry. Here's another example: om_qu_customer_to_orders_form. This is a master/detail one-to-many form derived from a prebuilt query with one customer shown with the corresponding orders.

Let us try this one: customer_query. Can you guess what type of presentation style and data source this one has? If you said none, you are right! Remember, queries do not have a presentation style or a data source.

Following this type of naming convention will help you find the objects you want quickly and will give other InfoMaker developers a roadmap to follow when they work on your systems.

Naming tables and columns

When you name tables, the only requirement other than the 40-character limit is to be sure that the name is descriptive. Column names should be prefaced with the name of the table in which they reside. This way, when you build a form with columns from several different tables, the column's table is immediately recognizable.

Interface Guidelines

When you are developing an application, the interface should be considered one of the most important factors. If a screen is cluttered and hard to manage, people will find the application difficult to work on. Build a screen cluttered with columns and controls, and you will hear lots of complaints.

Basic screen design

Screens should appear orderly, clean, and clutter-free. Provide only the information that is essential to making a decision or performing an action. Do not flood a user with information. Screens should provide only relevant information because the more information thrown at someone, the greater the competition among the screen components for the person's attention. If the screen is overly cluttered, visual search times will be longer and meaningful patterns will be more difficult to perceive. If necessary, use multiple windows to display all the necessary information, instead of placing everything on one screen. But if you do have to use multiple screens, provide all the information needed to complete the screen so the user does not have to remember data from one screen to the next.

The user's eye will naturally read a screen from top left to bottom right. Use this progression to your advantage by placing the natural business order of the information entered or read on the screen in this same way. The tab order of the columns should also follow this flow—even though users can use the mouse to interrupt this natural progression.

There should be an obvious indication of what is being shown and what should be done with it. There should also be a clear indication of what relates to what (headings, labels, static text, etc.). Users expect information to be located where it should be. There should be a simple way of finding what is in the system and getting it out. When an action could make a permanent change in data, the user should have a clear indication of the action.

Fonts, colors, and spacing should be the same on all screens in an application and across all applications in an organization. Use common labels such as *OK, Close,* and *Cancel* on buttons. These types of things help users learn an application much more quickly, and users do not have to struggle with a new environment as they enter each application.

Controls

There are many controls that can be placed on a window. Knowing the type of control to use and when it is appropriate is an art that comes more easily with experience. The object of good screen design and use of controls is to communicate all the available screen functionality to users in the least time and screen real estate. One way to do this is to limit the number of controls placed on a window to avoid overwhelming the user. Each window should have lots of white space to avoid a cluttered look. Let us take a look at the controls available in InfoMaker and how to optimize their use in forms and reports.

Command and picture buttons

Command and picture buttons are used primarily as a launching point for some processing. A command button should represent only one action. Use ellipses on a command button to indicate that further information is required before processing an action. When several command buttons are placed on a window, the buttons should be aligned vertically on the right side of the window or horizontally along the bottom. The exception to this rule occurs when a button is related to another control on the screen. In this case, it is more appropriate to place the button close to the related control.

The first letter of each word on a command button, with the exception of prepositions such as *for, of,* etc., should be capitalized. In addition, the same font and size should be used on multiple command buttons within an application and across applications.

If a screen has many command buttons on it, try to use toolbar items instead. Placing the actions on the toolbar and menu saves screen real estate. Figure 4.1 demonstrates how command buttons may be placed on a screen.

Single- and multiple-line edits

The single- and multiple-line edit controls are used to type information into the database from the keyboard. The column border should be long enough so no data displayed in the column is truncated. And borders are generally in the 3D lower style.

When you design the column label, keep the distance between the column label and the data column about an average character length. The column label should be located to the left of a free-form column. Column labels in vertical groups should be left-aligned with other labels. Entry fields and labels are vertically aligned. When there are two columns of data on a screen, leave about five spaces between the longest entry column and the text label in the adjacent column. See Fig. 4.2 for an example of how to design entry columns.

Spin controls

Spin controls are normally used when sequential numbers are needed in an entry field. Choosing the up or down arrow on the control increments or decrements the number. If possible, limit the number of spin control values to a maximum of 10 items. Limiting the number of items enhances user comprehension. The values in a spin control should not change and should be ordered. Figure 4.3 shows an example of a spin control on a window.

Figure 4.1 This is an example of command buttons on a screen, with the proper spacing and text.

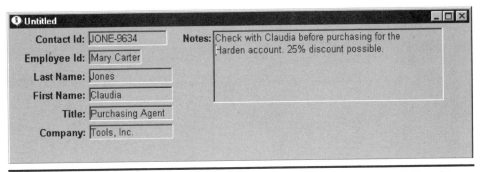

Figure 4.2 This window shows a column of single-line edits on the left and a multiple-line edit column on the right. Note how the columns and labels are spaced and aligned horizontally and vertically to provide an easy path for users to follow.

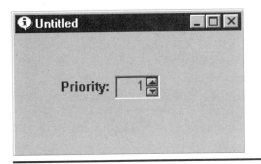

Figure 4.3 This is an example of a spin control.

Drop-down list box and drop-down DataWindows

List boxes typically allow users to choose from a list of static options. A drop-down list box looks like a single-line edit with an arrow to the right. The arrow allows the user to drop down a list of available choices. The user can select only one choice from the list. The list box should hold no more than about 30 or 40 choices. If the list is short, about five items, consider using a radio button.

When a list of options will change over time, use a drop-down DataWindow. Checking the Always show arrow option when defining the DataWindow tells users that there is additional data to display.

On both drop-down list boxes and drop-down DataWindows, use vertical scroll bars. Avoid using horizontal scroll bars because it is easier to comprehend lists in a vertical format. In addition, list items alphabetically or in the order of the highest probability of selection. This avoids unnecessary scrolling. Display a maximum of 10 items in the list without the use of a scroll bar. Size the window or box to prevent entries from being truncated horizontally or vertically. In general, use a full description for options, instead of codes. And finally, the default option should be displayed when the window is opened.

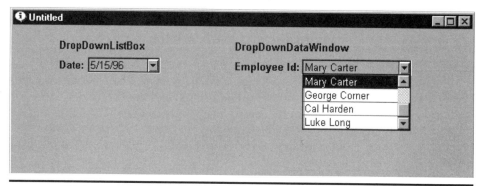

Figure 4.4   This is an example of a drop-down list box on the left and a drop-down DataWindow on the right. In the drop-down list box, a specific set of data is displayed each time. The drop-down DataWindow retrieves information from the database.

The difference between a drop-down list box and drop-down DataWindow is that when you are building a form or report, you enter the explicit values that will display in the list box. In the drop-down DataWindow, you build a report that retrieves the data from the database and displays it in the drop-down DataWindow. Figure 4.4 displays a window with both a drop-down list box and a drop-down DataWindow. You will notice that visually, there is not much difference between the two.

Check boxes

Check boxes control individual logical choices. The choice is either on or off. The user can change the state by clicking on the check box. Use check boxes for up to four selections. When an on/off type of choice is required, a check box should be used instead of two radio buttons. Check box text should be located to the right of the check box and should not change. Check boxes should be aligned vertically. Figure 4.5 shows a window with a check box on it.

Group boxes (oval, rectangle, round rectangle)

Group boxes can greatly enhance groups of information and direct the viewer's eye in the required direction. Group boxes organize a screen into functional groups. This establishes structure and groups related information together. Place the group box label in the upper left corner of the group box, and generally use a 3D lowered style border. See Fig. 4.6 for an example of a group box.

Radio buttons

Radio buttons are used for selecting one out of a limited set of mutually exclusive options. The user can only select one option at a time. When an option is

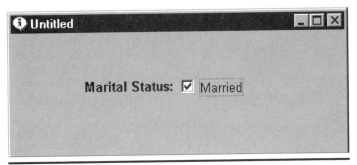

Figure 4.5 The check box contains values that represent on and off logical settings. If checked, the setting is on; if not checked, the setting is considered off.

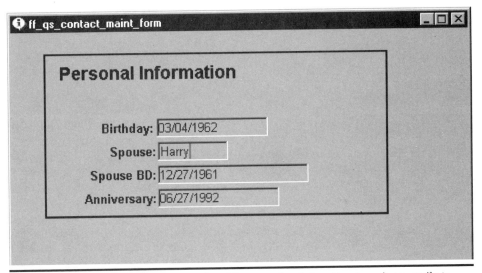

Figure 4.6 This is an example of a group box. The group box brings the viewer's eye easily to a group of related information.

selected, the circle is full. When it is not selected, the circle is empty. If you find you need more than five options, consider using a drop-down list box.

When radio buttons are aligned horizontally, use a minimum of five spaces between each radio button. This gives the screen a less crowded look. The radio button text should not change. A default radio button should be displayed when a window containing radio buttons is opened. Where applicable, provide a general choice such as "none" as part of the selection values to allow the user an alternative. Figure 4.7 shows an example of how a radio button should appear.

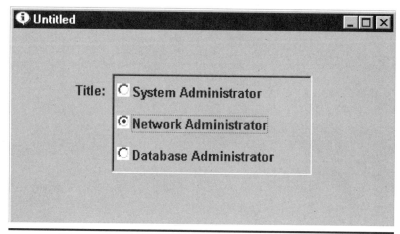

Figure 4.7 This is an example of a radio button. Only one option can be chosen at a time.

Error messages

When building validation rules, you have control over the message that displays when a user enters the wrong information. Provide good feedback to users. When applicable, include corrective action in the message text. A message stating, "XYZ is an invalid entry" is much less informative than a message reading, "You must enter a digit between 1 and 5 in the credit level column." And one final reminder: Always keep user messages simple, polite, and friendly.

MicroHelp

MicroHelp displays on the status bar at the bottom of the InfoMaker workspace. You have complete control over the MicroHelp messages that display for buttons in your applications. Make effective use of them. Instead of saying, "Open a form," a more descriptive entry is, "This button opens the Client Entry form." MicroHelp is an easy technique you can use to keep users informed while working with your application.

Fonts

Limiting the number of fonts to one or two in an application is a perfect example of the principle of less is more. Using more fonts detracts the eyes from the application and brings attention to the fonts. To make it easier on yourself, use one of the fonts installed with Windows. Otherwise when you distribute the application, users may not have the necessary fonts installed on their machines. Use bold text for labels, headings, and static text. Do not use bold for data columns. All text labels should be followed by a colon and be left aligned.

Color

Use color judiciously. Color-blind people or monochrome monitors make color on a screen illegible. Generally, screens should have the Windows default colors of black text on a gray background. Color is most effective for bringing out those portions of a window that you want the user to see most readily, such as a negative account balance displaying in red.

Graphs

Graphs should be used for larger data sets. Graphs should not be wasted on simple linear changes or situations where one or two numbers would summarize the result better. Minimize redundant data and maximize data density. In graphs, more information is better than less. The greater the amount of information displayed on a graph, the larger the number of visual comparisons that can be made, which improves comprehension. And finally, clearly label each axis and segment, and give the graph a title.

Pie charts should be used with caution because they provide no means of absolute measures, they cannot represent totals greater than 100 percent, and they can only represent a fixed point in time. If you decide to use a pie chart, use five segments or less and avoid very small segments. Segments should take at least 5 percent. Used in the right situations, pie charts can be very effective in displaying data graphically.

Text case

In most situations throughout an application, mixed case is the best option. This is because mixed case is easier and faster to read. Mixed case occurs when the first letters of important words are capitalized and the rest are lowercase. Capitalize all important words including the first word. Use mixed case for static text, messages, menu bars, and command buttons. No punctuation should be used with field labels. Being aware of the text case in your applications will make them easier for your users to read.

Abbreviations and symbols on windows

Text on application screens should be clear, unambiguous, and free of computer jargon. GUI standards call for the full spelling of words whenever possible. If you cannot use the full spelling because of space limitations, use a standard abbreviation. Consistent use of abbreviations and hyphens promotes user understanding and eases development decisions and maintenance.

Number formats

When you are using numbers in an application, there are several things to keep in mind. Dollar figures should be displayed in whole numbers with cents rounded. All dollar figures should be capable of displaying $999,999,999,999.99

as the largest figure. And dollar figures may be positive or negative. Display negative numbers in a red font within parentheses.

When you place a calculated column on a screen, the calculated column itself is not updateable. To change the calculated figure, the user must update the figures used in the calculation. In addition, percentage change calculations should be rounded to the nearest hundredth. Again, display negative percentages in a red font within parentheses.

There are also some miscellaneous items regarding other types of numbers to be aware of. When you enter dates, use the standard date format of `mm/dd/yyyy` and do not require the user to enter the slashes. Times should be entered using a standard time format `hh:mm am/pm`. Phone numbers should be formatted with parentheses around the area code and a dash between the phone number and prefix and suffix. And Zip codes should be displayed with a dash between the first five and the last four digits. Following these simple numeric rules will make it easier for users to move between applications in an organization.

Summary

We covered naming conventions for forms, reports, queries, and pipelines in this chapter, in addition to offering some suggestions for naming tables and columns. Although naming conventions may be cumbersome to deal with at first, they will truly pay off in the long run. Interface guidelines are also important when you are building an application. These guidelines enforce consistency, which makes learning and using an application much easier.

5

Project Development in InfoMaker

What You Will Learn

Chapter 5 discusses how to plan and implement an InfoMaker project. Whenever you start a new InfoMaker project, there are many factors that must be taken into account to ensure that the application you build meets your users' needs. This chapter will give you some guidelines to follow to guarantee that every project you work on is a success.

Project Development

Many of the concepts we cover in this chapter apply equally to any software development project. Although building an application in InfoMaker is a much less involved process than that using a complete development environment such as PowerBuilder, many of the same types of factors are involved and must be given careful thought before you proceed.

Applications built in InfoMaker are usually on a small to medium scale of magnitude. By this I mean that the "application" may consist of only one report that is run once a month. Other applications may be on the medium end of the scale, where custom forms built in PowerBuilder are brought into InfoMaker to enforce company standards, query libraries are accessed, data is transferred on a regular basis from another data source, and so on. There may be several forms, reports, data pipelines, and queries housed on a network and accessed by many people in the company in this type of application. Even if an application consists of one report, it is always a good idea to at least take a cursory look at each of the steps to project development outlined in this chapter. These steps will keep you on the right path and help you build better applications faster. What follows is a proven and time-tested method of project development.

Every application goes through what is commonly called, in the computer industry, a *project life cycle*. The application evolves through several phases during its lifetime, until eventually it is discarded and a new application is written to take its place. During each phase of the life cycle, there are certain things that you can do as an InfoMaker developer to prolong the life of an application, build applications faster, and build applications that do what users need them to do. Projects following these guidelines will be less expensive to maintain, more reliable, and acceptable to users. The larger the application, the more important it is to follow the procedures listed in this chapter.

The project life cycle is composed of the following phases:

1. Define the requirements.

2. Determine how to solve the problem.

3. Determine the database and object layouts.

4. Build the database.

5. Build and test a prototype.

6. Is the prototype acceptable? If so, continue with development; otherwise, go back to step 5 and work on the prototype again.

7. Finalize and test the application.

8. Is the application acceptable to users? If so, continue; otherwise, go back to step 7 and make modifications.

9. Distribute the application.

10. Maintain the application. If changes are requested, go back to step 1.

Before you build an InfoMaker application, define the system requirements. These requirements outline exactly what the application will accomplish and the things that will have to be in place before you actually create any InfoMaker objects. Once it is determined what the system must do, you must decide how it is going to accomplish its task. Ascertain if there are any modifications that can be made to existing databases or applications which will meet the system requirements. If there are existing processes in place, make the necessary modifications; otherwise, design and build a new database. Then build a prototype so that users have an opportunity to see how the final product will appear. Once the prototype is accepted, the system can be completed by making sure all the pieces of the system are properly in place and are tested thoroughly. During testing, users have a chance to go through the new system and work out any problems. Finally, the system is distributed to the user community. It is possible to go through several iterations of these steps before you finally enter the maintenance phase, where users or other circumstances may dictate continual changes to the system. Following the project life cycle ensures that all questions are answered, users are consulted, and the application is tested thoroughly before being deployed.

Defining the requirements

The requirements phase serves to

- Identify the scope of the current system
- Identify problems in the current system, either manual or automated
- Identify major objectives for the new system
- Estimate the costs of each possible solution to the user's problem
- Determine the advantages and disadvantages of each possible solution
- Develop outlines of how the project might be carried out
- Obtain a decision from management to support the project

Before you start building forms and reports, you should have a clear idea of what it is you're trying to accomplish. Ask yourself these types of questions:

Do I need to build an application that I can distribute over the network to coworkers to use, or will the application be used in a stand-alone environment?

Do I need to build one report that I will use only once?

Do I want to post forms on the Internet?

What types of information do I want to track?

Do I need to enter any information into a database?

What database will I need to access?

Do I have security access to the database?

Are there query or style libraries in existence that I can take advantage of?

Do I need to build tables to complete my project?

Will I be importing data to and exporting data from the system?

Will my application be used alone or with other applications?

Each of these questions will probably lead to a host of other questions. And that is good. The more questions you can confidently answer before you even touch InfoMaker, the more you will save lots of time and trouble down the line. You may need help from your network administrator, database administrator, and PowerBuilder developers before you begin. Other InfoMaker users in your organization will also be helpful and perhaps will have an application they have already built that you can use as a model for your application. You should be familiar with any company standards currently in place, and make sure you follow them. This will help not only you, but also others who follow you.

It is in this phase that either you or another person determines that there is a need for some type of system. The idea of developing a new system occurs when the user recognizes there is a problem in the way business is currently carried out or when an opportunity is identified to improve the business. The major goal here is to identify what problems have to be addressed. During this phase, problems and deficiencies in the user's environment are evaluated, with the assumption that they may provide the justification for developing new approaches. Establish what the new system should accomplish, determine if it is feasible to automate the business process requested, and suggest some possible solutions.

The system requirements can be outlined in four steps. First, interview the appropriate member(s) of the user community to identify the problems with the current system or procedure. On a small project, such as would normally occur in InfoMaker, this activity could require an interview with one or two users. Talking to users about their business processes is very important if the system is going to be successful.

Second, establish the system goals. For example, the user may point out that one of the deficiencies of the current system or procedure is that IS does not have time to build a report to retrieve information from the corporate database. So a goal of the new system would be to retrieve information from the database. Having a clearly defined goal keeps you heading in the right direction as you develop the new application.

Third, outline what can be done to solve the problem. Present the user with more than one solution, with advantages and disadvantages to following a particular route. This allows the user to make a choice. Additionally, there may be a time or money constraint on the project which may limit one solution or another. When you recommend a particular solution, determine whether any new hardware or software must be available before the system can be put in place. Outlining several possible solutions ensures that everyone can make an informed decision when building the new application.

Fourth, produce a document stating a working plan. Describe what you are going to build and what it will solve. For a simple project it may be a short sentence such as "I'm going to build a report to retrieve employee hire dates from the corporate database so human resources can build a seniority list." On larger projects, the requirements document may span several pages with a more formal template. This requirements document is used throughout the project.

Once the requirements are defined, you can decide how to put your plan of action into place. If there is currently a database or application in existence, decide what changes will have to be made to get the system to do what you want it to do. Determine database and object layouts. If the database layout is conducted well, then anyone can write the system; but if it is done poorly or not at all, you will have nothing but grief down the road. And finally, make sure that any system built does not affect the operations in another area of the organization. Once you have defined the system objectives, chosen a course of action, and decided how to implement the system, you are well on your way to deploying a successful application.

Build the database

Before you can build any forms or reports, you must have an underlying database to build upon. If the database already exists, so much the better. Make sure you have security access to all the tables you will be using in the application. If the database management system (DBMS) that you will be accessing is something other than SQL Anywhere, you must have all the correct drivers installed on your machine and a profile created in InfoMaker.

If the database does not exist, the first thing to do is to follow the system requirements previously gathered and determine the database layout. Define the relationships between tables and any necessary indexes. One of the hardest things for beginning InfoMaker users to learn is relational database design. Chapter 7, Working with Databases, gives a general overview of database design and how to create a database. For more information, there are many books on the market covering this subject in depth, and I highly recommend that you consult one before proceeding.

Once the tables are created, make sure the extended attributes are set the way you prefer. It is easier to use the default settings when you are building forms and reports than to set each column's attributes manually in each object. At this point, you know what you are going to build and how you are going to build it, and you have the database in place as a foundation for the rest of the application. Now it is time to build the InfoMaker objects.

Build and test the prototype

For any application, large or small, you may want to consider building a prototype. Prototyping is a process of creating a working model of a new application. This working model is created so the user can interact with the application to get a more realistic feeling for the system functions. InfoMaker lends itself well to this type of environment because building forms and reports can be done quickly. Once a prototype is complete, it can be used in meetings to discuss any modifications needed before it is actually distributed. Prototyping enables InfoMaker developers to build applications that do a better job of meeting an organization's needs in a short time span and at a lower cost.

Finalize and test the application

Now that we have the underlying tables, and possibly a prototype, in place, it is just a matter of making sure that all the pieces of the puzzle are in place to ensure the application is successfully deployed.

If there are company standards regarding forms, consult a PowerBuilder or other InfoMaker developer in your organization. If you need any special functionality that InfoMaker cannot provide, work with a PowerBuilder developer to create any forms you will need. If you decide the system is large enough to warrant doing so, you may want to include a Help system with the application. You will need the help of a PowerBuilder developer to link your InfoMaker application to the Help system.

Before testing, you will want to determine the type of things to test. This is called a *test plan*. The nature of the test plan will obviously vary from project to project, but without some kind of organized plan, there is little hope of building a well-tested system. Testing should answer the question, Does this system do what it was built to do? The test plan should cover the people needed to test the system, testing guidelines and criteria for determining when the test is completed. One criterion for determining when testing is complete may be that every form, report, or other object in the application must be invoked at least once. Results of all the test cases where the actual results differed from the expected result are analyzed, and appropriate action is taken.

The initial goal of the test plan should be the establishment of a person or a group responsible for testing the system. For obvious reasons, the person responsible should be someone other than the developer. Testing should be done by someone who understands that the process has the express intention of finding errors; that is, the test should be a thoroughly diabolical attempt to cause system failures. Where can one find such devious minds? Certainly not among members of the development group. The users may be a good source of error test cases.

Standards need to be developed for the construction of test cases, and it is a goal of the test plan to establish procedures and standards for testing. There should also be standards for the documentation of test cases and results, naming conventions for files of test data, and standards for storing and retrieving sets of test data.

When you are putting the finishing touches on an application, do not forget system and user documentation. System documentation is used by other InfoMaker or PowerBuilder developers who may have to make modifications to the system. Each column's description should be placed in the system documentation, as well as the purpose for each object, any libraries accessed, where custom forms reside, etc. User documentation consists of some type of manual describing how to use the system. Even if it is just a small system running one report, if there is the possibility that someone else may have to run the report, write up a quick reference sheet outlining the steps necessary to complete the report. This will make using the system much faster and easier for someone who may not be as familiar with computers as you are.

If you are writing an InfoMaker application for yourself, you have been testing as you built each module. You have made sure your queries are retrieving the information you want and displaying it in the way you want. But if you are developing an application that will be used by many people on a network, you will want users to put your application through the paces so they can be assured that everything works just as they want. Evaluate their feedback and make any necessary changes. If users are involved in the project from the beginning, they will accept the application much more readily.

Distributing the application

The details of implementation are unique for each project; however, the following issues will almost certainly have to be addressed. First, the detail of when the system will be installed must be settled. Careful planning is usually required to ensure that the installation of the new system does not disrupt the users' day-to-day business.

Second, one must determine when the old system will be dismantled. No matter how thorough the testing, the user will almost certainly insist that the new system be run in parallel with the old system for some period of time. The old system is a safety net in case something goes wrong. The user also realizes that the parallel operation is frustrating, especially for the person who has to verify that the new system is operating properly. But the user knows that pulling the plug on the old system is probably an irrevocable act.

Finally, it is essential to decide how the users should be trained. On a small project, training can be informal. The system is usually intrinsically simple, the user manual is adequate, and the developer is available if questions or problems arise.

Once the application is built and you are ready to deploy it, create an executable and distribute it, using InfoMaker's Install Builder. For more information on how to complete this task, see Chap. 16, Creating and Distributing a Complete Application.

Installation is the end of the road. It is the final joining of the application, user manual, and new database. In a small project, installation should be almost anticlimactic. If the previous activities have been carried out properly, the project should end not with a bang, but with a whisper. The system is officially declared operational, and the users begin typing transactions. Anything that happens to the system from this point on is called *maintenance.*

Maintaining the system

Just when you thought you were finished with the application, someone comes back and says something to the effect, "This is nice, but can it do X?" These are words that developers come to dread. You have to go back in and figure out how you got that negative balance to display in asterisks and on which screen it appeared, for instance. This is where the standards you implemented from Chap. 4, Standards and Guidelines, and the documentation put in place earlier will save you time and frustration.

A few years after the delivery of a traditional system, changes during maintenance become extremely tedious, error-prone, and expensive. Ideally, management recognizes the problem and does a feasibility study to replace the old system with a new one. Thus the cycle begins anew.

Project development in InfoMaker is not a difficult task. Most of the applications built in InfoMaker are on the smaller side, which makes managing them easier. But being aware of the project life cycle and following these proven methods to project development ensure that the applications you deploy are readily accepted by your users. This all translates to another success story to add to your resume.

Project Directory Structures

Every application, no matter how large or small, goes through an iterative process of modification, testing, and production once it has been deployed. You may end up with several different versions of an application residing on the network. One version may be the one that is currently installed and being used. Another version may be a beta version that is currently being tested. And finally, another version may be currently in the development process where you are adding new forms, changing reports, etc.

It would be very easy to lose track of these different versions and inadvertently install perhaps the development version in the current working environment. One way to track all the versions is to use specific subdirectory structures.

To use this method, have a directory or folder set up on the network for an application. Under this main directory are the three subdirectories DEVL, BETA, and PROD. Each version resides in the appropriate subdirectory until it is time to copy it to the next level. So, for instance, a developer works on a new application in the DEVL subdirectory. When the application is completed and ready to be user-tested, it is copied into the BETA directory. This is where users will access it for testing. Once the application is thoroughly tested and users are satisfied with it, it is copied into the PROD directory.

After it is put into production, users may want a new report or some other change. The InfoMaker developer makes changes to the DEVL directory, and the application follows the same progression as before. Using this type of directory scheme keeps all the different versions of the applications organized and thus easy to find.

Summary

We discussed some of the issues you should keep in mind as you plan your InfoMaker project. Each project has a life cycle that it follows, from determining there is a need for a system, to maintaining a system. Following the project development methods in this chapter ensures successful application delivery. We also discussed one way to track multiple versions of an application within the corporation. You now have the tools you need to start planning your InfoMaker projects.

6

The Environment Painter

What You Will Learn

Chapter 6 is an overview of the Environment painter. This chapter explains what a library is and how to maintain one. You will learn how to manipulate and access objects from the Environment painter. You will learn how to copy, move, and delete objects and to define style and query libraries. We will also cover how to open and delete a library. By the end of this chapter, you will be completely comfortable with the Environment painter.

The Library

InfoMaker holds all the forms, reports, queries, and pipelines you create in a *library*. You can have only one library open at a time. Using the Environment painter, you can manipulate objects in a library, move them from one library to another, and create and open libraries. Figure 6.1 shows an example of the Environment painter with objects in an open library displayed.

Maintaining a library

Maintaining libraries in InfoMaker consists of modifying objects to maintain consistency, such as adding comments, or deleting those objects which are no longer needed. Within the Environment painter it is also possible to create a library to contain a new application's objects or to open a different library. Think of the Environment painter as InfoMaker's File Manager or Explorer. It is simply a way to manage all the objects placed in an InfoMaker pibble, or library, file.

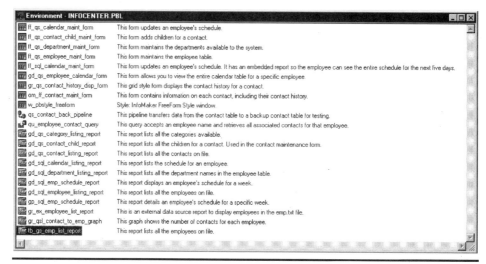

Figure 6.1 This is the Environment painter showing all the InfoMaker objects in a library.

Creating a new library

When you begin a new project, a directory or folder must be created. Then the library is created and placed in the directory. Finally, objects are created and placed in the new library. All objects for a particular project should be placed in the same library. This makes finding and working with objects within an application much easier.

To create a directory by using Windows 3.1, do the following:

1. Double-click on File Manager in the Main window.
2. Select the root directory on your computer, normally c:\ , by clicking on it with the mouse to highlight it.
3. Select File | Create Directory... from the menu.
4. In the Create Directory dialog box that displays, type the directory name.
5. Click OK.

To create a folder using Windows 95, do the following:

1. Select Explorer from the Program Start menu.
2. Make sure c:\ in your root directory on the local drive is highlighted.
3. Select File | New | Folder from the menu.
4. Type the folder name.
5. Press Enter to accept the new name.

Now that a directory exists in which to place a library, using the Environment painter, create the new library in the directory which will contain the InfoMaker objects.

To create a new library:

1. Enter the Environment painter, by clicking on the Environment painter button on the PowerBar.
   or
   Select the Environment painter item from the PowerPanel.
   or
   Press the key combination SHIFT + F5.
   or
   Select the Environment painter button in the PowerBar's drop-down toolbar.

2. Select the New button on the Environment painter's toolbar, or select File | New from the menu.

3. The Select Library dialog box displays, as shown in Fig. 6.2. Move to the desired subdirectory.

4. Name the library.

5. Click on Save.

Deleting a library

Once a library is no longer needed, it can be deleted from the computer. Removing outdated libraries saves disk space. However, a library cannot be deleted from within InfoMaker. A library is deleted from either File Manager or Explorer.

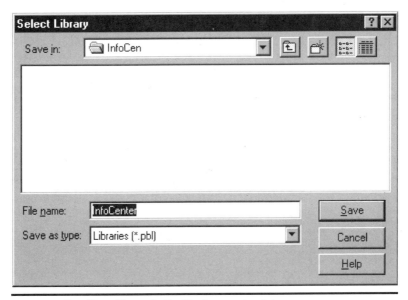

Figure 6.2 Creating a library in the Environment painter.

To delete an InfoMaker library using Windows 3.1, do the following:

1. Enter the File Manager.
2. Select the directory containing the library.
3. Select the .pbl file to delete.
4. Press the Delete key on the keyboard.

To delete an InfoMaker library using Windows 95, do the following:

1. Enter the Explorer.
2. Select the folder containing the library to delete.
3. Select the .pbl file to delete.
4. Press the Delete key on the keyboard, or choose File | Delete from the menu and when prompted, confirm the delete.

Opening a library

Since only one library can be open at a time, as soon as another library is opened, the first library is automatically closed. You will want to change libraries whenever you work on a different project.

To open a library, do the following:

1. Select File | Open from the menu.
   or
   Choose the Open button on the Environment painter bar.
2. Go to the desired folder and select the library file, as Fig. 6.3 demonstrates.
3. Now click on Open. The library opens, and you can work there.

Showing comments and modification dates

In the Environment painter, it is possible to view the comments and the modification dates for objects in a library. The comments are a sentence or two that you have entered to describe a particular object. The modification date is the date stamp InfoMaker places on an object each time it is changed. The last date it was changed displays as the modification date. The Environment painter workspace can be customized to show comments, the modification date, or both. These options are toggled on and off.

To view the Comments or Modification Date in the Environment painter, choose Design | Comments or Modification Date from the menu, or right-click on the Environment workspace and choose the Comments or Modification Date option from the pop-up menu, as shown in Fig. 6.4.

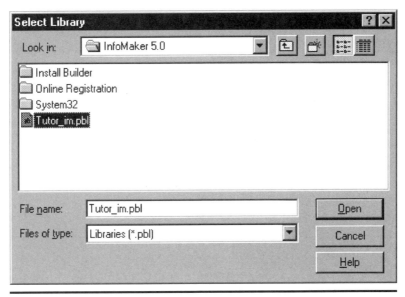

Figure 6.3 Opening a library using the Environment painter.

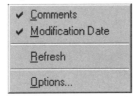

Figure 6.4 The Design Menu in the Environment painter contains options to toggle the Show Comments and Show Modification Dates for objects in the Environment painter workspace.

Creating executables

It is from within the Environment painter that executable files are created for distribution to the user community. Since this is such a large topic, it is covered in depth separately in Chap. 16, Creating and Distributing a Complete Application.

The Form Style Library

A form style library is created by the PowerBuilder developers in your organization. A form style library is simply a library containing additional form presentation styles which are made available when you build InfoMaker forms.

Remember that InfoMaker comes with four presentation styles: free-form, grid, master/detail one-to-many, and master/detail many-to-one. Using a form style, additional types of forms are available. Before you use a style library, it must be identified from within InfoMaker.

To identify a form style library:

1. Select Design | Options from the Environment painter's menu. The Environment property sheet displays, as in Fig. 6.5.

2. Click the Browse... button on the property sheet.

3. The Open dialog box displays. Select the library containing the form styles.

4. Click OK. The library appears in the library search path list on the Environment property sheet.

5. Click OK to accept the changes.

Query Library

Within the Environment painter is also the ability to define query libraries. Query libraries are a collection of SQL queries built previously by using either InfoMaker or PowerBuilder. Using a query library speeds up development time

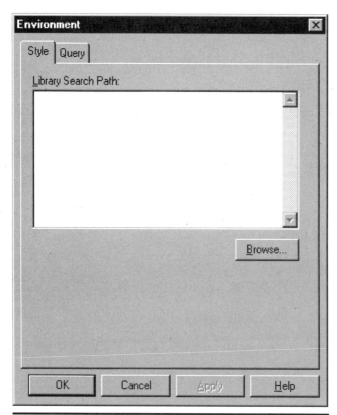

Figure 6.5 The Environment painter property sheet.

because you do not have to keep creating the same query repeatedly to retrieve data from the database.

To define a query library, do the following:

1. From within the Environment painter, select Design | Options from the menu.

2. The Environment property sheet displays. Select the Query tab. The screen should look like Fig. 6.6.

3. Press the Browse... button and select the library containing the prebuilt queries.

4. Click OK to accept the changes. When you are finished, the property sheet should look similar to Fig. 6.7.

Unassigning Style and Query Libraries

When a style or query library is no longer needed for a particular project, the library can be removed from the project definition. The library still exists; however, it can no longer be accessed from the open application.

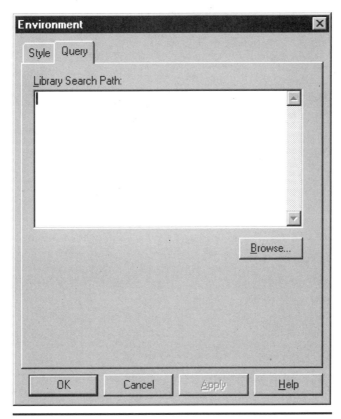

Figure 6.6 Defining a Query library using the Environment painter property sheet.

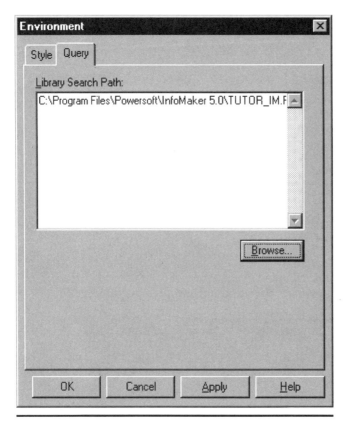

Figure 6.7 Defining a Query library for use within an Info-Maker application.

To unassign a style or query library:

1. In the Environment painter, select Design | Options to open the Environment property sheet.

2. Select either the Style or the Query tab, and highlight the library no longer needed, as shown in Fig. 6.8.

3. Press the Delete key.

4. Press OK to accept the changes.

Accessing InfoMaker Objects

From within the Environment painter you can also open and preview existing forms, reports, queries and pipelines. The Environment painter is not capable of creating new objects here. Objects can only be created from their respective painters. Within the Environment painter, objects can only be opened.

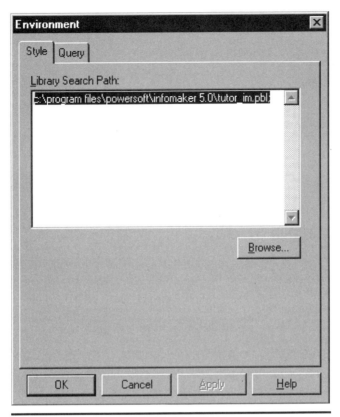

Figure 6.8   Removing a Style Library from the current project using the Environment painter property sheet.

Opening objects

To open an object in the Environment painter, do the following:

1. Double-click on the object in the Environment painter workspace.
    or
    Choose the Open button on the Environment painter bar.
    or
    Right-click on the item in the Environment painter. The Environment painter's pop-up menu displays, as shown in Fig. 6.9.

2. To open the object in Design mode, choose the Edit option from either the pop-up menu or the Environment Entry menu.
    or

3. To open the object in Preview mode, choose the Run/Preview option from the pop-up menu or the Environment Entry menu.

Figure 6.9 From the pop-up menu in the Environment painter, an InfoMaker object can be opened in either Edit mode or Preview mode.

Copying, moving, and deleting objects

In addition to working with the libraries themselves, we can work with the objects in a library from the Environment painter. Using the Environment painter, we can copy and move objects to different libraries, and we can delete objects that are no longer needed.

To copy an object to a different library:

1. Select the object(s) to copy from the current library, using the mouse.

2. Select Entry | Copy from the Environment painter menu.
   or
   Select the Copy button on the Environment painter bar.
   or
   Right-click on the object(s) in the workspace, and choose Copy from the pop-up menu.

3. The Select Library dialog box opens. Open the library to copy the object(s), as shown in Fig. 6.10.

4. Click on Open. InfoMaker copies the object to the destination library.

Moving an object to a different library deletes the object in the current library and copies it to the new library. Deleting an object removes it from the library entirely. The Move and Delete options in the Environment painter are used for these actions. The Move and Delete options work exactly the same way as the Copy option. Just highlight an object in the source library (the library where the object currently resides) and select the appropriate action (move or delete). When moving objects, InfoMaker prompts for the destination library (the library to which you want to move the object).

Modifying comments

When saving a new object, you have the opportunity to enter a short description about the object. Comments are a useful way to see at a glance an object's

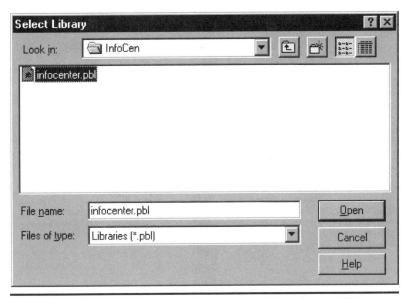

Figure 6.10 Selecting the destination library to copy objects from one library to another.

purpose. It is good practice to have comments for each object. Once you have entered comments associated with an object, it is very easy to modify them.

To modify object comments, do the following:

1. Select the object to change by clicking on it once with the mouse.

2. Right-click on the object and select Modify Comments... from the pop-up menu or Select Entry | Modify Comments from the Environment painter menu, as shown in Fig. 6.11.

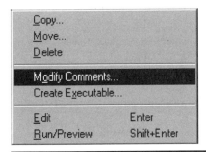

Figure 6.11 Select Entry | Modify Comments from the Environment painter menu to change the comments on an object.

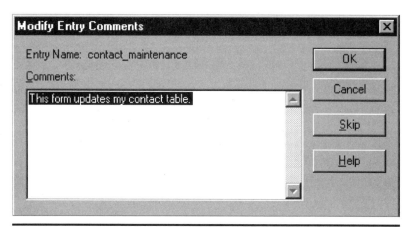

Figure 6.12 The Modify Entry Comments dialog box can be used to change the comments on an InfoMaker object.

3. The Modify Entry Comments dialog displays, as shown in Fig. 6.12.

4. Change the comments.

5. Press OK to accept the changes.

   If you have selected several objects on which to change the comments, modify the first object's comments and then press the Skip button on the Modify Entry Comments dialog box. This will open the next item in the list so you can change the comments.

Putting It All Together

In this section we will put into practice what we discussed in this chapter. We will create a directory in which to place our InfoCenter application files and a library in that directory to contain our forms, reports, queries, and pipelines.
   To create a directory using Windows 3.1, do the following:

1. Double-click on File Manager in the Main window.

2. Select the root directory on your computer, normally c:\, by clicking on it with the mouse to highlight it.

3. Select File | Create Directory... from the menu.

4. In the Create Directory dialog box that displays, type in "InfoCen."

5. Click OK. The directory is now on your system.

   To create a directory using Windows 95, do the following:

1. Select Explorer from the Programs Start menu.

2. Make sure c:\ in your root directory on your local drive is highlighted.

3. Select File | New | Folder from the menu.

4. Type "InfoCen" as the directory name.

5. Press Enter to accept the new name.

Now, using the Environment painter, we create a new library in our InfoCen subdirectory to contain the objects we will be building for the InfoCenter application throughout this book.

1. Start the Environment painter by clicking on the Environment painter button on the PowerBar.
    or
    Select the Environment painter item from the PowerPanel.
    or
    Press the key combination SHIFT + F5.
    or
    Select the Environment painter button in the PowerBar's drop-down toolbar.

2. Choose the New button on the Environment painter's toolbar, or select File | New from the menu.

3. The Select Library dialog box displays. Move to the InfoCen subdirectory.

4. Name the library "InfoCenter."

5. Click on Save.

Summary

Chapter 6 provides an overview of the Environment painter. This chapter explains what a library is and how to maintain it. How to manipulate and access an object in InfoMaker is also covered. We discussed the things you can do in the Environment painter, including how to create and move objects between libraries. We also talked about how to copy, move, and delete objects in a library. We discussed what a form and query library was and why you would use one. You should now be familiar with the Environment painter.

7

Working with Databases

What You Will Learn

Chapter 7 discusses how to work with databases in the InfoMaker environment. There is a short database design primer which gives you a basic understanding of databases, tables, columns, and views. You will learn how to create tables, display formats, edit styles, and validation rules. We will also talk about implementing some basic security on database tables. You will understand how to index and create keys on tables. When you finish this chapter, you will be well on your way to understanding the underlying functionalities behind InfoMaker objects.

Database Design Primer

As we discussed in Chap. 1, data is information about something. That something could relate to customers, such as their names and addresses, or inventory, such as product and quantity on hand. Data is anything you want to track. Each item of information, such as customer name, product, etc., is placed in a column in a table. A collection of data related to something, such as a customer, is held in a table. And a database is simply a collection of related tables.

All the information about one customer in a table—the name, address, phone number, etc.—is called a *row*. Each table has many rows of information, so you can have information on file for Josephine Smith, John Doe, and every other customer in an organization. Figure 7.1 shows a graphical example of a database structure. Notice that a database is composed of several tables, each containing related information about a logical grouping of data. Each of these tables, in turn, is composed of columns, which are individual items of information.

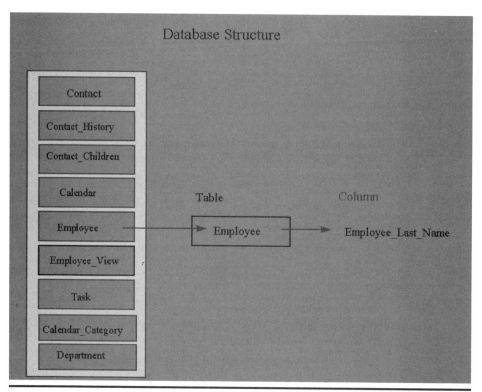

Figure 7.1 This is an example of a database hierarchy showing a column, table, and a database.

The tables in a database sometimes have relationships with other tables. For instance, an employee is usually related to a specific department within an organization. This type of relationship is denoted with the use of primary and foreign keys. A *primary key* is a column in a table which makes the row unique. The primary or foreign key can be anything—a social security number, an employee identification, or a department number. The keys can even be generated by the system if necessary. All that is required is that a column be identified in each table which differentiates one column from another. This enables the database system to recognize each individual row of information.

InfoMaker is bundled with a product called SQL Anywhere. SQL Anywhere is a database management system (DBMS). InfoMaker provides a graphical interface to work with data in a database. Regardless of whether the DBMS containing your data is SQL Anywhere, Oracle, Sybase, or one of a dozen other products, you can access the database through the graphical interface. This makes it much easier to manipulate data within InfoMaker systems.

How the Database Painter and Table Painter Work Together

The Database painter is used primarily to manage entire tables. The Table painter's purpose is to create the table structure and any extended attributes related to the columns. The Database painter and the Table painter are independent of each other, but when they are both open at the same time, they work together. For example, when you are creating and saving a table definition in the Table painter, the Table painter notifies the Database painter that a new table exists and the new table displays in all instances of the Database painter. If an index is added in the Database painter, you can see the change in the Table Properties property sheet in the Table painter.

Creating a New Database

Before you start any project, one of the first things to do is create a database. Remember, a database contains all the information needed for an application, or several applications if necessary.

To create a new database:

1. From the PowerBar or the PowerPanel, select the Database painter button.

2. When the Select Tables dialog box displays (see Fig. 7.2), click on Cancel.

3. Select File | Create Database from the Database painter menu, as shown in Fig. 7.3.

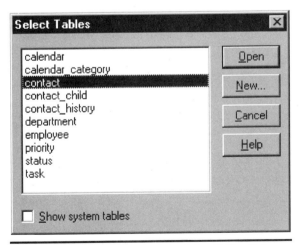

Figure 7.2 This is an example of the Select Tables dialog box.

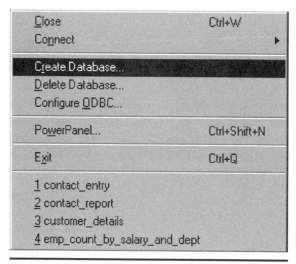

<u>C</u>lose	Ctrl+W
Co<u>n</u>nect	▶
C<u>r</u>eate Database...	
<u>D</u>elete Database...	
Configure <u>O</u>DBC...	
Po<u>w</u>erPanel...	Ctrl+Shift+N
E<u>x</u>it	Ctrl+Q
<u>1</u> contact_entry	
<u>2</u> contact_report	
<u>3</u> customer_details	
<u>4</u> emp_count_by_salary_and_dept	

Figure 7.3 This is the File menu in the Database painter menu. Choosing the Create Database... option creates a new SQL Anywhere database.

4. The Create Local Database dialog box displays. For a discussion of the proper entries for this dialog box, please refer to the section "Create Local Database" in this chapter.

5. Click OK to create the database.

Create Local Database

The Create Local Database dialog box, shown in Fig. 7.4, is accessed whenever a new database is created in InfoMaker. This section discusses the available options on this dialog box and the purpose of each of the settings.

Create Local Database		
<u>D</u>atabase Name:	c:\infocen\infocen.db	OK
<u>U</u>ser ID:	DBA	Cancel
<u>P</u>assword:	xxx	Browse...
<u>S</u>tart Command:	dbeng50	Help
☐ Prompt for Password during <u>C</u>onnect		More>>

Figure 7.4 This is an example of the Create Local Database dialog box. Filling out information in this box gives the path name and start parameters for a new database.

Database name

When you create a database, the actual filename must be specified before InfoMaker can access it. In the Database Name area of the Create Local Database dialog box, enter the path name and the name of the database to create. If there is no path name, the database is created in the current directory.

User id and password

When creating a new database, InfoMaker automatically enters the default database user id and password of DBA and SQL. The security in your environment depends on how security is authorized in your organization. See your network or database administrator for more information.

Start command

Before InfoMaker can send the command to SQL Anywhere to start the database, it must be sent the appropriate command. This command is specified in the Start Command area of the Create Local Database dialog box. The Start Command for an SQL Anywhere database is dbeng50. Each DBMS has a different start command. For the command needed in your DBMS, consult your DBMS documentation.

Prompt for password during connect

It is possible to have SQL Anywhere prompt for a password each time you connect to the database. This is specified with the Prompt for Password During Connect option on the Create Local Database dialog box when you create a new database.

Use case-sensitive names

To ensure that table and column names are case-sensitive, choose the More≫ button on the Create Local Database dialog box to access additional database create options (see Fig. 7.5). If the case-sensitive option is enabled, a column named employee_id is different from a column called EMPLOYEE_ID. Leaving the Use case-sensitive names check box blank sets the database to case-insensitive.

Use ANSI Blank Behavior

If you want the database to ignore trailing blanks when doing comparisons between string items in a database, select the Use ANSI Blank Behavior check box on the Create Local Database dialog box. Setting the Use ANSI Blank Behavior means that "Internal Revenue Service" and "Internal Revenue Service   " are the same.

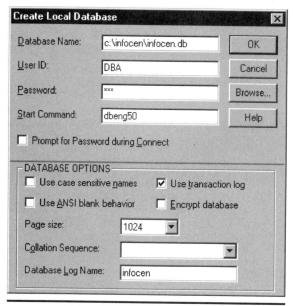

Figure 7.5 Additional options on the Create Local Database dialog box enable more specific settings when you create a new database.

Use Transaction Log

To record every change made to the database, select the Use Transaction Log check box on the Create Local Database dialog box. This option is useful for backup and recovery purposes. InfoMaker has this check box enabled by default and you can enter the log name in the Database Log Name box. If the Use Transaction Log box were not checked, then the Database Log Name box would be disabled and you would not be able to specify the log name.

Encrypt database

It is possible to encrypt a database. When a database is encrypted, it is much more difficult for someone to access the data in it. This option is enabled by checking the Encrypt database check box on the Create Local Database dialog box.

Page size

The page size refers to the amount of space the database requires to contain information. For small databases, accept the default size. For larger databases, contact your database administrator for more information.

Collation sequence

The Collation Sequence box is used to tell SQL Anywhere about any special considerations for string comparisons in the database. There are many options available in this drop-down list box to select different code pages for a specific country. Normally, we can leave this set at the default.

Database Profiles

A database profile is used within InfoMaker to create a fast way to move between databases. It contains the connection information necessary for SQL Anywhere and InfoMaker to access a database. InfoMaker provides the tools necessary to create, change, and delete the profiles.

Creating and editing a database profile

InfoMaker automatically creates a database profile for SQL Anywhere databases when the database is created with either InfoMaker or PowerBuilder. However, for other database products, the profile will have to be created manually.

To create a database profile for an SQL Anywhere database, do the following:

1. Select the DB Profs button on the Database painter bar.
   or
   Choose File | Connect | Setup from the menu. The Database Profiles dialog box displays, as shown in Fig. 7.6.

2. To create a new profile, choose the New... button. To edit an existing profile, select the Edit... button. The Database Profile Setup dialog box displays, as shown in Fig. 7.7.

3. Give the profile a name, and select the DBMS. For SQL Anywhere, choose ODBC.

4. Choose OK. The SQL Data Sources dialog box displays, as shown in Fig. 7.8.

5. Select the database.

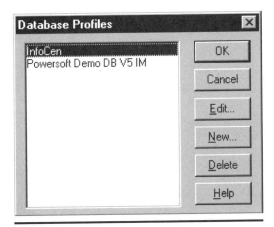

Figure 7.6 The Database Profiles dialog box is used to create, edit, and delete database profiles.

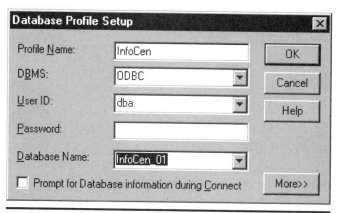

Figure 7.7   The Database Profile Setup dialog box is used to set attributes in a database profile.

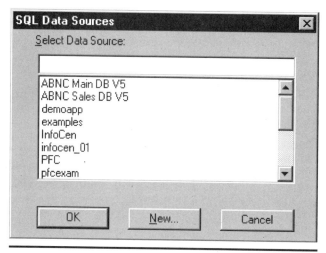

Figure 7.8   Choose a database for setting the profile in the SQL Data Sources dialog box.

6. Choose OK. InfoMaker automatically extracts the information it needs to complete the profile.

7. When you have finished entering information, choose OK to exit.

For more information on creating database profiles, see the InfoMaker documentation.

Deleting a database profile

When a database profile is no longer needed on the system, it is possible to remove it. Make sure that the database to which it refers is not on the system and will not be needed before you delete the profile.

To delete a database profile, do the following:

1. Select the DB Profs button on the Database painter bar.
   or
   Choose File | Connect | Setup from the menu. The Database Profiles dialog box displays.

2. Choose the Delete button on the Database Profiles dialog box. There is no confirmation here, so be careful where you click.

3. When you have finished, choose OK.

Working with Database Tables

Once the database is created and a profile is defined to access the database, you can start creating the database tables to contain information. When you design the tables, they should contain some type of related information. For more information on proper table and database design, refer to any number of database design books on the market.

Creating database tables

Once the actual database is created, add tables and columns which will contain the data. Tables are created within the Table painter. The Table painter is accessed either from the Database painter or from the PowerBar.

To create a database table from within the Database painter, do the following:

1. Click the Table button in the Database painter bar.
   or
   Select Object | New | Table from the menu, as shown in Fig. 7.9. The Create Table window appears, as shown in Fig. 7.10.

2. Fill out the necessary information for all the column attributes. For more information on each of the entries available on this window, see the section on the Table painter in this chapter.

3. When you have finished defining the columns for the table, do one of the following:
   Choose the Close button from the Table painter bar.
   or
   Choose the Close option from the File menu.
   or
   Choose SaveAs from the File menu.
   or
   Choose the Save button from the Table painter bar.

Opening existing tables

Once a table is created, it can be opened in the Database painter at any time for viewing or additional manipulation.

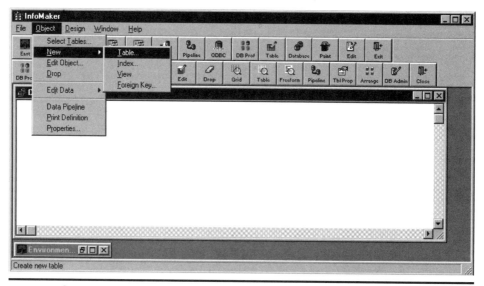

Figure 7.9 One way to create a new database table is to select Object | New | Table from the Database painter menu.

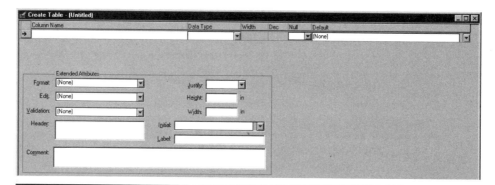

Figure 7.10 The Table painter's Create Table window contains areas to add columns and extended attributes to a column.

To open a table in the Database painter, do the following:

1. Choose the Open button on the Database painter bar, or choose Objects | Select Tables...from the menu.

2. Select the tables to open by clicking on them with the mouse.

3. Choose Open when you have finished.

Editing existing tables

After a table is opened in the Database painter, it is possible to open the table in the Table painter and to modify extended attributes, add and delete columns, etc. However, when you modify an existing table, the data type and null column are inaccessible and cannot be changed.

To edit an existing table from the Database painter, do the following:

1. Select the table in the Database painter workspace by clicking on it with the mouse. The title bar indicates when the table is selected.

2. Select Object | Edit Object from the menu.
   or
   Click on the Edit button on the Database painter bar.
   or
   Right-click on the title bar of the table and choose Alter Table from the menu.

For more information on modifying a table, see the section "The Table Painter" in this chapter.

Deleting a table

When a table is no longer needed, it can be dropped from the database. When a table is deleted, the data contained in the table and the table definition are deleted. Once a table is deleted, it cannot be retrieved.

To delete a table in the Database painter, do the following:

1. Open the table to delete.

2. Right-click on the table's title bar, and choose Drop Table from the pop-up menu.
   or
   Select Object | Drop from the Database painter menu.
   or
   Choose the Drop button on the Database painter bar. InfoMaker displays a message to verify the deletion.

3. Choose Yes to delete the table or No to return to the Database painter.

Editing Data

To quickly access data in a table without having to create a form or report, access the Data Manipulation painter from the Database painter. There are three different views available to work with the data: table, grid, or free-form. These three buttons are accessible from the Database painter bar or from the Object | Edit Data menu item. For more information about the Data Manipulation painter, see Chap. 8, Working with Data in InfoMaker.

Data Pipeline

The Data Pipeline is a tool to transfer data between two tables in a database or between two different databases. For more information about the Data Pipeline, see Chap. 15, The Data Pipeline.

To access the Data Pipeline, do one of the following:

Choose the Pipeline button on the Database painter bar.

or

Choose Object | Data Pipeline from the Database painter menu.

Display Format Maintenance

A display format is a column definition that specifies how the data in a column displays on a form or report. Before a display format can be specified for a column in the Table painter or from a form or report, it must be created. Accessing the Display Format Maintenance option in the Database painter reveals the options necessary to complete this task.

To add a display format to the current database, do the following:

1. In the Database painter, select Design | Display Format Maintenance from the menu, as shown in Fig. 7.11. The Display Formats dialog box displays, as in Fig. 7.12.

2. Click on the New... button on the Display Formats dialog box. The Display Format Definition dialog box displays, as shown in Fig. 7.13.

3. Enter the name of the new display format.

4. Choose a display type. There are five different types to choose from in the Type drop-down list box: string, number, date, time, and datetime.

5. In the Format box, enter the format for the display.

6. Enter a test value.

7. Click on the Test button. The way the column appears is displayed in the Test box. An example is shown in Fig. 7.14.

8. Click OK in the Display Format Definition box.

9. Click on Close in the Display Formats box.

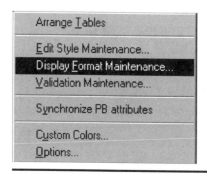

Figure 7.11 The Display Format Maintenance option from the Design menu in the Database painter.

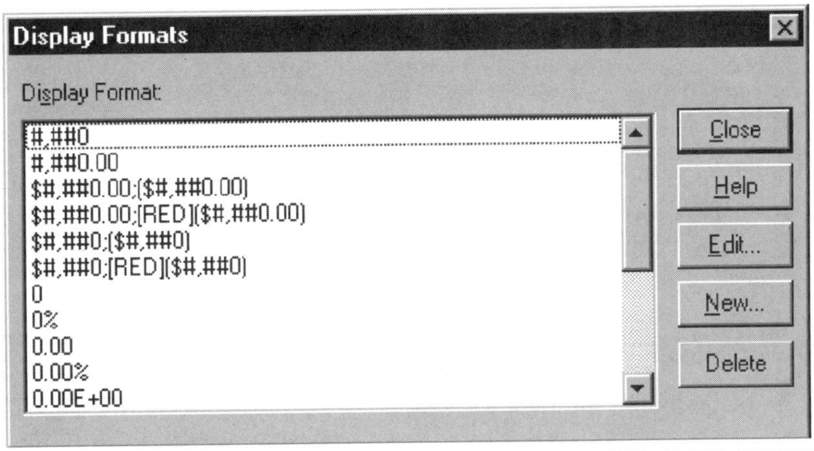

Figure 7.12 The Display Formats dialog box shows all the display formats available from which to choose.

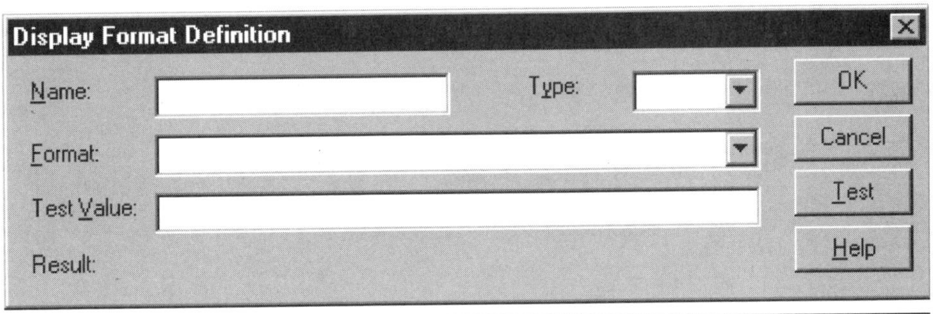

Figure 7.13 The Display Format Definition dialog box. Enter a new display format and test it here.

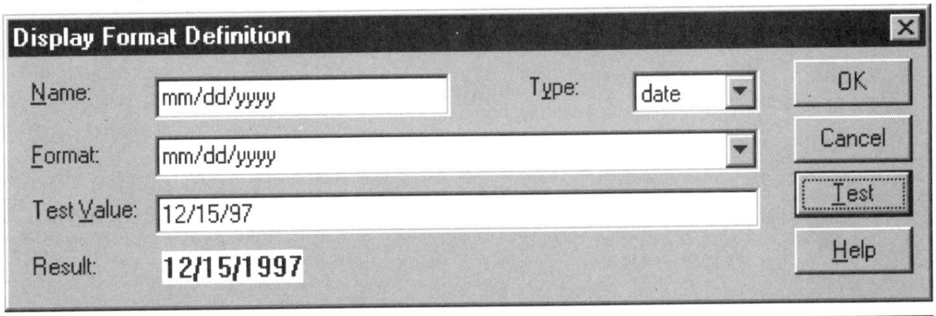

Figure 7.14 Entering a value in the Test value area and choosing the Test button display how the data appears.

Edit Style Maintenance

An edit style specifies how data in a column must be entered on a form or report. Before an edit style can be used for a column in the Table painter, or on a form or report, it must be defined. This is accomplished by accessing the edit style maintenance options in the Database painter.

To add an edit style, do the following:

1. Select Design | Edit Style Maintenance from the Database painter menu. The Edit Styles dialog box displays, as shown in Fig. 7.15.

2. Click on the New... button on the Edit Styles dialog box. The Edit Style dialog box displays.

3. Fill out the desired options. For a complete discussion of all the available options on the Edit Styles dialog box, see the section "Edit Style Options" in this chapter.

4. Choose OK on the Edit Style dialog box when you have finished setting options.

5. Choose OK on the Edit Styles dialog box when you have finished adding edit styles.

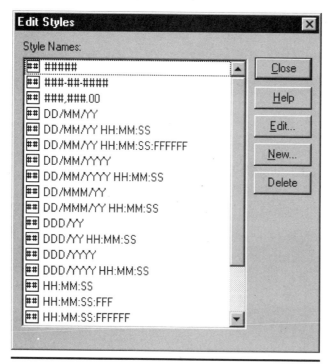

Figure 7.15 The Edit Styles dialog box displays all the available edit styles currently defined.

Edit Style Options

When defining an edit style for a column in the Edit Styles dialog box, you will notice that there are several choices in the Style Names drop-down list box. Each of the styles is distinct from the others and serves a specific purpose. The type of data being displayed and the easiest way to enter data into the column determine which edit style to use. There are five edit styles available in InfoMaker. Edit, which is the default, displays a value in a box. It accepts a value typed in from the keyboard. The DropDownListBox option displays a value in a drop-down list on a report or form. When you enter data, a value is selected from a list. The CheckBox style displays a column as a check box, with the value either checked or unchecked. Think of a check box as either a yes-or-no, or on-or-off option. The RadioButton edit style defines a column having several choices. Only one choice can be made at a time. The Edit Mask style displays data in a specific format and when data is entered, it only allows specific characters. A DropDownDataWindow displays a value from a drop-down DataWindow. Data is retrieved from the database and displayed in an InfoMaker report. These options make the display and entry of data on forms and reports much easier. We now go through all the edit styles in detail and describe the options available for each.

The Edit edit style

The Edit edit style is used to place an entry area on a form. The edit style accepts information from the keyboard. This type of edit style can contain any type of data. When you select the Edit Style, the dialog box looks like Fig. 7.16.

Name.   Enter the name of the edit style in the Name box.

Limit.   The Limit box contains the maximum number of characters allowed in a column. The maximum is 32,767. If the user tries to enter more characters than what is specified here, he or she receives an error message.

Case.   The Case box sets the case in which data must be entered into the column. The available options are uppercase, lowercase, or any case.

Accelerator.   The Accelerator box assigns an accelerator key, also called a *hot key,* to the column. Enter the letter to use as the accelerator key. The accelerator key can display with the label or a text object associated with the column by entering an ampersand (&) before the letter used as the accelerator key.

Password.   The Password box converts anything entered in the column to asterisks. This is used for sensitive data.

Required.   The Required box sets the column to required. The row cannot be saved until the column data has been entered into it.

Figure 7.16   The Edit edit style options are available to configure a specific column.

Format.   The Format area is used to specify a display format. The display mask must be valid for the data type of the column. For example, # is used for numbers and @ for alphanumeric. For more information about the types of mask characters, refer to the InfoMaker documentation.

Auto Selection.   When the Auto Selection box is checked, InfoMaker automatically selects the contents of the column when the cursor is moved to that column.

Display only.   The Display Only option sets a column to read only. No changes can be made to the information in that column.

Use Code Table.   If the Use Code Table box is checked, the Code Table option appears at the bottom of the Edit Style dialog box. It is here that display and data values are entered which will appear on a form or report. Also when this box is selected, the Validate Using Code Table displays, which sets data validation by using a code table.

Show Focus Rectangle. When the Show Focus Rectangle option is checked, there is a rectangle around the column when it has focus.

Empty String is NULL. The Empty String is NULL option sets the column to NULL if there is nothing in the column. NULL does not mean 0 or blank; it just means nothing is there.

Validate Using Code Table. The Validate Using Code Table option uses a code table to validate entered data. Also see Use Code Table.

Auto Horz Scroll. Auto Horz Scroll prevents the column from scrolling horizontally automatically when data is entered.

Auto Vert Scroll. Auto Vert Scroll prevents a column from scrolling vertically automatically when data is entered in the column.

Horz Scroll Bar. Horz Scroll Bar displays a horizontal scroll bar in the column.

Vert Scroll Bar. Vert Scroll Bar displays a vertical scroll bar in the column.

CheckBox style

The CheckBox style is available to place check boxes on a form or report. When this style is selected, the Style window changes to look like Fig. 7.17.

Text. The Text area is used to specify a label for the check box.

On and off data values. The On and Off data value areas contain the values that will be saved to the database when the option is either checked or unchecked.

Left Text. The Left Text option specifies that text will display to the left of the check box.

Scale. The Scale option specifies that the size of the check box will scale to the size of the text.

3 States. The 3 States option enables the check box to have three states: on, off, or neither on nor off.

3D Look. The 3D Look option displays a three-dimensional check box.

DropDownDW style

To define a child window for a column, use the DropDown DataWindow edit style. To use a DataWindow, first create a report that contains the column to use as a display on the form or report and another column to save the infor-

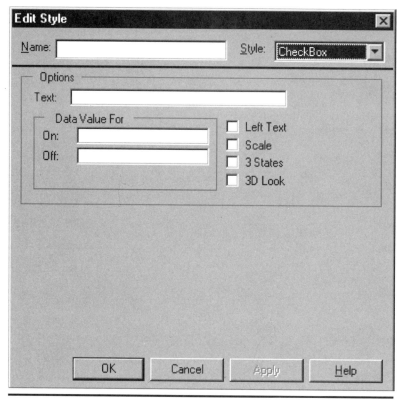

Figure 7.17   The Edit Style dialog box with the CheckBox edit style.

mation to the database. For instance, to choose an employee by name but save the employee id to the database, the report contains just the employee id and the employee name columns. When you are defining a DropDownDW style in the Edit Style dialog box, the window looks like Fig. 7.18.

DataWindow.   The DataWindow area contains the name of a previously defined report. This is also called a *DataWindow object*.

Display Column.   Display Column is the name of the column in the Data-Window object to display when you select a row from a form or report.

Data Column.   Data Column is the name of the column containing the value to store in the database.

Lines in DropDown.   The Lines in DropDown option specifies the number of lines that appear in the DropDownDataWindow before you have to scroll to see more information.

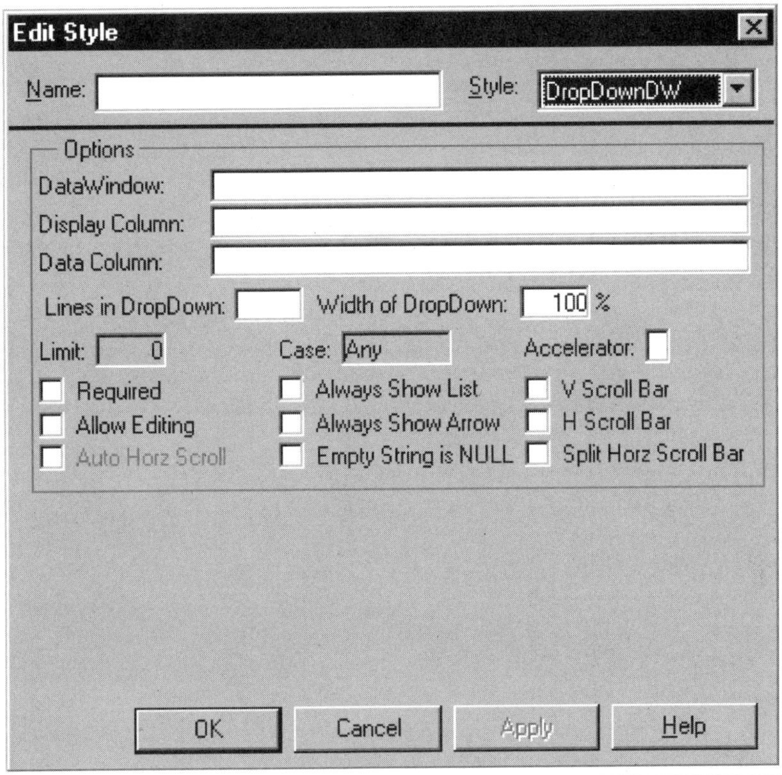

Figure 7.18 TheEdit Style dialog box with the DropDown DW style activated.

Width of DropDown. The Width of DropDown option specifies the default width of the drop-down portion of the DataWindow. This can be changed in individual forms or reports as required.

Limit. The Limit option specifies the number of characters or numbers that can be entered in the column.

Case. The Case option specifies the case in which data must be entered. There are three options: uppercase, lowercase, and any case.

Accelerator. The Accelerator option assigns an accelerator key to the DropDownDataWindow. If an accelerator key is assigned to the column, when you enter data on a form, pressing ALT and the assigned accelerator key will move the cursor directly to that column.

Required. The Required option makes the DropDownDataWindow required. The form cannot be saved unless a row has been selected in the Drop-DownDataWindow.

Allow Editing. The Allow Editing option permits values to be entered into the DropDownDataWindow.

Auto Horz Scroll. The Auto Horz Scroll option specifies that the column will scroll horizontally automatically when data is entered into the column.

Always Show List. When the Always Show List option is selected, the drop-down portion of the DropDownDataWindow opens whenever the field has focus.

Always Show Arrow. When the Always Show Arrow option is selected, the arrow at the end of the editable area of the column is always shown. If Always Show Arrow is checked, the Always Show List option is disabled.

Empty String is NULL. The Empty String is NULL option sets the column to null when the column is blank.

V Scroll Bar. When the V Scroll Bar option is selected, a vertical scroll bar is displayed.

H Scroll Bar. When the H Scroll Bar option is selected, a horizontal scroll bar is displayed.

Split Horz Scroll Bar. The Split Horz Scroll Bar option allows the user to divide the DataWindow object into two windows.

DropDownListBox

The DropDownListBox edit style has many of the same types of options as the DropDownDataWindow. However, the difference between them is that Drop-DownListBox displays static information, whereas DropDownDataWindow displays dynamic information because the information is retrieved from the database. As the information is changed in the database, DropDownDataWindow retrieves the new data. The DropDownListBox Edit Style dialog box is shown in Fig. 7.19.

Limit. The Limit option specifies the maximum number of characters or numbers that can be entered in the column. The maximum is 32,767.

Case. The Case option specifies the case in which data must be entered. There are three options: uppercase, lowercase, and any case.

Accelerator. The Accelerator option assigns an accelerator key to the Drop-DownDataWindow. If an accelerator key is assigned to the column, when you enter data on a form, pressing ALT and the assigned accelerator key will move the cursor directly to that column.

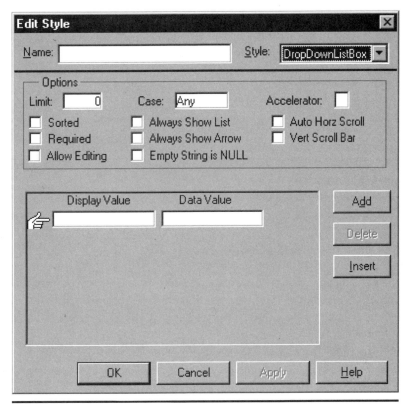

Figure 7.19 The Edit Style dialog box with the DropDownListBox style enabled.

Sorted. The Sorted option specifies that the data displays in sorted order.

Required. The Required option makes the DropDownDataWindow required. The form cannot be saved unless a row has been selected in the DropDown-DataWindow.

Allow Editing. The Allow Editing option permits values to be entered into the DropDownDataWindow.

Always Show List. When the Always Show List option is selected, the drop-down portion of the DropDownDataWindow opens whenever the field has focus.

Always Show Arrow. When the Always Show Arrow option is selected, the arrow at the end of the editable area of the column is always shown. If Always Show Arrow is checked, the Always Show List is disabled.

Empty String is NULL. The Empty String is NULL option sets the column to null when the column is blank.

Auto Horz Scroll.   The Auto Horz Scroll option specifies that the column will scroll horizontally automatically when data is being entered into the column.

Vert Scroll Bar.   When the Vert Scroll Bar option is selected, a vertical scroll bar displays.

Display Value and Data Value.   Display Value is the information that displays when you select a row from a form or report. Data Value is the name information to store in the database.

The EditMask edit style

The EditMask edit style is used as a type of formatting technique on a data column. The edit mask is useful when you enter data that is easier to read when it has a specific format, such as telephone or social security numbers. The EditMask Style window is displayed in Fig. 7.20.

Mask.   The Mask area contains the characters used in the mask. The mask can be either typed from the keyboard or selected from the Masks drop-down list box and pasted into the Mask box.

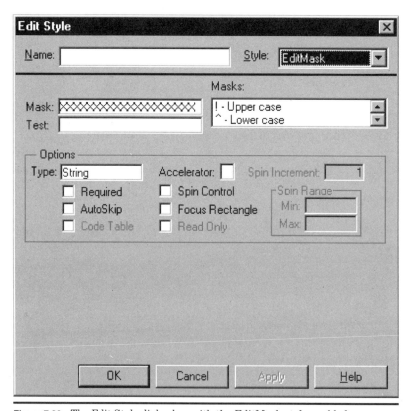

Figure 7.20   The Edit Style dialog box with the EditMask style enabled.

Test. The Test area is used for testing how the mask works. Simply enter a value, such as a telephone or social security number, to make sure the dashes and parentheses are placed correctly.

Masks. The Masks list box has several types of characters to choose from when you build a mask, including uppercase and lowercase, numeric, and string masks.

Type. The Type drop-down list box contains all the data types available for the column. The data types are string, number, date, time, and time stamp. The type should match the data type for the column.

Accelerator. The Accelerator option assigns an accelerator key to the DropDownDataWindow. If an accelerator key is assigned to the column, when you enter data on a form, pressing ALT and the assigned accelerator key will move the cursor directly to that column.

Spin Increment. The Spin Increment option specifies the increment by which the spin control values are increased or decreased when the up or down arrow is selected on numeric data. See also "Spin Control."

Required. The Required option makes the entry in the Mask column required. The form cannot be saved unless an entry matching the Mask has been entered.

AutoSkip. The AutoSkip option sets the form to automatically skip the column when the user is tabbing on columns.

Code Table. The Code Table option is enabled when the Spin Control option is selected. When the Code Table option is enabled, the Display Value and Data Value area displays. Enter the values to display on the form or report and the values to store in the database.

Spin Control. Spin Control is used to set a spin control, allowing the user to spin through the valid values for a column. See also "Code Table," "Spin Increment," and "Spin Range."

Focus Rectangle. The Focus Rectangle option displays a dotted rectangle around a column when it is selected or has focus.

Read Only. The Read Only option specifies that any values displayed from the code table cannot be modified on the form. They cannot be updated. See also "Display Value and Data Value."

Spin Range. The Spin Range group box has Minimum and Maximum options. To set the minimum and maximum values to display in a spin control, enter the appropriate values in these areas. See also "Spin Control."

Display Value and Data Value.   The Display Value is the information that displays when you select a row from a form or report. Data Value contains the actual information to store in the database.

The RadioButton edit style

The RadioButton edit style creates a radio button that can be displayed on a form or report. The RadioButton Edit Style window looks like Fig. 7.21.

Columns Across.   The Columns Across option specifies the number of radio buttons to display horizontally.

Left Text.   The Left Text option sets the radio button label to display to the left of the radio button.

Scale Circles.   The Scale Circles option scales the radio buttons to the size of the text on the form.

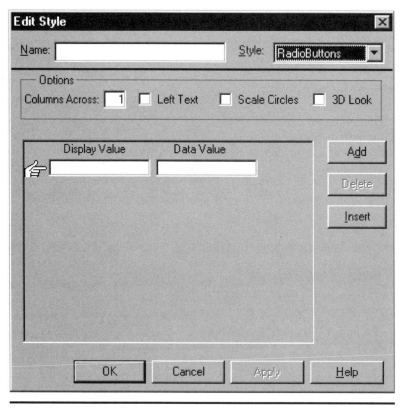

Figure 7.21 The Edit Style dialog box with the RadioButton edit style enabled.

3D Look. The 3D Look option gives the radio button a three-dimensional look.

Display Value and Data Value. Display Value is the information that displays when you select a row from a form or report. Data Value contains the actual information to store in the database.

Validation Maintenance

Validation is a set of rules that data entered into a column must satisfy before it can be saved into the database. For instance, a rule might be defined that specifies only California customers can be entered into the database. In this section we discuss how to maintain validation rules in the InfoMaker environment. Validation rules can be added, changed, or deleted from the current database.

Adding and editing validation rules

The processes of adding and editing validation rules in InfoMaker work in much the same way. However, once a validation rule is defined, the name cannot be changed. To change the name, you have to delete it and create a new one.

To add or edit validation rules, do the following:

1. In the Database painter select Design | Validation Maintenance... from the menu, as shown in Fig. 7.22. The Validation Rules dialog box displays, as shown in Fig. 7.23.

2. Click on either the New... or Edit... button on the Validation Rules window. The Input Validation Window appears, as shown in Fig. 7.24.

3. Enter the name of the validation rule. If you are editing an existing rule, the name cannot be changed.

4. Select the data type. There are the usual data types to choose from, including string, number, date, time, and date time.

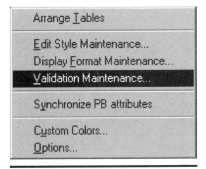

Figure 7.22 The Validation Maintenance menu option on the Database painter Design menu.

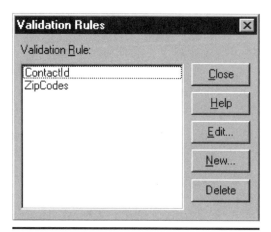

Figure 7.23 The Validation Rules dialog box is used to view existing validation rules or to create new ones.

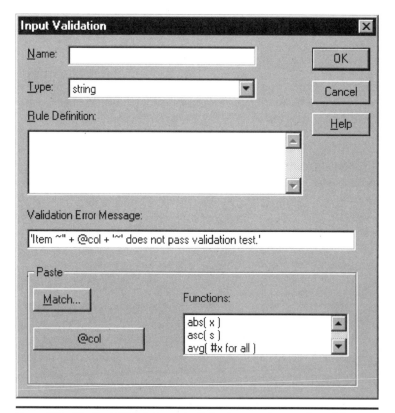

Figure 7.24 The Input Validation rule dialog box creates or edits validation rules.

5. Define the rule and the error message to display when information is incorrectly entered. The Input Validation dialog box will look similar to Fig. 7.25.

6. When you have finished, click OK on the Input Validation window.

7. When you are satisfied with the validation rule, choose Close on the Validation Rules dialog box.

Deleting a validation rule

When a validation rule is no longer needed in a database, it can be removed from the system. Before you delete a validation rule, make sure that no columns in the database use it. Otherwise you will get errors when you try to enter data into the system.

To delete a validation rule, do the following:

1. In the Database painter, select Design | Validation Maintenance... from the menu. The Validation Rules dialog box displays.

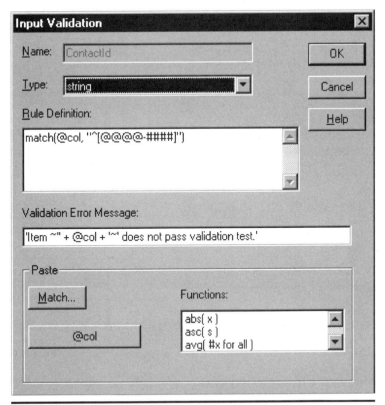

Figure 7.25 The Input Validation dialog box with a validation rule defined.

2. Select the validation rule to delete by clicking on it with the mouse.

3. Choose the Delete button.

4. When you have finished, choose the Close button on the Validation Rules dialog box.

Primary Keys

Keys are unique identifiers to a database table. A primary key is one column or several columns combined that uniquely identify each row on a database table. For example, if there are two employees in a table with the same first and last names, we need a way to uniquely identify them. For this reason, we would add a column called `employee_id,` which contains an identifier for each person. So, for instance, we may have two people named Joe Smith. One may work in accounting and the other in purchasing. By assigning Joe Smith from accounting the `employee_id` of SMIT-1234 and Joe Smith from purchasing the `employee_id` of SMIT-5678, we are able to maintain information on both employees without confusion.

One thing to keep in mind when you define columns that will be used as primary and foreign keys: The data types, widths, and number of decimal places must match exactly. If they do not, when you define a foreign key, InfoMaker will not allow you to proceed and will display an error message, as shown in Fig. 7.26.

Creating a primary key

Before a table can be updated by using SQL Anywhere, a primary key must be defined for the table; otherwise, InfoMaker will not allow updates on the table.

To create a primary key from the Database painter, do the following:

1. From the Database painter, open a table. The table displays in the Database workspace, as shown in Fig. 7.27.

2. Right-click on the table name in the Database painter workspace, as shown in Fig. 7.28.

3. Select Properties... from the pop-up menu to open the table property sheet, as shown in Fig. 7.29.

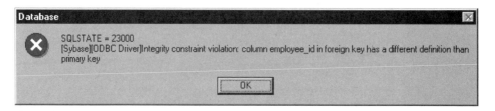

Figure 7.26 The columns defined as primary and foreign keys must match exactly, or InfoMaker will not allow you to continue.

Figure 7.27 Displaying a table in the Database painter.

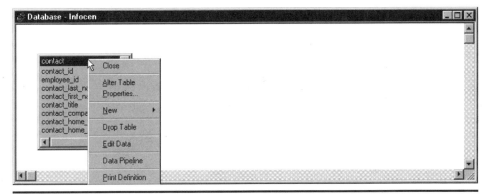

Figure 7.28 Right-clicking on a table name opens a pop-up menu to change options on the table.

4. Click on the Primary Key tab, which displays the Primary Key sheet.

5. Select the column(s) for the primary key by clicking on them in the Table Columns list box. The column(s) appear in the Key Columns box, as shown in Fig. 7.30.

6. Click on OK to accept the changes. InfoMaker now returns to the Database painter. You will notice a change in the table. There is now a primary key icon linked to the table, as shown in Fig. 7.31.

Changing a primary key

After a primary key is defined, it is possible to modify it. You may decide to add another column to the primary key or to remove a column. InfoMaker allows you to change the key as often as necessary.

To change a primary key, do the following:

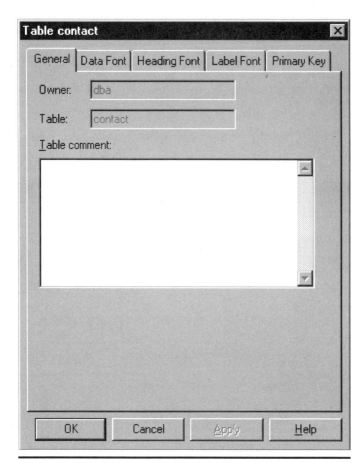

Figure 7.29 This is an example of opening the Table property sheet in the Database painter. The property sheet has many options to set for a table.

1. Right-click on the primary key icon for a table in the Database painter workspace.
   or
   Right-click on the table's title and select Properties from the pop-up menu.

2. Select Properties... from the pop-up menu.

3. Modify the primary key.

4. Choose OK when you have finished.

Dropping a primary key

Removing a primary key entirely from the table is very simple.
   To drop a primary key from a table, do the following:

Working with Databases 113

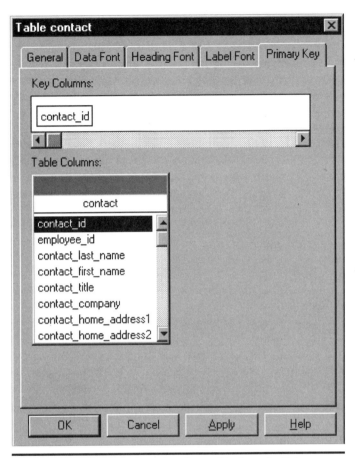

Figure 7.30 Select the primary key for a table from the Primary
Key tab on the Table property sheet.

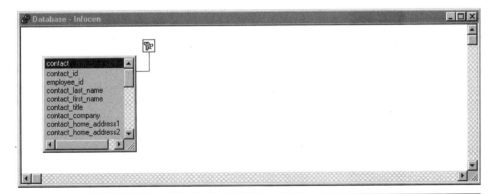

Figure 7.31 Once a primary key is assigned to a table, the primary key icon displays in the
Database painter workspace.

1. Right-click on the primary key icon on the Database painter workspace.

2. Select Drop Primary Key from the pop-up menu.

3. InfoMaker displays a dialog box asking you to confirm the deletion. Select Yes to delete the primary key, and select No to return to the Database painter workspace.

Foreign Keys

A *foreign key* is a key to another table within a primary table. For instance, let us take a look at the Joe Smith example again. Within a table we have a column entitled employee_id, which assigns to a specific employee a unique identifier. This is our primary key. Now we want to link the employee to a specific department. We create a table called department with a primary key called department_id. Within the employee table we assign each employee a department_id. This effectively links the employee to a department. The department_id in the employee table is a foreign key. Foreign keys are simply links to other tables. We build these links to cut down on the amount of duplicate data stored in a database, which saves room. If we did not have an employee table and a department table, we would have to save all the information related to a department possibly several hundred times. With a foreign key, the departments are stored once, and we only have to store the numeric identifier hundreds of times, saving hard drive space.

Creating a foreign key

Before a table can refer to the unique identifier in another table, one of its columns must be defined as a foreign key.

To define a foreign key, do the following:

1. Click once on a table in the Database painter to select it.

2. Then click on the Create FK button on the Database painter bar. The Foreign Key Definition window displays, as shown in Fig. 7.32.

3. Enter a Foreign Key Name.

4. Next select the Primary Key Table. This is the table in which the foreign key is a primary key. Once selected, the primary key defined for the table displays in the Primary Key Columns box below the Primary Key Table.

5. Define the column in the table you want as a foreign key. Click on the column in the Select Columns box.

6. And finally, we need to tell InfoMaker what to do when a row is deleted on the primary table. We have three selections available in the On Delete of Primary Table Row group box: Disallow if Dependent Rows Exist (RESTRICT), Delete any Dependent Rows (CASCADE), and Set Dependent Columns to NULL (SET NULL). RESTRICT, which is the default, will generate an error if you try to modify a primary key value and do not finish it.

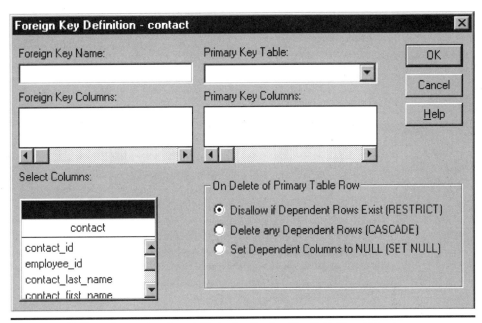

Figure 7.32   Define a foreign key for a table in the Foreign Key Definition dialog box.

When CASCADE is used with ON DELETE, all rows are deleted which contain foreign keys that reference the deleted primary key. This is for SQL Anywhere only. For other databases, check the database documentation. Choose one of these options and choose OK.

Deleting a foreign key

Once a foreign key is no longer needed, it can be deleted.
To drop a foreign key from a table, do the following:

1. Right-click on the foreign key icon on the Database painter workspace.
2. Select Drop Foreign Key from the pop-up menu.
3. InfoMaker displays a dialog box asking you to confirm the deletion. Select Yes to delete the foreign key, and select No to return to the Database painter workspace.

Opening Dependent Tables

When you have one table open with tables that are linked by foreign keys, it is possible to open all these dependent tables at once, instead of having to search for them and open them individually. This is accomplished with the Open dependent tables option in the Database painter.
To open dependent tables, do the following:

1. Right-click on the primary key icon on the Database painter workspace.

2. Select Open Dependent Tables from the pop-up menu. All the dependent tables are opened in the Database painter workspace.

Indexes

Indexes are used to improve search times on those columns that are neither a primary nor a foreign key. Do not set an index on a column that is a primary or foreign key. These keys are already optimized for quick access. If you run a specific search often, you may want to set an index.

Creating an index

Before you do any searches on a specific column in a table quickly, the index must be created.

To add an index to a table, do the following:

1. Open the table to add the index to the Database painter.

2. Click once on the table's title in the Database painter workspace to select it.

3. Then select the Index button on the Database painter bar.
   or
   Choose Object | New | Index from the menu. The Create Index window appears, as shown in Fig. 7.33.

4. Give the index a name.

5. Choose either Unique or Duplicate values in the index.

6. Set the sort order to either ascending or descending.

7. Select the column(s) to include in the index. The column then appears in the Index Columns box. An example of a completed index is shown in Fig. 7.34.

8. When the index is created, the table displays the Index key in the Database painter workspace, as shown in Fig. 7.35.

Dropping an index

When an index is no longer needed, it can be dropped. Once dropped, the index is removed from the system and can no longer be accessed.

To drop an index, do the following:

1. Right-click on the index icon for a table in the Database painter workspace. The Index pop-up menu displays, as shown in Fig. 7.36.

2. Select Drop Index... from the pop-up menu that displays.

3. InfoMaker prompts for confirmation. Once you click Yes, InfoMaker deletes the index for you.

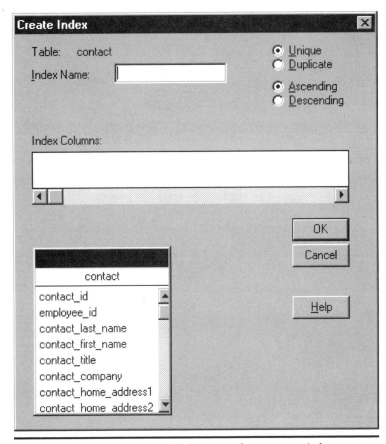

Figure 7.33 The Create Index dialog box is used to create an index on a Database table.

Views

A *view* is a modified table of a master table employed either for ease of use or security reasons. Take, for example, an employee table. Normally employees' salaries are not available to the public. A database can be set up so the employees' names and departments are available, but not allow anyone outside a specific list to see the salary, social security number, birthdate, etc. To accomplish this goal, create what is called a *view*. Think of a view as another table. It is a subset of the master table. However, unlike a regular table, you cannot create primary and foreign keys for a view.

A view does not physically exist in a database as a regular table does. Each time a view is accessed, an SQL statement is executed and the view is created. Views are used to give names to frequently run SELECT statements, combine information in multiple tables for easy access, or limit access to data in a table.

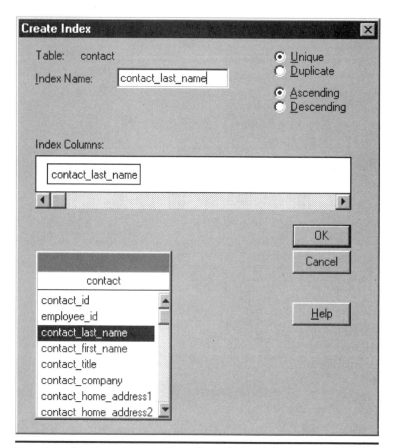

Figure 7.34 This is an example of the Create Index dialog box.

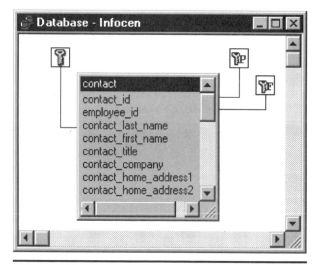

Figure 7.35 Once an index is created on a table, the index icon displays in the Database painter.

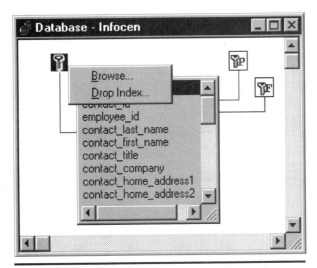

Figure 7.36 The Index pop-up menu has options to drop an index.

Creating database views

A view must be created in much the same way as a database table before it is used in an application.

To create a view to a table, do the following:

1. In the Database painter, select the View button on the painter bar. The View painter opens and displays the Select Tables dialog box, as shown in Fig. 7.37.

2. Select a table and click on Open.

3. Select the table column(s) to add to the view, as shown in Fig. 7.38.

4. When you have finished defining the view, click on the Return button on the View painter bar.

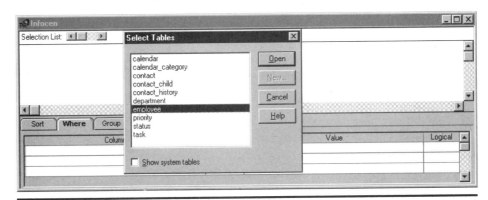

Figure 7.37 When you create a view, the Select Tables dialog box displays, which allows you to choose the table(s) to include in a view.

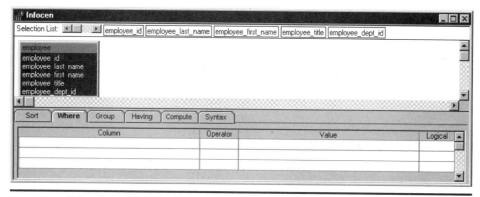

Figure 7.38 Select the columns in the Master table you want to add to a view.

5. The Save View Definition dialog box displays, as shown in Fig. 7.39. Enter the view name and click on Create.

The Database painter workspace now should display both the master and the view tables, similar to what is shown in Fig. 7.40.

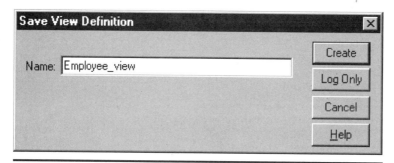

Figure 7.39 The Save View Definition dialog box allows you to name a view.

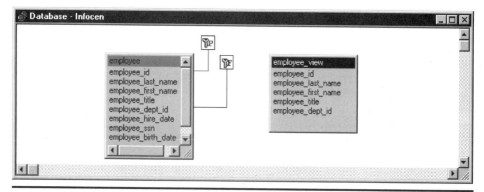

Figure 7.40 This is an example of a view created from a Master table.

Opening existing views

Once a table view is created, it can be accessed just as any other table in the Database painter, as demonstrated in Fig. 7.41.

Joining tables in a view

For more complex views, it is possible to join more than one table to create a view. Joining tables in a view this way makes it easier to build some reports and forms which have complex selection criteria.

To join tables in a view, do the following:

1. Open the tables in the View painter, as shown in Fig. 7.42.

2. Choose the Join button on the View painter bar. InfoMaker automatically creates the join based on the primary-foreign key relationship.

When you have finished, choose Return from the View painter bar.

Dropping a view

When a table view is no longer needed, it may be deleted from the database. Before you delete it, make sure that no forms, reports, queries, or any other InfoMaker objects access this view.

To drop a view, do the following:

1. Open the view in the Database painter workspace.

2. Select the view by clicking on its title bar.

3. Drop the view by either choosing the Drop button from the Database painter bar, or right-clicking on the view and choosing Drop View from the pop-up menu.

4. Choose Yes when InfoMaker asks you to confirm the delete.

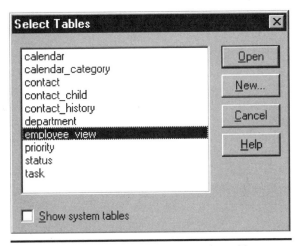

Figure 7.41 A view is accessible, as any other table.

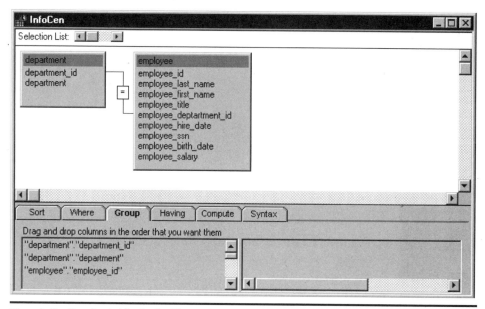

Figure 7.42   Opening tables in the View painter.

The Table Painter

The Table painter is used to define the columns and column attributes for tables in a database within a graphical interface. The Table painter can be accessed either directly from the PowerBar or PowerPanel or from within the Database painter. This section describes all the available options and settings in the Table painter. For information on how to access the Table painter, see the section "Creating Database Tables" in this chapter.

How the Table painter works

The Table painter creates a new table definition or alters an existing table definition. It is possible to open the Table painter multiple times to work on more than one table at a time. Each time the Table painter is opened, you can select one table definition to change or create one new table definition.

Although the Table painter is not an editor, it has some features that are similar to those of an editor. But instead of working with text, you work with table columns. For example, you can copy a column and paste that column in the current table definition or in a different table definition.

Column name

The column name area in the Table painter workspace contains the name of the actual column.

Data types

To create or alter a table, you must have a clear understanding of each of the various data types available in your DBMS. Data types vary with each database product. SQL Anywhere, which is bundled with InfoMaker, contains several different data types. We will concentrate on SQL Anywhere here. For other databases, read the documentation for your particular database. But since data types are similar, this section will give you a basic understanding of data types.

The column's data type affects the maximum size of the column. The larger the column, the more room it needs to store the data on your computer's hard drive or on a network drive. There are several different categories of data types in SQL Anywhere: character, numeric, binary, and date and time.

Character data types.   Character data types are used to store strings of characters, including letters, numbers, and symbols. These data types in SQL Anywhere are *char, varchar,* and *long varchar.* SQL Anywhere treats columns with these data types the same, with some exceptions. The maximum size of a char data type is 32,767. Varchar is considered the same as char. However, the maximum size of a long varchar data type is limited by the maximum size of the database file, which currently is 2 Gbytes in SQL Anywhere.

Numeric data types.   SQL Anywhere also has numeric data types. These are used to store numeric data. Included in this category are *integer, numeric, smallint, tinyint, double,* and *float.*

Integer.   The maximum value of an integer data type is 2,147,483,647. This type requires 4 bytes of storage.

Numeric.   Numeric data types are considered a decimal number.

Smallint.   The maximum value of a smallint data type is 32,767, which requires 2 bytes of storage.

Tinyint.   A Tinyint is a value less than 255.

Double.   A double-precision floating-point number is stored in 8 bytes. The range of values is $2.225073858550720160e - 308$ to $1.79769313486231560e + 308$. A double-precision number is accurate to 15 significant digits, but may be subject to roundoff errors beyond the 15th digit.

Float.   A single-precision floating-point number is stored in 4 bytes. Float data type values range from $1.175494351e - 38$ to $3.402823466e + 38$. It's accurate up to six significant digits, but may be subject to roundoff errors beyond the sixth digit.

Date and time data types.   Date and time data types are used for storing dates and times in SQL Anywhere. The data types in this category are *date, time,* and *timestamp.*

Date. A date is stored in the Windows default date format, such as `mmddyy`. The year can be from 0001 to 9999. This data type requires 4 bytes of storage.

Time. The time of day is stored in the Windows default time format, such as `hh:mm:ss`.

Time stamp. A time stamp is composed of both the date and time.

Binary data types. Binary data types store binary data such as images or word processing documents in the database. It can hold anything the database cannot recognize. These are also commonly called *binary large objects,* or *BLOBs.* The binary data types in SQL Anywhere are binary and long binary.

Binary. When creating a binary data type, you can specify the maximum size of the column.

Long binary. The long binary data type has an arbitrary length. It grows or shrinks to any size to contain the data placed within it.

Width

The width of a column defined in the Table painter contains an integer which defines the column size.

Decimal

The decimal column specifies the number of places to the right of the decimal point in the number.

Null

The null column is defined with either a yes or a no. *Yes* means that the column can be left blank when a row of data is saved. *No* means it must contain some data.

Default

There are several different choices available when you specify a default value for a column. Default means that when a new row is created, such as adding a new employee to a table, you can specify how this column is initially set. There are several default values available in an SQL Anywhere database: none, autoincrement, current date, current time, current timestamp, timestamp, null, and user.

None. When none is selected as the default value, there is no default value specified for the column. If any information is contained in this column, it must be entered.

Autoincrement. Autoincrement means a column is set to automatically increment by 1. For instance, to create a unique identifier for a column with 100 contacts in it, the next time a contact is added to the table, the id is incremented by 1, becoming 101.

When you work with the autoincrement feature of the SQL Anywhere database, only use autoincrement on primary key columns or those columns with a UNIQUE constraint or columns that are first in a compound index. If you try to use autoincrement on another type of column, performance may be affected. Deleting rows does not decrement the autoincrement counter. The only way to fill the gaps in the numbers is to explicitly insert rows with the specific numbers which are missing. Autoincrement can be used only on columns with a data type of integer, smallint, float, or double because autoincrement generates a number.

Current date.   The current date default value initializes a column to the current date.

Current time.   The current time default value initializes a column to the current time.

Current timestamp.   The current timestamp default value initializes a column to the current date and time.

Timestamp.   The timestamp data type is used in SQL Anywhere for transaction processing. This means when you create a column named timestamp and specify timestamp as the data type, SQL Anywhere will automatically check for this column when updating a row in the table. If two people are modifying the same row of information and one person saves it, the other person will not be able to save his or her version of the row because the time stamps will be different.

Null.   The null default value initially sets a column to empty.

User.   The user default value initially sets a column to the user id of the person creating the row.

Format extended attributes

A display format is a way to specify in InfoMaker how information displayed on a report or form appears. For instance, if a phone number has a display format of (###) ###-#### set on the column, when the column is displayed, the phone number appears as (800) 555-1111. If there was no display format specified on the column, the number will appear as 8005551111. A display format makes viewing information much easier.

When you define display formats, a mask is used. A mask is simply a series of characters representing string and numeric characters, dates, and times. The @ symbol represents string or alphabetic characters. The pound sign # represents numbers; d represents a day, m represents a month, and y represents a year in a date; and so on. For a complete description of all the available display masks, see the InfoMaker User's Guide.

Display formats are stored in the repository. For more information about the repository see Chap. 3, Setting Preferences.

For a discussion of how to add display formats to the InfoMaker environment, refer to the section "Display Format Maintenance" in this chapter.

Edit extended attribute

The Edit style extended attribute formats data as it is entered onto a form. For instance, to enter a phone number, normally it looks something like (123) 456-7890. Without an edit mask defined for a phone number column, the number would appear as 1234567890 as it was entered on the form. An edit extended attribute makes reading the column much easier. An edit style extended attribute is added to the InfoMaker environment much as a display format.

Edit styles are stored in the repository. For more information about the repository, see Chap. 3.

For a complete discussion of how to add edit styles to the InfoMaker environment, see the section "Edit Style Maintenance" in this chapter.

Validation

Validation is a set of rules that data entered into a column must pass before it can be saved into the database. For instance, a rule might be defined that specifies only California customers can be entered into the database.

Validation rules are stored in the repository. For more information about the repository see Chap. 3.

For a complete discussion of how to add validation rules to the InfoMaker environment, see the section "Validation Maintenance" in this chapter.

Header

When you define a column in the Table painter, the heading area is used to specify column headings in reports.

Justify

The Justify area in the Table painter is used to set the column justification in a form or report. The data can be set to the left, the right, or centered.

Height

The Height area is used to define the height of the column in a form or report in inches. InfoMaker automatically creates a default height based on the default font set in the environment.

Width

The Width area is used to define the width of a column in inches. InfoMaker automatically creates a default height based on the default font set in the environment.

Initial

The Initial box in the Table painter extended attribute area sets an initial value on a column. The available choices are to fill the column with spaces, set the column to an empty string, or set the column to null.

Label

The Label area is used to set a label for the column which is displayed when the column is used on a form.

Comment

The Comment area is used to describe the column. This is a good place to explain the type of information the column contains.

Copy, cut, and paste columns

Within the Table painter there is the capability to copy columns from one place to another within a table or to an entirely different painter. To complete these types of actions, there are buttons available on the Table painter bar.

To copy or cut a column, do the following:

1. Select a column.
2. Select the Cut button on the Table painter bar or Edit | Cut Column from the menu to remove a column and place it elsewhere.
   or
   Select the Copy button on the Table painter bar or Edit | Copy Column from the menu to leave the column and copy it elsewhere.

To paste a column, do the following:

1. Choose the Insert button on the Table painter bar or select the Edit | Insert column from the menu.
2. Place the cursor on the new column, and select Paste on the painter bar or select Edit | Paste column from the menu.

Inserting columns

It is possible to add columns to an existing table. However, columns can only be appended after the last column in the table. Columns cannot be inserted elsewhere within the table.

To insert a column, do the following:

1. Place the cursor on the last column in the Table definition.
2. Select the Insert button on the Table painter bar, or choose the Edit | Insert Column from the menu.

Deleting columns

If a column is no longer necessary, it can be removed from the table. Before you remove a column, however, make sure that there are no forms, reports, or other InfoMaker objects that access the column.

To delete a column, do the following:

1. Place the cursor on the column to delete.

2. Press the Delete button on the Table painter bar, or select Edit | Delete Column from the menu.

Changing a table name

After a table has been created, it is possible to change its name in the Table painter. Before you change the name, make sure any forms or reports are also changed.

To change a table name, do the following:

1. Select the Props button on the Table painter bar.

2. Choose the General tab on the property sheet, as shown in Fig. 7.43.

3. Choose OK when you have finished.

Creating and modifying a primary key in the Table painter

Besides being able to create a primary key in the Database painter, it is possible to create a primary key from within the Table painter.

To create or edit a primary key from the Table painter, do the following:

1. Select the Props button on the Table painter bar.
   or
   Select Edit | Table Properties… from the Table painter menu.

2. Choose the Primary Key tab on the Table Properties sheet.

3. Define the primary key.

4. Choose OK when you have finished.

For more information on primary keys, see the section on primary keys in this chapter.

Creating and modifying a foreign key in the Table painter

A foreign key can be created in the Database painter, but it can also be created in the Table painter.

To create or edit a foreign key in the Table painter, do the following:

1. Select the Props button on the Table painter bar.

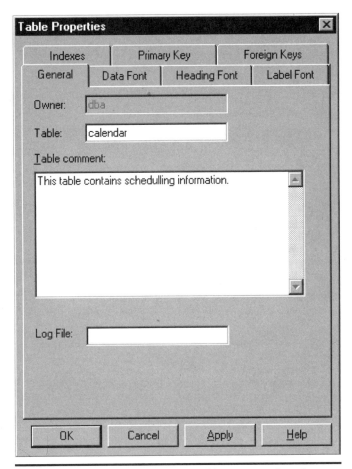

Figure 7.43 The General tab on the Table property sheet has options to change the table name and set a log file for the table.

or

Select Edit | Table Properties... from the Table painter menu.

2. Choose the Foreign Keys tab on the Table Properties sheet.

3. Define the foreign key.

4. Choose OK when you have finished.

For more information on foreign keys, see the section on foreign keys in this chapter.

Indexing columns in the Table painter

While it is possible to create an index in the Database painter, it is also possible to do so in the Table painter.

To create an index in the Table painter, do the following:

1. Select the Props button on the Table painter.
   or
   Select Edit | Table Properties... from the Table painter menu.

2. Choose the Indexes tab on the Table Properties sheet.

3. Define the index.

4. Choose OK when you have finished.

For more information on indexing, see the section on indexing in this chapter.

Changing fonts

Within the Table painter, it is possible to change fonts for specific items such as data, headings, and labels. For instance, to set the label headings which display on a form to bold, it would work best if it were changed in the Table painter. This way, the font is stored in the repository and does not have to be redefined each time a form is created. This saves time when you are creating applications.

To change data, heading, and label fonts, do the following:

1. Select the Properties button on the Table painter bar.
   or
   Select Edit | Table Properties... from the Table painter menu.

2. Select the appropriate tab on the Table painter property sheet; Data Font, Heading Font, or Label Font. All three font sheets are similar to the one shown in Fig. 7.44.

3. Define the font.

4. Choose OK when you have finished defining fonts.

Setting table comments

Comments relating to a table can be helpful when the table must be modified later. A comment is simply one or two sentences describing what information the table contains and its purpose. These comments can be modified at any time.

To modify table comments, do the following:

1. Select the Properties button on the Table painter.
   or
   Select Edit | Table Properties... from the Table painter menu.

2. Choose the General tab on the Table Properties sheet.

3. Define the comments.

4. Choose OK when you have finished.

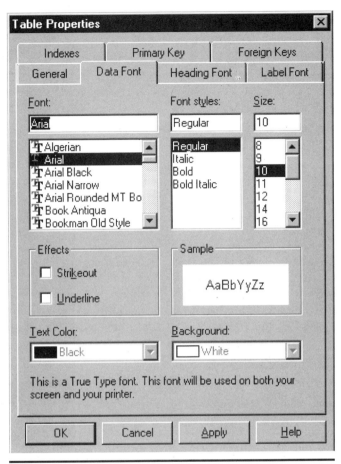

Figure 7.44 This is the Data Font property sheet in the Table painter where the font for all data in the specified table is changed.

Viewing SQL syntax in the Table painter

Within the InfoMaker environment it is possible to view the commands Info-Maker generates to make changes to database tables. If you are trying to learn SQL, this is a good way to do so.

To view the SQL commands, do one of the following:

Select the SQL Syntax button on the Table painter bar.

or

Choose Design | Syntax from the menu. The Pending Changes window appears, as shown in Fig. 7.45.

Figure 7.45 This window displays the commands InfoMaker creates to make changes to a database table.

The Database Administration Painter

The Database Administration painter is used to administer the database by controlling security access. Within the Database Administration painter you can also create SQL statements which are executed immediately. This painter is for advanced users who are familiar with SQL and who understand the current database structure. The Database Administration painter uses an editor very similar to InfoMaker's File Editor, which was discussed in Chap. 3, Setting Preferences. It is possible to cut, copy, and paste text, in addition to accessing some options which are only available in the Database Administration painter.

Accessing the Database Administration painter

To access the Database Administration painter, choose the DB Admin button on the Database painter bar. The Database Administration painter workspace opens in the File Editor.

Table security

By accessing the Database Administration painter it is possible to selectively give permissions to people. You can authorize users to access or not access specific tables or specific columns within those tables, or you can give them permission to complete certain tasks such as update authorization but not deletion.

To set table security, do the following:

1. In the Database Administration painter, select the Design | Table Security item from the menu. The Table Security dialog box displays, as shown in Fig. 7.46.

2. Select the groups or users, the tables, and the privileges to grant.

3. To grant access to only specific columns within a table, choose the Update button. The Column Security—Update dialog box displays, as shown in Fig. 7.47.

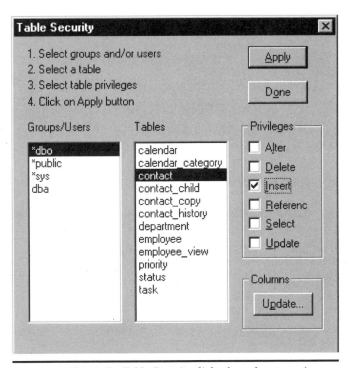

Figure 7.46 This is the Table Security dialog box where permissions to tables are granted.

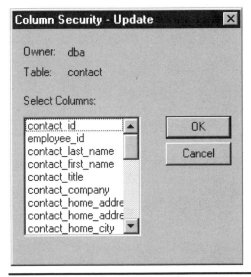

Figure 7.47 This is an example of the Column Security—Update dialog box. Select the columns to which the user has access.

4. Select the columns to which to give the user(s) access by clicking on them with the mouse.

5. Choose OK when you have finished.

6. Choose Done on the Table Security dialog box when you have finished.

Maintaining users.   Before users can be granted specific privileges, they must be entered into the security system. The Database Administration painter has the functionality to add, delete, and modify users in the security system.

Adding users to the security system.   To add users to the security system, do the following:

1. Choose Design | Maintain Users... from the Database Administration painter. The Maintain Users dialog box displays, as shown in Fig. 7.48.

2. Choose the New... button. The Create User dialog box displays, as shown in Fig. 7.49.

3. Enter the user id and the password.

4. When you have finished, choose OK.

5. Choose Done on the Maintain Users dialog box.

Editing existing users.   When a user is in the security system and she or he needs to change the password, this can be done from the security system.
To change the password for a particular user, do the following:

1. Choose Design | Maintain Users... from the Database Administration painter. The Maintain Users dialog box displays.

2. Choose the Modify... button. The Create User dialog box displays.

Figure 7.48 This is the Maintain Users dialog box where users are added to and deleted from the security system.

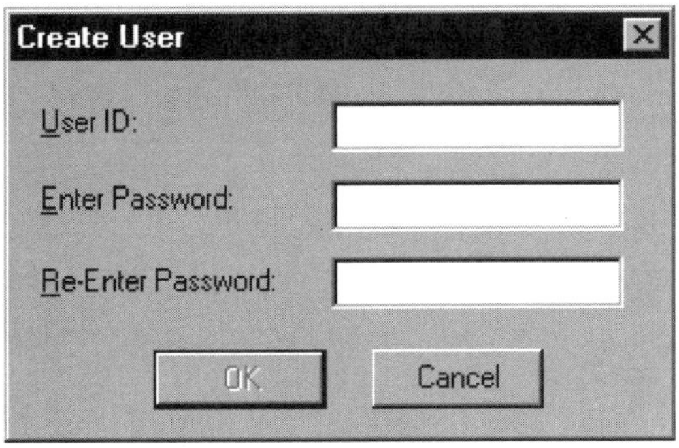

Figure 7.49 This is the Create User dialog box where users and their passwords are entered into the security system.

3. Enter the new password.

4. When you have finished, choose OK.

5. Choose Done on the Maintain Users dialog box.

Deleting users from the security system.   When users are no longer accessing the system, they can be deleted from the security system.

To delete users from the security system, do the following:

1. Choose Design | Maintain Users... from the Database Administration painter. The Maintain Users dialog box displays.

2. Choose the Delete... button. InfoMaker deletes the user immediately without confirmation.

3. When you have finished, choose OK.

4. Choose Done on the Maintain Users dialog box.

Maintaining groups.   When a large number of users have access to an application, it is easier to grant permissions to many users at once than to do so individually. This is where the maintaining groups functionality in the Database Administration painter comes in handy. Add users to the system, and then add them to a specific group in the security system.

Creating a group.   To create a new group, do the following:

1. Choose Design | Maintain Groups... from the Database Administration painter menu. The Maintain Groups dialog box displays, as shown in Fig. 7.50.

2. Choose the New Group... button on the Maintain Groups dialog box. The Group Id dialog box displays.

3. Enter the name of the new group.

4. Choose Done when you have finished.

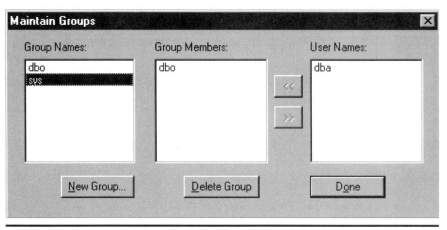

Figure 7.50 This is the Maintain Groups dialog box. Users are added to and deleted from groups in the security system.

Deleting a group.   When a group is no longer needed, it can be deleted from the system.

To delete a group, do the following:

1. Choose Design | Maintain Groups... from the Database Administration painter menu. The Maintain Groups dialog box displays.

2. Select the group to delete in the Group Names list by clicking on it with the mouse.

3. Choose the Delete Group button. InfoMaker does not confirm the deletion.

4. Choose Done when you have finished.

Adding users to and removing users from a group.   Once a group is created and users are added to the security system, users can be placed in a group. When users leave the company or are moved to another department, they can be removed from a particular group also.

To add users to and remove users from a group, do the following:

1. Choose Design | Maintain Groups... from the Database Administration painter menu. The Maintain Groups dialog box displays.

2. Choose a group in the Group Names list. All the users in the list display in the Users list.

3. Highlight a user and click on the right-headed arrow or the left-headed arrow to add or remove the user from the group.

4. Choose Done when you have finished.

Executing SQL

The Database Administration painter can execute SQL statements directly from its workspace. Enter an SQL statement by typing it from the keyboard, pasting it from the Windows Clipboard, or importing it from an .sql file. When you are satisfied with the command, press the Execute button or the Design | Execute SQL menu item. The SQL command is executed immediately.

Explaining SQL

Before running a SQL command against a large database, you can access the Explain SQL command in the Database Administration painter. This function calculates the resources needed to execute the command. If a large amount of resources are needed to run the SQL command and will tie up your machine or the network for a time, you have the option of running it at night or at another time when it will not affect system performance. This is also a good way to determine if there is a more efficient way to code the SQL statement.

To run the Explain command, do the following:

1. Enter a SQL command into the Database Administration workspace.
2. Select the Design | Execute SQL item from the Database Administration menu. The SQL Statement Execution Plan is created and displayed on screen.
3. Choose OK when you have finished viewing it.

Viewing stored procedures

Stored procedures can be viewed within the Database Administration painter. To view an existing stored procedure, do the following:

1. Select the Design | View Syntax from the Database Administration painter. The Procedures dialog box displays, as shown in Fig. 7.51.
2. Select the stored procedure to view in the Select Procedure list by clicking on it with the mouse. The code in the stored procedure is displayed in the Syntax window.
3. When you have finished viewing the stored procedure, choose OK.

Viewing views

From the Database Administration painter, it is possible to view the SQL command that generates a table view. This SQL statement is executed each time the view is accessed.

To display a view, do the following:

1. Select Design | View Syntax from the Database Administration painter menu. The Views dialog box displays, as shown in Fig. 7.52.

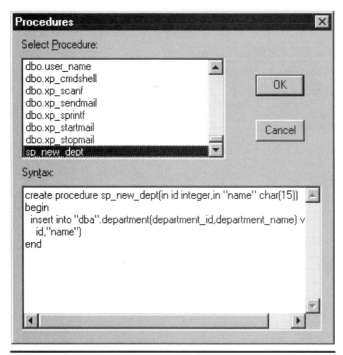

Figure 7.51 This is an example of a stored procedure being viewed in the Procedures dialog box.

Figure 7.52 This is the Views dialog box to examine SQL commands which generate a view.

2. Select the view to examine in the Select View list by clicking on it with the mouse. The code for the view displays in the Syntax list.

3. When you have finished, choose OK.

Setting colors

Each of the different types of words which make up a SQL command is color-coded for easier reading. For example, comments are in one color and SQL commands are in another. These can be changed from the InfoMaker default to anything you prefer.

To change the SQL command color scheme, do the following:

1. Choose Design | Options... from the Database Administration painter menu. The Properties for Editor property sheet displays, as shown in Fig. 7.53.

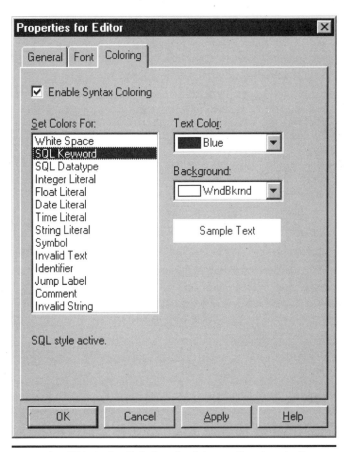

Figure 7.53 This is the Coloring sheet to specify colors in the Database Administration painter's workspace.

2. Choose the Coloring tab.

3. Change the colors for the objects you want.

4. Choose OK when you have finished.

Commenting and uncommenting text

When a large SQL Command is entered into the Database Administration painter, it is sometimes helpful to add comments explaining what the code does. At other times, when the code is not executing properly, it is helpful to comment out part of the code to determine where the problem is. The Database Administration painter includes tools to comment and uncomment text in SQL commands.

To comment and uncomment text, do the following:

1. Highlight the text in the workspace to be affected.

2. Choose the Comment or Uncomment button on the Database Administration painter bar, or choose Edit | Comment Selection or Edit | Uncomment Selection from the menu. Slashes are placed on the line containing the affected code.

Putting It All Together

In this section we will create a database. Then we create the tables and define the attributes for each of the columns in the table. Finally, we create the primary and foreign keys for each of the tables.

Let us begin by creating the database for our InfoCenter application.

1. If you have not already done so, start InfoMaker.

2. From the PowerBar or the PowerPanel, select the Database painter button.

3. When the Select Tables dialog box displays, click on Cancel.

4. Select File | Create Database from the Database painter menu. The Create Local Database dialog box displays.

5. In the Database Name area, enter the path name and the name of the database you are creating. In this case it is `c:\infocen\infocen.db`. If you do not enter a path name, the database will be created in whichever directory is current.

6. InfoMaker automatically enters the default database and password of DBA and SQL.

7. The start command is `dbeng50`. This is the command needed to start SQL Anywhere. For other databases, consult your DBMS documentation.

8. If you click on More on the Create Local Database dialog box, additional database options appear.

9. Check the Use transaction log box.

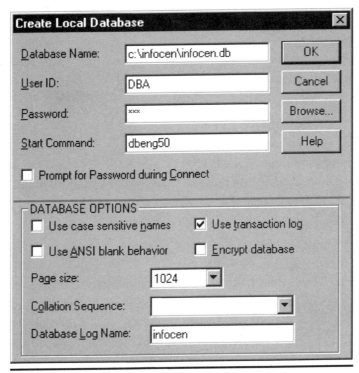

Figure 7.54 The completed Create Local Database dialog box.

10. In the Database Log Name area, enter "infocen." InfoMaker will create the log file in the InfoCenter directory since you specified that is where you want the database file. InfoMaker automatically gives the file a .log extension. The completed screen should look like Fig. 7.54.

11. Click on OK to create the database.

Creating database tables

Now that our database is created, we can start adding the tables we will need for our project. Let us start with the Contact table.

1. You should still be in the Database painter at this point.

2. To create a table, click the Table button in the Database painter bar or select Object | New | Table from the menu. The Create Table window appears.

3. In the Column Name area, enter `contact_id`.

4. Enter `varchar` for the type.

5. The width is 10.

6. No decimals.

7. No for null.

8. Default is none.

9. Format is ContactId.

10. Edit style is @@@@-####.

11. Validation is none.

12. Header is Contact Id.

13. Left justification.

14. Label is Contact Id:.

15. Enter the comment "This is the contact table's unique identifier."

16. Now that you have completed one column in the contact table, you can finish entering the table definitions by following Table 7.1.

Creating primary keys

Let us set up some primary keys for our InfoCenter tables.

1. From the Database painter, open the Contact table, if it is not already open.

2. Right-click on the table name. The table pop-up menu appears.

3. Select Properties... to open the Contact Table property sheet.

4. Click on the Primary Key tab, which displays the Table Contact Primary Key sheet.

5. To specify the contact_id column as the primary key, click on the contact_id column in the Table Columns list box. Contact_id appears in the Key Columns box.

6. Now click on OK to accept the changes.

Now that you know how to add primary keys to a table, define the primary keys for the rest of the tables in the InfoCenter database, following the values in Table 7.2.

Defining foreign keys

Now let us define the foreign keys for our tables. Let us look at the Contact table again. We want to define the column employee_id, as a foreign key. This means all the information for an employee is stored in another table, Employee in this case.

1. To define a foreign key, click once on the Contact table to select it.

2. Then click on the Create FK button on the Database painter bar. The Foreign Key Definition window displays.

3. First, enter a Foreign Key Name. In this case we name it employee_id.

4. Next select the Primary Key Table. In this case, the table containing the employee_id column resides in the Employee table. Select the Employee table from the Primary Key Table drop-down list box. Once selected, the pri-

TABLE 7.1 All the Columns for the Tables in the InfoCenter Application

Table name	Column name	Data type	Width	Dec	Null	Default	Format	Extended attributes edit	Validation	Header	Initial	Label
Contact	contact_id	varchar	10		No	None	ContactId	@@@-####	dddw_employee_listing	Contact Id		Conta ct Id:
	employee_id	integer			Yes	None	General	None	None	Employee Id		Employee Id:
	contact_last_name	varchar	25		No	None	None	None	None	Last Name		Last Name:
	contact_first_name	varchar	25		No	None	None	None	None	First Name		First Name:
	contact_title	varchar	25		Yes	None	None	None	None	Title		Title:
	contact_company	varchar	25		Yes	None	None	None	None	Company		Company:
	contact_home_address1	varchar	25		Yes	None	None	None	None	Home Address		Home Address:
	contact_home_address2	varchar	25		Yes	None	None	None	None	Home Address		Home Address:
	contact_home_city	varchar	25		Yes	None	None	None	None	City		City:
	contact_home_state	char	2		Yes	None	None	None	None	State		State:
	contact_home_zip	varchar	9		Yes	None	None	None	None	Zip		Zip:
	contact_home_country	varchar	20		Yes	None	None	None	None	Country	USA	Country:
	contact_work_address1	varchar	25		Yes	None	None	None	None	Work Address		Work Address:
	contact_work_address2	varchar	25		Yes	None	None	None	None	Work Address		Work Address:
	contact_work_city	varchar	25		Yes	None	None	None	None	City		City:
	contact_work_state	char	2		Yes	None	None	None	None	State		State:
	contact_work_zip	varchar	9		Yes	None	None	ZipCodes	None	Zip		Zip:
	contact_work_country	varchar	20		Yes	None	None	None	None	Country	USA	Country:
	contact_home_phone	varchar	10		Yes	None	None	(###)###-####	None	Home Phone		Home Phone:
	contact_work_phone	varchar	10		Yes	None	None	(###)###-####	None	Work Phone		Work Phone:
	contact_email	varchar	20		Yes	None	None	None	None	E-mail		E-mail:
	contact_cell_phone	varchar	10		Yes	None	None	(###)###-####	None	Cell phone		Cell phone:
	contact_birthday	date			Yes	None	None	mm/dd/yyyy	None	Birthday		Birthday:
	contact_spouse	varchar	15		Yes	None	None	None	None	Spouse		Spouse:
	contact_spouse_birthday	date			Yes	None	None	mm/dd/yyyy	None	Spouse BD		Spouse BD:
	contact_anniversary	date			Yes	None	None	mm/dd/yyyy	None	Anniversary		Anniversary:
	contact_notes	long varchar			Yes	None	None	None	None	Notes		Notes:

TABLE 7.1 All the Columns for the Tables in the InfoCenter Application (*Continued*)

Table name	Column name	Data type	Width	Dec	Null	Default	Format	Extended attributes edit	Validation	Header	Initial	Label
contact_history	contact_id	varchar	8		No	None	None	None	ContactId	Contact Id		Contact Id:
	contact_history_id	numeric	5	0	No	Auto-increment	General	None	None	History Id		History Id:
	contact_date	date			No	None	None	None	None	Date		Date:
	contact_time	time			No	Current time	None	None	None	Time		Time:
	contact_history_subject	varchar	15		Yes	None	None	None	None	Subject		Subject:
	contact_history_notes	long varchar			Yes	None	None	None	None	Notes		Notes:
Contact_Child	contact_id	varchar	10		No	None	None	None	ContactId	Contact Id		Contact Id:
	contact_child_id	numeric	5		No	Auto-increment	General	None	None	Child Id		Child Id:
	contact_child_name	varchar	15		No	None	None	None	None	Child Name		Child Name:
	contact_child_bday	date			Yes	None	None	None	None	Birthdate		Birthdate:
calendar	calendar_id	numeric	5		No	Auto-increment	General	None	None	Calendar Id		Calendar Id:
	employee_id	varchar	10		No	None	None	None	None	Employee Id		Employee Id:
	calendar_date	date			No	None	None	None	None	Date		Date:
	calendar_start_time	time			Yes	None	None	None	None	Start Time		Start Time:
	calendar_end_time	time			Yes	None	None	None	None	End Time		End Time:
	calendar_desc	varchar	5	0	Yes	None	None	None	None	Desc		Desc:
	calendar_category_id	numeric			Yes	None	General	ddww_category_listing	None	Category		Category:
employee	employee_id	integer	5	0	No	None	General	None	None	Employee Id		Employee Id:
	employee_last_name	varchar	15		No	None	None	None	None	Last Name		Last Name:
	employee_first_name	varchar	15		No	None	None	None	None	First Name		First Name:
	employee_title	varchar	15		No	None	None	None	None	Title		Title:
	employee_department_id	numeric	5	0	No	None	General	ddww_department_	None	Department Id		Department Id:

144

TABLE 7.1 All the Columns for the Tables in the InfoCenter Application (*Continued*)

Table name	Column name	Data type	Width	Dec	Null	Default	Format	Extended attributes edit	Validation	Header	Initial	Label
employee	employee_hire_date	date			No	None	mm/dd/yyyy	None	None	Hire Date		Hire Date:
	employee_ssn	numeric	9	0	No	None	General	None	None	SSN		SSN:
	employee_birthdate	date			No	None	mm/dd/yyyy	None	None	Birthdate		Birthdate:
employee view	employee_salary	numeric	6	2	No	None	General	###.###.00	None	Salary		Salary:
	employee_id	integer	5	0	No	None	General	None	None	Employee ID		Employee ID:
	employee_last_name	varchar	15		No	None	None	None	None	Last Name		Last Name:
	employee_first_name	varchar	15		No	None	None	None	None	First Name		First Name:
	employee_title	varchar	15		No	None	None	None	None	Title		Title:
	employee_department_id	numeric	5	0	No	None	General	dddw_department_list	None	Department Id		Department Id:
task	task_id	numeric	5	0	No	Auto-increment	General	None	None	Task Id		Task Id:
	employee_id	numeric	5	0	No	None	General	None	None	Employee Id		Employee Id:
	task_date	date			No	Current date	None	None	None	Date		Date:
	task_priority_id	numeric	2	0	Yes	None	General	None	None	Priority		Priority:
	task_name	varchar	15		Yes	None	None	None	None	Task Name		Task Name:
	task_due_date	date			Yes	None	None	None	None	Due Date		Due Date:
	task_status_id	numeric	2	0	Yes	None	General	None	None	Status		Status:
	task_notes	long varchar			Yes	None	None	None	None	Notes		Notes:
status	task_category_id	numeric	2	0	Yes	None	General	None	None	Category		Category:
	task_project	varchar	25		Yes	None	None	None	None	Project		Project:
	status_id	numeric	2	0	No	Auto-increment	General	None	None	Status Id		Status Id:
calendar_category	status_name	varchar	15		No	None	None	None	None	Status		Status:
	calendar_category_id	numeric	2	0	No	Auto-increment	General	None	None	Category Id		Category Id:
	calendar_category	varchar	1	5	No	None	None	None	None	Category		Category:

TABLE 7.1 All the Columns for the Tables in the InfoCenter Application (*Continued*)

Table name	Column name	Data type	Width	Dec	Null	Default	Format	Extended attributes edit	Validation	Header	Initial	Label
department	department_id	numeric	5	0	No	Auto-increment	General	None	None	Department Id		Department Id:
	department	varchar	15		No	None	None	None	None	Department		Department
Priority	priority_id	numeric	2	0	No	Auto-increment	General	None	None	Priority Id		Priority Id:
	priority	varchar	15		No	None	None	None	None	Priority		Priority:

TABLE 7.2   All the Primary Keys for the InfoCenter Application

Table	Primary key
Contact	contact_id
contact_history	contact_id
	contact_history_id
contact_child	contact_id
	contact_child_id
calendar	calendar_id
	employee_id
employee	employee_id
task	task_id
	employee_id
status	status_id
calendar_category	calendar_category_id
department	department_id
priority	priority_id

mary key defined for the Employee table displays in the Primary Key Columns box below the Primary Key Table.

5. Now let us define the column in the Contact table we want as a foreign key. Click on `employee_id` in the Select Columns box. The `employee_id` column displays in the Foreign Key column box.

6. Since we want to be able to delete employees and not delete their contacts since they may be reassigned to another employee, let us choose SET NULL. The screen should look like Fig. 7.55.

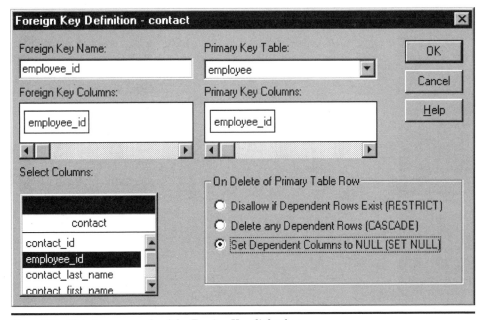

Figure 7.55   This is an example of the Foreign Key dialog box.

TABLE 7.3   All the Foreign Keys for the InfoCenter Application

Contact	employee_id	
Calendar	calendar_category_id	
Employee	employee_dept_id	
Task	task_priority_id	Linked to Priority table
	task_status_id	Linked to Status table
	task_category_id	Linked to Category table

Now go ahead and define the foreign keys for the rest of the database tables, using Table 7.3 as a guide.

Once you have defined all the foreign keys in the InfoCenter database, the Database painter workspace should look similar to Fig. 7.56.

Summary

We covered a lot of ground in this chapter. You should now have a good understanding of what a database is and how to create the tables, keys, indexes, and views as a basis for building your forms, reports, queries, and pipelines. We talked about the Database painter, the Table painter, and the Database Administration painter and the purpose of each in the InfoMaker environment.

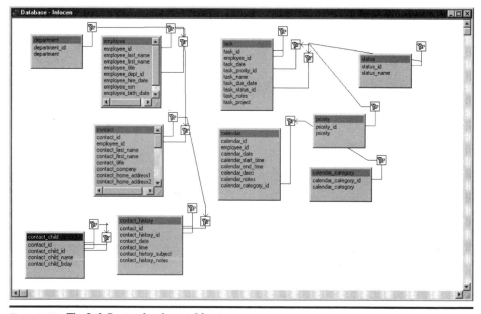

Figure 7.56 The InfoCenter database table structure.

8

Working with Data in InfoMaker

What You Will Learn

Chapter 8 talks about working with actual data in a database. You will learn how to retrieve, change, sort, filter, and import data without having to build a form or report. By the end of this chapter, you will feel comfortable loading new database tables, manipulating the data by using a variety of methods, and exporting data to other formats.

The Data Manipulation Painter

The Data Manipulation painter is used to import, enter, and view data as well as test validation rules, display formats, and edit styles. The Data Manipulation painter's sole purpose is to get information into and out of a database and view it, all without building a single form or report. Of course, the results are not as pleasant as if the data were displayed using a form or report, but the Data Manipulation painter is a useful tool to access data in a database quickly, nonetheless.

To access the Data Manipulation painter, do the following:

1. Start the Database painter by selecting the Database button on the Power-Bar.
   or
   Select the Database painter option on the PowerPanel.

2. When the Select Tables dialog box appears, choose the table to view. The Database painter workspace should look similar to Fig. 8.1.

3. Choose the type of view to open: Grid, Table, or Freeform. The Data Manipulation painter opens.

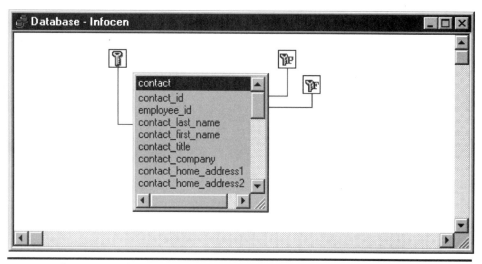

Figure 8.1   Accessing a table in the Database painter workspace.

Working with the Data Manipulation painter

On the Database painter bar, there are three different options available with these types of views to use in the Data Manipulation painter: Grid, Table, and Freeform. Using one of these three different types of views enables you to get a quick look at your data, enter or change small sets of data, test validation, edit styles, and display formats. If you will be making many changes to the data, I highly recommend you learn how to build forms rather than work in the Data Manipulation painter exclusively. Forms are much easier to work with in comparison to using the Data Manipulation painter and forms can be customized to display specific columns. There are several types of form styles to choose from; in addition, you have the capability to build custom form styles from PowerBuilder to access in InfoMaker.

It is difficult to enter data into a table by using the Data Manipulation painter. If there are many columns in a table, you are unable to see all the columns because they scroll off the window to the right. You also have a difficult time entering foreign keys to other tables. You need a list of all the code tables and what each value represents in order to enter them into the system correctly. Data entry is slow and error-prone. Let's take a look at the views available in the Data Manipulation painter.

The Grid view presents data in a spreadsheetlike format with grid lines separating rows and columns, as shown in Fig. 8.2.

The Table view is another type of view available in the Data Manipulation painter. The difference between the Grid and Table views is the Table view does

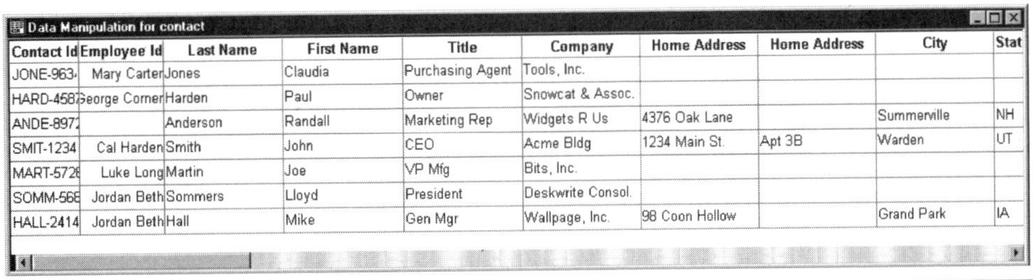
Data Manipulation for contact
Contact Id | Employee Id | Last Name | First Name | Title | Company | Home Address | Home Address | City | Stat
JONE-963 | Mary Carter | Jones | Claudia | Purchasing Agent | Tools, Inc.
HARD-458 | George Corner | Harden | Paul | Owner | Snowcat & Assoc.
ANDE-897 | | Anderson | Randall | Marketing Rep | Widgets R Us | 4376 Oak Lane | | Summerville | NH
SMIT-1234 | Cal Harden | Smith | John | CEO | Acme Bldg | 1234 Main St. | Apt 3B | Warden | UT
MART-572 | Luke Long | Martin | Joe | VP Mfg | Bits, Inc.
SOMM-568 | Jordan Beth | Sommers | Lloyd | President | Deskwrite Consol.
HALL-2414 | Jordan Beth | Hall | Mike | Gen Mgr | Wallpage, Inc. | 98 Coon Hollow | | Grand Park | IA

Figure 8.2 This is an example of the Data Manipulation painter in Grid view.

not have the grid pattern separating rows and columns. An example of a table shown in Table view is displayed in Fig. 8.3.

The Freeform view is a little better but not by much. You'll find that the data doesn't scroll to the right of the screen anymore. It now scrolls down the bottom of the screen (see Fig. 8.4).

Retrieving data

Retrieving data in the Data Manipulation painter is very simple. Upon entering the Data Manipulation painter, data is retrieved from the database and displayed automatically in the view. Additionally, it is possible to retrieve data at any time into the view.

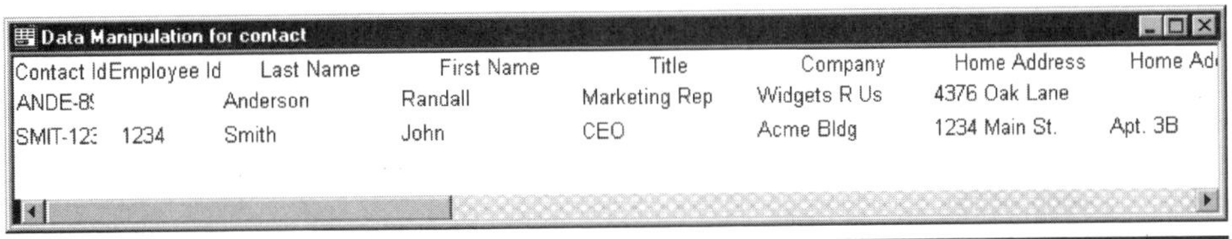
Data Manipulation for contact
Contact Id Employee Id Last Name First Name Title Company Home Address Home Ad
ANDE-8 Anderson Randall Marketing Rep Widgets R Us 4376 Oak Lane
SMIT-12 1234 Smith John CEO Acme Bldg 1234 Main St. Apt. 3B

Figure 8.3 Viewing the data in Table view using the Data Manipulation painter.

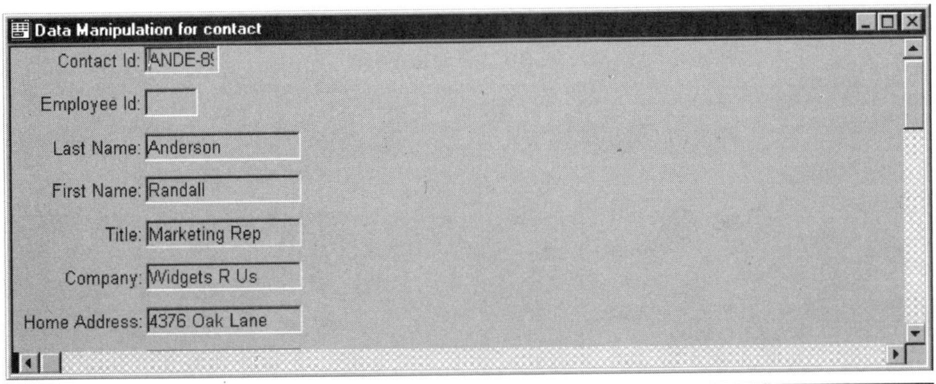
Data Manipulation for contact
Contact Id: ANDE-8
Employee Id:
Last Name: Anderson
First Name: Randall
Title: Marketing Rep
Company: Widgets R Us
Home Address: 4376 Oak Lane

Figure 8.4 Viewing the data in Freeform view using the Data Manipulation painter.

To retrieve data, do the following:

1. Start the Database painter.

2. Click on one of the Data Manipulation buttons on the Database painter bar: Grid, Freeform, or Table. The Data Manipulation painter displays after retrieving data from the table.

Notice that the data is automatically retrieved when the Data Manipulation painter is started. To retrieve data at any time from the database, click on the Retrieve button on the Data Manipulation painter bar. If there are several hundred rows in the table, it may take a few moments for InfoMaker to retrieve them all. In this case, the Retrieve button changes to Cancel. Choosing the Cancel button stops the process.

Changing data

Most data at one time or another will be changed. The Data Manipulation painter facilitates this process without having to build a form. However, if there is a large amount of data to change, build a form. Data entry will be much easier and faster.

To change data, do the following:

1. Enter the Data Manipulation painter, using the Table, Freeform, or Grid view.

2. Place the cursor on the column to change.

3. Type the changes.

4. Move the cursor to another column.

Adding a new row

Since information is constantly changing, there will come a time when data must be entered into a table. The Data Manipulation painter has the capability to add new rows to a table. However, if there are many rows to add or if information is added on a regular basis, build a form.

To add a new row, do the following:

1. Click on the Insert Row button in the Data Manipulation painter. A new row is added to the table, as shown in Fig. 8.5.

Contact Id	Employee Id	Last Name	First Name	Title	Company	Home Address	Home Address	City	State
.									
ANDE-897		Anderson	Randall	Marketing Rep	Widgets R Us	4376 Oak Lane		Summerville	NH
SMIT-1234	1234	Smith	John	CEO	Acme Bldg	1234 Main St.	Apt. 3B	Warden	UT

Figure 8.5 Demonstration of how a table appears with a new row inserted.

2. The cursor is placed in the first column. Enter information in the column, and press the Tab key once. The cursor moves to the next column.

Deleting a row

When information is no longer needed, it can be deleted from the table. Keep in mind, however, that until the table is actually saved, the information is not removed from the table and can be retrieved. If there are many rows to delete or if information is deleted on a regular basis, build a form.

To delete a row, do the following:

1. Move the cursor to the row to delete.
2. Now click on the Del Row button in the Data Manipulation painter bar. InfoMaker deletes the row without asking for confirmation.

Maneuvering within a table

For tables that contain more rows than can fit on a screen (and most do), InfoMaker moves the cursor throughout the table by using these buttons. The Last button moves the cursor to the last screen of data in the table, Prior goes to the previous screen, Next moves the cursor to the next screen, and of course First goes to the first screen of data stored in the table.

To maneuver within a table, select the First, Prior, Next, or Last button on the Data Manipulation painter bar, or choose First Page, Prior Page, Next Page, or Last Page from the Data Manipulation Rows menu.

Saving data

When making changes to a table in the Data Manipulation painter, you must keep in mind that changes are not permanent until the information is saved to the database. There are many possible ways to save data.

To save changes in a database table, do one of the following:

Choose the Close button from the Data Manipulation painter bar.

or

Choose the Updt DB button on the Data Manipulation painter bar.

or

Choose File | Close from the menu.

or

Choose File | Save Changes to Database... option on the menu.

Saving data in other formats

The Data Manipulation painter has the ability to save rows in a different format, such as text, an Excel or Lotus spreadsheet, an HTML file, a Powersoft report, and some others. Saving data to some of these other formats allows you to extend the power of InfoMaker by manipulating data using other tools.

To save data to another format, do the following:

1. Choose File | Save Rows As... from within the Data Manipulation painter, as shown in Fig. 8.6.

2. The Save As dialog box appears. Select the output file format, and give the file a name.

3. Click on the Save button on the Save As dialog box. InfoMaker saves the file.

Sorting data

To view table rows in a particular order, use the sorting functionality available in the Data Manipulation painter. Rows are sorted in either ascending or descending order on a specific column or on several columns.

To sort data, do the following:

1. Select Rows | Sort... from the Data Manipulation painter menu, as shown in Fig. 8.7.

2. The Specify Sort Columns dialog box displays, as shown in Fig. 8.8. The Source Data list box on the left side of the dialog box displays all the columns available in the table.

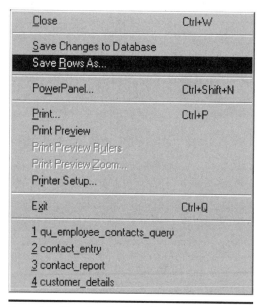

Close	Ctrl+W
Save Changes to Database	
Save Rows As...	
PowerPanel...	Ctrl+Shift+N
Print...	Ctrl+P
Print Preview	
Print Preview Rulers	
Print Preview Zoom...	
Printer Setup...	
Exit	Ctrl+Q
1 qu_employee_contacts_query	
2 contact_entry	
3 contact_report	
4 customer_details	

Figure 8.6 Choosing the Save Rows As... menu option on the file menu allows you to save rows from a table in another format for further manipulation.

Figure 8.7 The Sort menu available in the Data Manipulation painter allows you to set sort options.

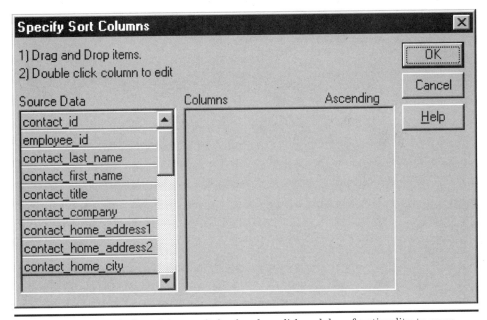

Figure 8.8 The Specify Sort Columns dialog box has click-and-drag functionality to move columns for sorting.

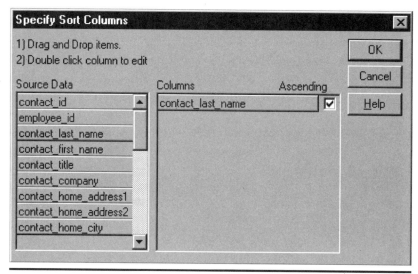

Figure 8.9   The Specify Sort Columns dialog box with a sort order selected.

3. To sort on a specific column, drag the column to the Columns area. The Specify Sort Columns dialog box should look similar to Fig. 8.9.

4. An ascending sort order is selected automatically. To sort by descending order, remove the check mark in the Ascending column.

5. Now click on OK. The dialog box closes, and the rows in the table are sorted according to the specified column, as shown in Fig. 8.10.

To remove the sort order, do the following:

1. Choose Rows | Sort... from the Data Manipulation painter.

2. When the Specify Sort dialog box displays, drag the sort column from the Columns area to the Source Data list box.

3. Now choose OK. The rows are not redisplayed in their original order when you return to the view. Select the Retrieve button in the painter bar to display the rows in their original order.

Contact Id	Employee Id	Last Name	First Name	Title	Company	Home Address	Home Address	City
ANDE-8972		Anderson	Randall	Marketing Rep	Widgets R Us	4376 Oak Lane		Summerville
HARD-4587	5689	Harden	Paul	Owner	Snowcat & Assoc.			
JONE-9634	4763	Jones	Claudia	Purchasing Agent	Tools, Inc.			
SMIT-1234	1234	Smith	John	CEO	Acme Bldg	1234 Main St.	Apt 3B	Warden

Figure 8.10   The sorted data by last name in the Data Manipulation painter.

Filtering rows

When you filter rows, an expression is defined to select only certain rows that meet a specific criterion. The Specify Filter dialog box provides a number of tools to help build an expression. It is possible to build quite complex expressions. The filter functionality is useful when there are hundreds of rows in a database and you only want to see a small selection of rows and work with them.

To filter rows, do the following:

1. Select Rows | Filter... from the Data Manipulation painter while viewing a table, as shown in Fig. 8.11.

2. The Specify Filter dialog box displays, as shown in Fig. 8.12.

3. Build an expression. When the Specify Filter dialog box is completed, it should look something like Fig. 8.13.

4. Click on the Verify button on the Specify Filter dialog box. InfoMaker checks the expression and will let you know if there are any errors.

5. When you have the expression the way you want it, click on OK.

You'll see that InfoMaker will automatically remove from the view all those rows which do not have Jones as the last name, in this example. The rows have not been deleted, they just don't display. The Data Manipulation workspace would look similar to Fig. 8.14.

To remove the filter, do the following:

1. Select Rows | Filter... from the menu.

Figure 8.11 Select Rows | Filter to set selection criteria on the data.

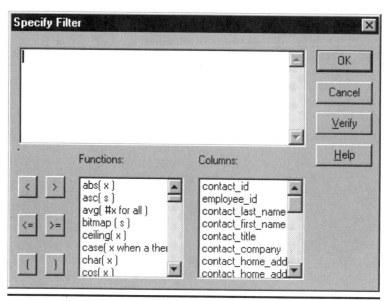

Figure 8.12 The Specify Filter dialog box is available to build a rule that sets selection criteria.

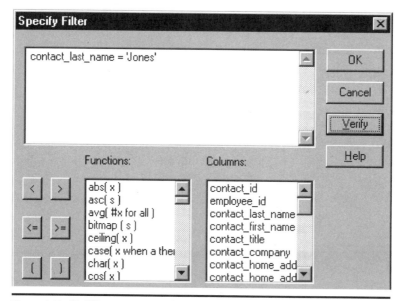

Figure 8.13 Building an expression to set selection criteria using the Specify Filter dialog box.

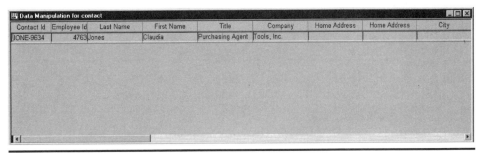

Figure 8.14 Filtering data from a table.

2. Delete the expression from the Specify Filter dialog box.

3. Press OK. The view returns to normal and shows all the rows in the database.

Importing data

InfoMaker has the ability to import data from another text or .dbf file format into a table. Having the ability to import data from other files makes loading new InfoMaker tables much easier and faster.

To import data, do the following:

1. From within the Data Manipulation painter in the table, select Rows | Import... from the menu. The Select Import File dialog box displays.

2. Enter the import file name.

3. Now click on the Open button. The rows from the text file are appended to the end of the table.

Displaying row information

Before you update the database, it is possible to review exactly how many rows have been deleted, how many rows have changed, and how many rows are currently displayed in the Data Manipulation painter by using InfoMaker's Described option. This information is helpful when we aren't exactly sure if we deleted the right number of rows or how many rows we filtered out of the current view. As soon as we update the database, however, these numbers are reset to zero.

To display row information, do the following:

1. Select Rows | Described from the Data Manipulation painter menu, as shown in Fig. 8.15.

2. The Describe Rows dialog box displays, as shown in Fig. 8.16.

Figure 8.15 Selecting the Described option to view the changes not saved to the database.

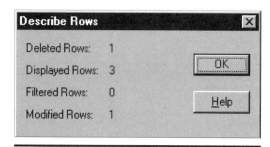

Figure 8.16 The Describe Rows dialog box displays the number of rows deleted, displayed, filtered, and modified in the current table.

Putting It All Together

In this tutorial you'll learn how to add, change, and delete information using the Data Manipulation painter. Additionally, you'll be able to save, filter, and sort data in a table.

Adding rows

Let's add a new row to the Contact table in our InfoCenter application.

1. If you haven't already done so, enter the Database painter.

2. Open the Contact table.

3. Select the Grid button on the Database painter bar to start the Data Manipulation painter in Grid view.

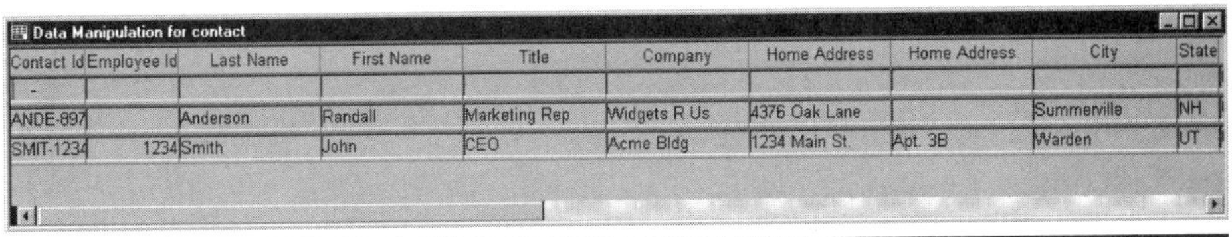

Figure 8.17   This is the Contact table with a new row inserted.

4. Click on the Insert Row button in the Data Manipulation painter. You'll see a new row added to the Contact table, as shown in Fig. 8.17.

5. The cursor is placed in the Contact Id column. Enter JONE-9634 and press the Tab key once. You'll move to the Employee_id column.

6. Now enter the rest of the information shown in Table 8.1 for the new contact, pressing the Tab key after each entry.

7. When you have finished, your screen should look like Fig. 8.18.

8. Now enter several more rows of data, adding names and addresses as we just did.

9. When you have finished, save your changes to the database by clicking on the Updt DB button in the painter bar.

TABLE 8.1   **All the Information Necessary to Add a New Contact to the Contact Table**

employee_id	4763
contact_last_name	Jones
contact_first_name	Claudia
contact_title	Purchasing Agent
contact_company	Tools, Inc.
contact_home_address1	
contact_home_address2	
contact_home_city	
contact_home_state	
contact_home_zip	
contact_home_country	
contact_work_address1	987 Loon Ave.
contact_work_address2	Floor 2
contact_work_city	Seattle
contact_work_state	WA
contact_work_zip	98501
contact_work_country	USA
contact_home_phone	
contact_work_phone	206 555-8574
contact_email	jonesc@tools.com
contact_cell_phone	206 555-9347
contact_birthday	
contact_spouse	
contact_spouse_birthday	
contact_anniversary	
contact_notes	Check with Claudia before purchasing for the Harden account. 25% discount possible.

Data Manipulation for contact									
Contact Id	Employee Id	Last Name	First Name	Title	Company	Home Address	Home Address	City	Stat
JONE-963	4763	Jones	Claudia	Purchasing Agent	Stuff & Puff Inc.				
ANDE-897		Anderson	Randall	Marketing Rep	Widgets R Us	4376 Oak Lane		Summerville	NH
SMIT-1234	1234	Smith	John	CEO	Acme Bldg	1234 Main St.	Apt. 3B	Warden	UT

Figure 8.18   Displaying the new row of information in the Contact table.

Changing data

We can now change some data. Let's say one of our contacts just got married. Let's add his wife's name to the row.

1. Find a contact without a spouse and click once on that row to select it.

2. Now tab to the Spouse column.

3. Enter Julie as the wife's name.

4. Tab to the Anniversary column and enter 7/25/1997, as shown in Fig. 8.19.

At this point, the changes you've made are not permanent. If you didn't want to save the changes, you could just click on the Close button in the Data Manipulation painter bar and exit the painter. The Data Manipulation painter would ask you if you wanted to save the changes, as shown in Fig. 8.20.

If you choose to save, the changes are made to the database. If you choose No, the changes aren't saved and you are returned to the Database painter. Last, you can select Cancel and return to the Data Manipulation painter.

Data Manipulation for contact												
Work Address	City	Country	Zip	Home Phone	Work Phone	Email	Cell phone	Birthday	Spouse	Spouse BD	Anniversary	No
uite 670	Summerville		01258	555 895-4254	555 259-857		-	00/00/00	Julie	00/00/0000	07/25/199E	
uite 310	Salt Lake City	USA	57958	555 123-4567	555 987-654	smith23@aol.cd	555 458-3	11/10/19	Paula	06/23/1976	06/01/1994	

Figure 8.19   Adding a new spouse in the Grid view of the Data Manipulation painter.

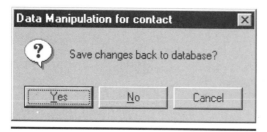

Figure 8.20   If changes have been made to a table, InfoMaker displays a dialog box to confirm saving before exiting the table.

Deleting a row

Now that we've added and changed data, let's delete a row. Remember that the changes we make are not permanent until we update the database. This gives us wide latitude to do "what if?" type of analysis.

1. Move the cursor to the row you want to delete in the Contact table.
2. Now click on the Del Row button in the Data Manipulation painter bar. InfoMaker deletes the row without asking for confirmation.
3. To get the row back, close the Data Manipulation painter.
4. When prompted to save the changes, select No.
5. Reenter the Data Manipulation painter. The row you deleted is still there.
6. Delete the row again.
7. Now choose the Updt DB button. The row is permanently deleted.

Sorting data

Now that we have several rows in the Contact table, let's try to sort them by the contact's last name.

1. Select Rows | Sort... from the Data Manipulation painter menu.
2. The Specify Sort Columns dialog box displays, as shown in Fig. 8.21. The Source Data list box on the left side of the dialog box displays all the columns available in the table.

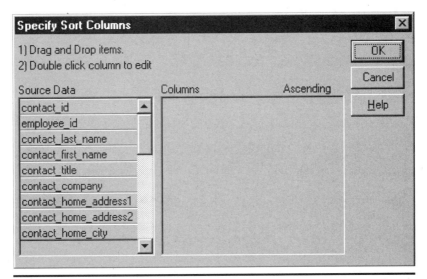

Figure 8.21   The Specify Sort Columns dialog box has click-and-drag functionality to move columns for sorting.

3. To sort on the contact's last name, drag the `contact_last_name` column to the Columns area. The Specify Sort Columns dialog box should look similar to Fig. 8.22.

4. Now click on OK. The dialog box closes, and the rows in the table are sorted according to the specified column. Your screen should look similar to Fig. 8.23.

Filtering rows

The filter functionality is useful when there are hundreds of rows in a database and you want to see only a small selection of rows and work with them. When you filter rows, basically what you're doing is setting some type of an expression to only see the rows that meet that criterion. So, let's say we want to see only those rows where the `contact_last_name` is Jones.

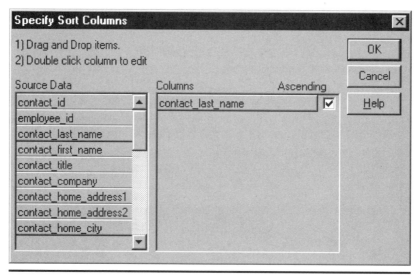

Figure 8.22 The Specify Sort Columns dialog box shows a sort order on a contact's last name.

Contact Id	Employee Id	Last Name	First Name	Title	Company	Home Address	Home Address	City
ANDE-8972		Anderson	Randall	Marketing Rep	Widgets R Us	4376 Oak Lane		Summerville
HARD-4587	5689	Harden	Paul	Owner	Snowcat & Assoc.			
JONE-9634	4763	Jones	Claudia	Purchasing Agent	Tools, Inc.			
SMIT-1234	1234	Smith	John	CEO	Acme Bldg	1234 Main St.	Apt 3B	Warden

Figure 8.23 The sorted data by last name in the Data Manipulation painter.

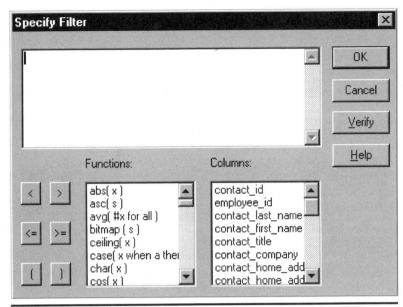

Figure 8.24 The Specify Filter dialog box is used to set selection criteria for viewing rows in a table.

1. Select Rows | Filter... from the Data Manipulation painter while viewing the Contact table. The Specify Filter dialog box displays, as shown in Fig. 8.24.

2. Click on the `contact_last_name` column from the Columns list box. When you click on it, the name of the column displays automatically in the expression area.

3. Now type an equals sign = after `contact_last_name`.

4. Type *Jones*. Remember that InfoMaker is case-sensitive at this point. If you just type *jones* with a lowercase j, no rows are filtered. When you've finished completing the Specify Filter dialog box, it should look similar to Fig. 8.25.

5. Click on the Verify button on the Specify Filter dialog box to ensure the expression is correct. InfoMaker checks the expression and will let you know if there are any errors.

6. When you have the expression the way you want it, click on OK.

You'll see that InfoMaker will automatically remove from the view all those rows which do not have Jones as the last name. The rows have not been deleted, they just don't show. Your Data Manipulation workspace should look like Fig. 8.26.

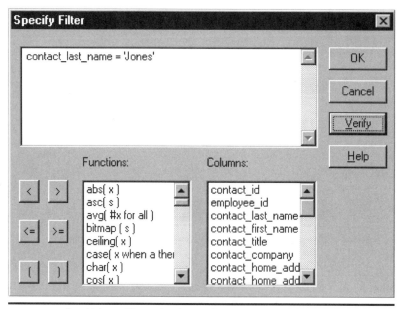

Figure 8.25 Specifying a filter criterion on Jones.

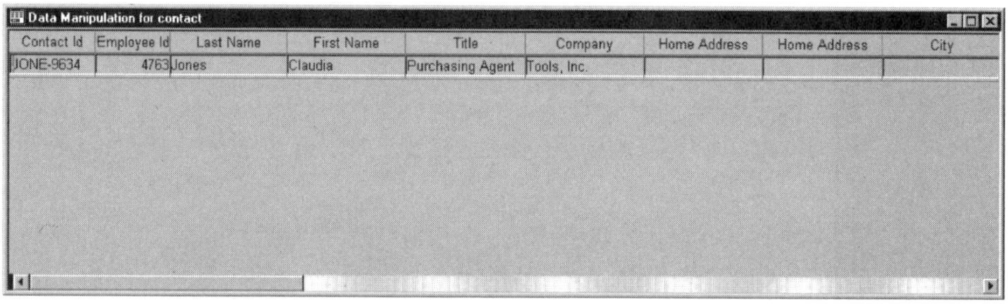

Figure 8.26 Displaying only those contacts with the last name of Jones.

Summary

In this chapter you have learned how to maximize the Data Manipulation painter's effectiveness. You've learned what it is and how to manipulate data, to retrieve data from the database and change it, to delete rows, and to sort and filter the data. You can now import data to and export data from a database. Now that you've read this chapter, you should feel confident accessing data by using the Data Manipulation painter.

9

Data Sources

What You Will Learn

Chapter 9 explains each of the data sources available in InfoMaker and the differences between the data sources for forms, reports, queries, and pipelines. We'll discuss in what situation each data source is used and how to implement it. By the time you finish reading this chapter, you will be able to create basic forms and reports, using each of the data sources.

Data Sources

A data source refers to how data is retrieved from the database to run forms, reports, queries, and pipelines. Each new form or report created in InfoMaker must have an associated data source. InfoMaker has five data sources available: Quick Select, SQL Select, Query, External, and Stored Procedures. Each of the different types of data sources can be used in reports. Only the Quick Select, SQL Select, and Query data sources can be used in forms. And when you build pipelines, only the Quick Select, SQL Select, Query, and Stored Procedure data sources are available. To create a query, there is no choice as to which data source can be used. The Query painter goes directly to the SQL Select data source. We'll discuss each of these data sources in depth.

The Quick Select data source is used for simple selection criteria and sorting. SQL Select is used for more advanced queries. Query is used to access a predefined SQL query created in InfoMaker's Query painter. An External data source is used to retrieve data from somewhere other than an InfoMaker database, such as a tab-separated text file (.txt) or an xbase file (.dbf). Stored Procedures can only be used if the database management system (DBMS) supports them. Stored procedures return result sets. Figure 9.1 shows all the data sources available in the Report painter.

Whenever a data source is defined, InfoMaker creates what is called an *SQL command* to execute the data selection. A SELECT statement tells the DBMS

Figure 9.1   The data sources available in InfoMaker.

what data to retrieve from the database. InfoMaker makes it easy to create complex selection criteria. You don't have to know SQL. InfoMaker has a graphical interface shielding you from the complexities of the SQL language. InfoMaker creates the SQL commands in the background.

Quick Select

With a Quick Select, data is selected from one table or from related tables linked with primary and foreign keys. The Quick Select data source is used to choose columns and specify simple sort and selection criteria.

To define a Quick Select data source, do the following:

1. Choose the Form, Report, or Pipeline painter from either the PowerBar or the PowerPanel. The Select Form dialog box displays, similar to Fig. 9.2.

2. Click on the New button on the Select Form dialog box. The New Form dialog box displays.

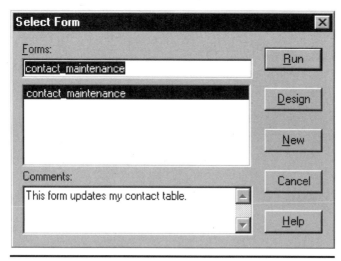

Figure 9.2   The Select Form dialog box displays whenever the Form, Report, or Pipeline painters is accessed.

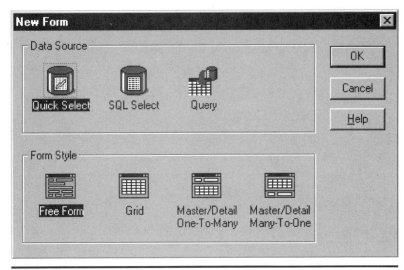

Figure 9.3 The New Form dialog box is used to select a data source and presentation style.

3. Choose the Quick Select Data Source.

4. If you are creating a form or report, select the presentation style, as shown in Fig. 9.3. If you're creating a pipeline, it is handled a little differently from this point. We'll discuss pipelines in greater detail in Chap. 15, The Data Pipeline.

5. Click OK on the New Form dialog box. The Quick Select dialog box displays, as shown in Fig. 9.4. This dialog offers several functionalities to create SQL statements when you are building a form, report, or pipeline.

6. Select the tables to use in the InfoMaker object. All the columns in the table appear in the Columns list box on the right side of the Quick Select dialog box.

7. Select the columns to appear on the object by clicking on them with the mouse, or choose the Add All button to add all the columns to the form.

8. Specify the sort order in the Sort drop-down list box, as shown in Fig. 9.5.

9. Specify the selection criteria from the criteria drop-down list box, as shown in Fig. 9.6.

10. Click OK. Now InfoMaker will continue and will build the form.

SQL Select data source

SQL Select is used in situations where more control is needed over the data. Within the Select painter, it is possible to set up more complex types of queries. SQL Select is also used to retrieve data from tables that aren't connected with a key.

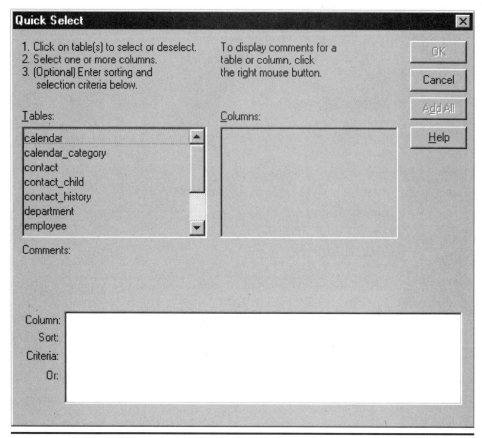

Figure 9.4 The Quick Select dialog box is used to select tables and columns.

To define an SQL Select data source:

1. Choose the Form, Report, or Pipeline painter button from the PowerBar or the PowerPanel.

2. In the Select dialog box, choose the New button.

3. In the New dialog box, choose the SQL Select data source.

4. Choose the presentation style for forms and reports. If you're creating a pipeline, it is handled a little differently from this point. We'll discuss pipelines in greater detail in Chap. 15.

5. Choose OK. The Select painter opens, displaying the Select Tables dialog box, as shown in Fig. 9.7.

6. Choose the table(s) to include in the SQL Select data source.

7. Click on the Open button on the Select Tables dialog box. The tables appear graphically in the Select painter workspace. There is an accompa-

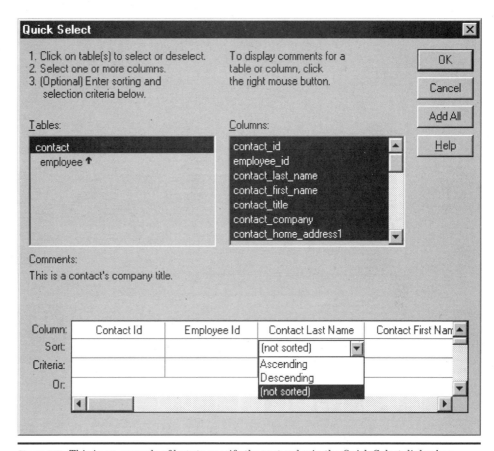

Figure 9.5 This is an example of how to specify the sort order in the Quick Select dialog box.

nying toolbar for specifying sort and selection criteria along a tab bar on the bottom, as shown in Fig. 9.8.

8. Select the columns to appear on the InfoMaker object. When you select tables in the Select painter, if there is a primary key–foreign key relationship between the two tables, then InfoMaker automatically joins them. If there is not this type of relationship, then join them by using the toolbox. When you have finished, the workspace should look similar to Fig. 9.9.

9. When you right-click on a table, a pop-up menu appears with the option to select all the columns in the table, to deselect them, or to close the table, as shown in Fig. 9.10.

10. Choose the SQL Select button on the Select painter bar to view the object in Design mode.

Adding sort criteria. To set the report to sort by a specific column you've chosen from the tables in the SQL Select workspace, click on the Sort button in the

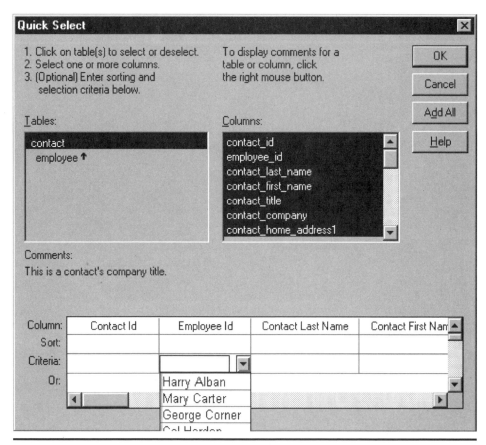

Figure 9.6 This is an example of how to specify selection criteria in the Quick Select dialog box.

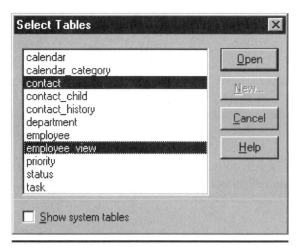

Figure 9.7 Choose the tables to include in the SQL Select data source using the Select Tables dialog box.

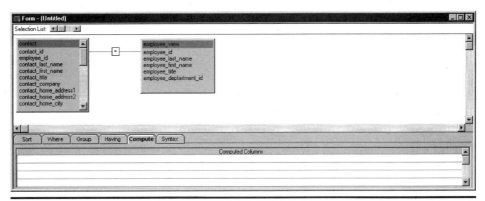

Figure 9.8 The Select painter is used to define an SQL Select data source. Additional options for specifying sort and selection criteria are available in the SQL Toolbox depicted by the tab bar.

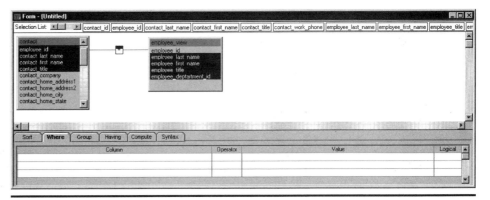

Figure 9.9 Selecting columns to appear in the SQL Select data source.

Figure 9.10 This is an example of the table pop-up menu.

SQL Toolbox. Then use the mouse to drag a column from the left to the right areas. Once you've selected the columns to sort on, your screen will look similar to Fig. 9.11.

In the example in Fig. 9.11, since `contact_last_name` is the first item in the right column, it will be the primary sort order. Then InfoMaker will sort the report by the `contact_first_name` column. Notice the sort order check boxes

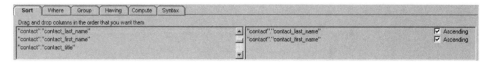

Figure 9.11 Specifying columns to sort on in the Select painter toolbox.

on the far right. These columns will both be sorted in ascending order. To sort in descending order, click on them to uncheck the box.

Setting selection criteria.   When specifying selection criteria, we are in essence telling InfoMaker to select specific rows in the database.

To set selection criteria, do the following:

1. Click on the Where tab in the Select painter Toolbox. There are four columns: Column, Operator, Value, and Logical.

2. Click in the first row under the column heading.

3. An arrow appears. Click on it. A drop-down list box appears, displaying all the columns from both tables, as shown in Fig. 9.12.

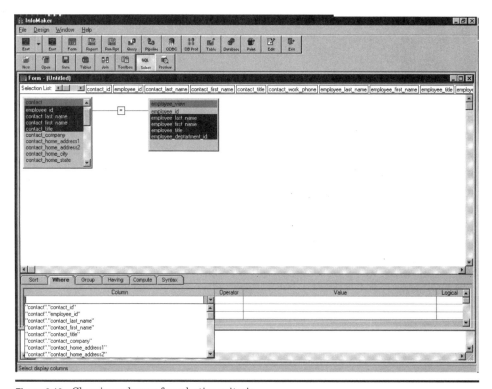

Figure 9.12 Choosing columns for selection criteria.

4. Select one of the column names.

5. The operator in the next column defaults to an equals sign = . If you click on the column, however, a list of operators appears, including less than, greater than, between, exists, etc.

6. Specify a value in the Value column by right-clicking on the first row of that column. The Value pop-up menu displays, as shown in Fig. 9.13. For more information on defining a value, see the section "Value Options for Selection Criteria" later in this chapter.

7. Select the Logical operator, if any. This is used to build an SQL statement with multiple criteria, such as with last name = "Jones" or state = "MN".

8. Press the Preview button to view the results.

Value options for selection criteria.   From the Value options pop-up menu in the Select painter, you can choose a column, a function, a specific value, or a query, or you can clear the current expression when specifying selection criteria. We discuss each of the options in this section.

  Setting selection to a column.   If the Columns… option is selected from the Value pop-up menu, the columns list box displays, as shown in Fig. 9.14. From this

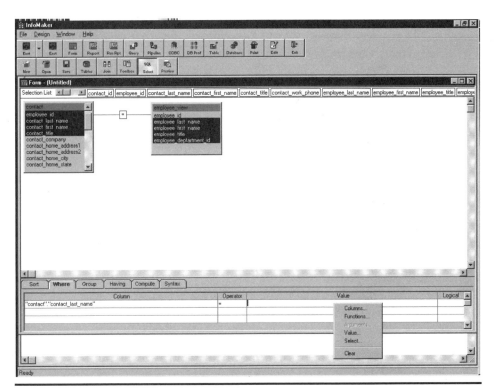

Figure 9.13 Setting a value for the selection criteria.

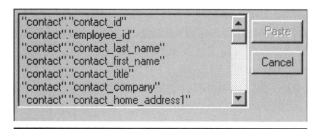

Figure 9.14 When you set criteria to equate to another column, select the columns from this list box.

list box, choose a column from one of the tables with which to equate. Put the column in the Value box by clicking on the Paste button.

Setting selection with a function. When the Function... option is chosen from the Value pop-up menu, the Function list box displays, as shown in Fig. 9.15. Use the Function list box to select a Function to equate to. Simply highlight one of the functions, and choose the Paste button. The function is pasted into the Value column in the Select painter toolbar.

Setting selection to a value. When the Value option is chosen from the pop-up menu, the Value list box appears, as shown in Fig. 9.16. For whichever column is selected as the primary select in the Column, all the values available are displayed. In the example from Fig. 9.16, we had chosen the contact_last_

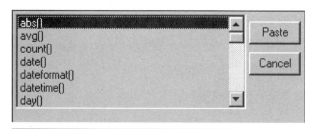

Figure 9.15 To set criteria to use a function, use this list box to choose from the available functions and paste it to the Select painter toolbar.

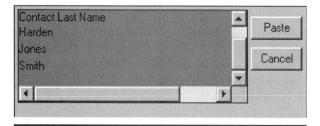

Figure 9.16 When you set criteria to equate to a specific value in a column, use this list box to choose from all the available values.

name column, so all the values in that column—Harden, Jones, etc.—display in the Value list box. If we want to equate to Jones, then we select it and click on the Paste button.

Setting selection to a nested Select statement. A nested SELECT statement is where the main SELECT statement uses another SELECT statement to retrieve data from a database. To create a nested SELECT statement, choose Select from the Value pop-up menu. A new SQL Select workspace appears to define another Select statement, as shown in Fig. 9.17.

Clearing selection criteria. To remove an entire Select expression from the tool-box, choose Clear from the Value pop-up menu. Once the expression is removed, a new expression can be built in its place.

Joining tables in SQL Select data sources. When more than one related table is available in the Select painter workspace, the join indicator displays to depict how the tables are joined. It is possible to change the equality of the join. Using the mouse, click on the equal box joining the tables. The Join dialog box shown in Fig. 9.18 appears.

You'll notice that the highlighted option contact.employee_id = employee_view.employee_id in Fig. 9.18 is the equality sign currently defined in the SQL Select workspace. To change the equality to less than or greater than or not equal to, click on the option and choose OK.

Grouping data. Grouping is a mechanism to associate certain information with things in common. Grouping is useful when you are building a report to group employees by department, for instance.

To group data, do the following:

1. Click on the Group tab in the toolbox. Notice that the Group tab is very similar to the Sort tab.

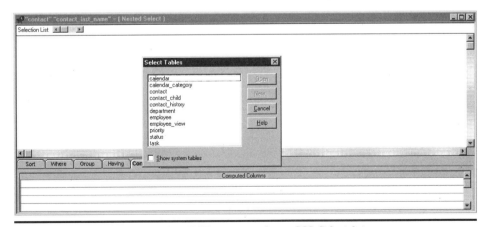

Figure 9.17 Setting up a nested SELECT statement for an SQL Select data source.

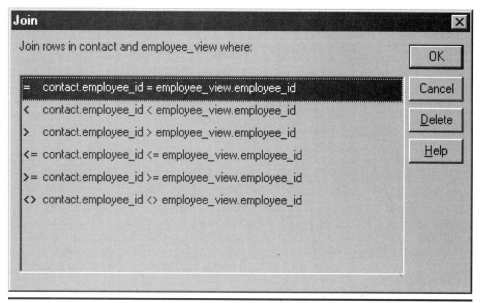

Figure 9.18 Changing the equality of related tables in the Select painter is as simple as selecting the join indicator between the tables in the workspace.

2. To group on a specific column, say, perhaps to group contacts by each state, simply drag the appropriate column into the right column, as shown in Fig. 9.19.

Setting Having clause. Having works in conjunction with grouping. The Having SQL clause only works when a Group clause is defined. Having criteria are much like setting up selection criteria.

For more information on defining a Having clause, see the section "Setting Selection Criteria" in this chapter.

Computed columns. Also available in the SQL Select toolbox is the Compute tab. It is here that computed columns are defined. Computed columns are made up of other values and cannot in and of themselves be updated. To change the value in a computed column, it is necessary to modify the values that make up the computed column.

To create a computed column:

1. Select the Compute tab in the toolbox.

Figure 9.19 Setting an SQL Select data source to group data.

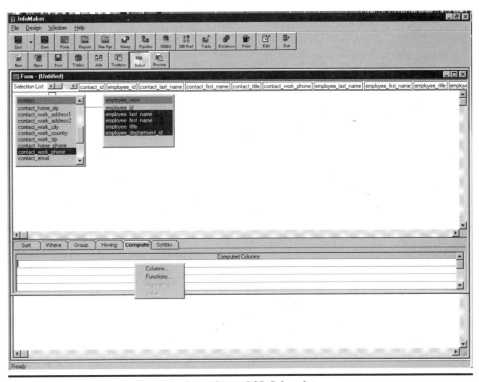

Figure 9.20 Setting up a computed column for an SQL Select data source.

2. Right-click on the first row in the Computed Columns column to bring up the Compute pop-up menu, as shown in Fig. 9.20.

3. Choose one of the options from the pop-up menu.

Viewing the syntax. If you want to learn SQL, viewing the SQL commands available in the Syntax workspace is a good way to start. SQL in the Syntax tab cannot be modified. However, as you become a more advanced SQL user, you can take the opportunity to modify the SQL statements you've created for a report or pipeline. In the Select painter, choose Design | Convert to Syntax from the Select painter menu. This converts the graphical representation of the current SQL statement, to an SQL statement command in the InfoMaker editor. It is possible to make any changes to the SQL by adding and removing columns and building more complex queries. See Fig. 9.21 for an example of an SQL statement.

Union. Union is a way to combine the results of one table with the results of another. It consists of two distinct SQL statements joined with an SQL Union clause. Each SELECT statement must contain the exact same number and type of data columns. InfoMaker allows you to create a Union by choosing Design | Unions from the SQL Select painter menu. When you choose this

```
Report - [untitled]
    SELECT "contact"."contact_id",
           "contact"."employee_id",
           "contact"."contact_last_name",
           "contact"."contact_first_name",
           "contact"."contact_title",
           "employee_view"."employee_last_name",
           "employee_view"."employee_first_name",
           "employee_view"."employee_title",
           "employee_view"."employee_deptartment_id"
      FROM "contact",
           "employee_view"
     WHERE ( "contact"."employee_id" = "employee_view"."employee_id" ) and
           ( ( "contact"."contact_last_name" = :contact_last_name ) )
```

Figure 9.21   This is an example of an SQL statement displayed using InfoMaker's editor.

option, it is possible to either change or delete an existing statement or to create a new one.

For more information on creating Unions, see your database documentation, since each database implementation has different functionalities.

Specifying retrieval arguments.   A retrieval argument defines information that the form or report needs before it can actually run. For instance, if you've built a report showing contacts in all states, a retrieval argument can be defined to retrieve only those contacts from a particular state. When retrieval arguments are defined for a report, InfoMaker displays a window prompting for the information to retrieve and then displays it in the report. Before you can actually use the retrieval argument, the argument must be referenced in either the Where or the Having tab in the SQL toolbox.

To specify retrieval arguments:

1. Choose Design | Retrieval Arguments from the Select painter menu. The Specify Retrieval Arguments dialog box displays, as shown in Fig. 9.22.

2. Enter the name of an argument here. The name must begin with an alpha character and can contain an underscore, numerals, or a dollar sign. When you have finished, the Specify Retrieval Arguments dialog box should look similar to Fig. 9.23.

3. Click OK to accept the new retrieval argument.

4. Select the Where tab in the Select painter.

5. In the Column area, select a column name from the table.

6. Set the operator.

7. In the Value column, right-click to bring up the Value menu.

8. Select Arguments…. The Arguments list box appears with the argument.

9. Select the argument and click on the Paste button. When you have finished referencing the argument, the SQL toolbox should look something like Fig. 9.24.

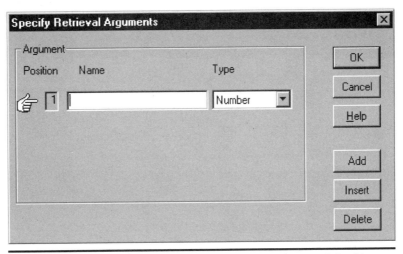

Figure 9.22 Before you access retrieval arguments, they must be defined by using the Specify Retrieval Arguments dialog box.

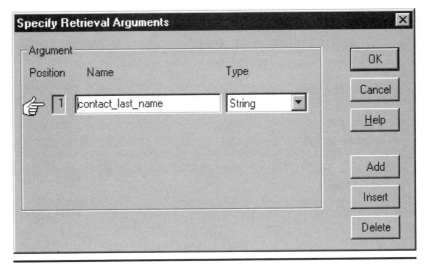

Figure 9.23 Specifying a retrieval argument.

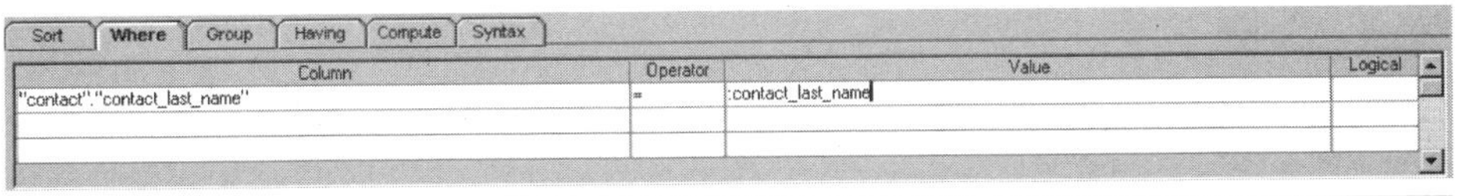

Figure 9.24 Setting up an SQL Select data source to use a retrieval argument.

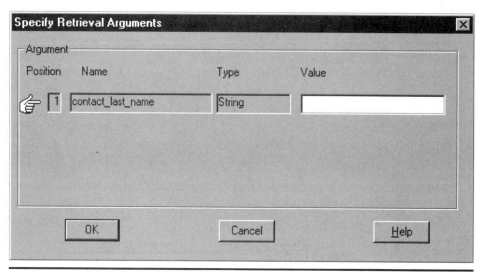

Figure 9.25 When a form or report has retrieval arguments defined, the Specify Retrieval Arguments dialog box displays before data is retrieved from the database.

Now, the first thing shown when the form or report is started is a dialog box for the retrieval arguments specified, as in Fig. 9.25. When a value is entered, for example, "Jones," only those people matching Jones are retrieved and displayed in the report.

Changing select painter options.   To change how the tables display in the Select painter workspace, experiment with the Show options. The Design | Show menu in the Select painter contains five different options. The first one, Datatypes, displays the data types next to each column in a table. If the next option, Labels, is checked, the labels associated with a column as defined in the Database painter display. Comments are also available as defined in the Database painter. The next option, SQL Toolbox, shows the toolbox in the Select painter, when checked. And last, the Joins option shows the joins graphically between tables showing the equality box.

Query data source

When a Query data source is selected, a form or report uses a predefined query to retrieve the data. Once a query has been created and thoroughly tested, it can be used repeatedly throughout an organization, saving development time. Using the Query data source is useful for creating forms or reports quickly and easily based on selection criteria that are used frequently.

To create a query, do the following:

1. Open the Query painter from the PowerBar. The Select Query dialog box displays, as shown in Fig. 9.26.

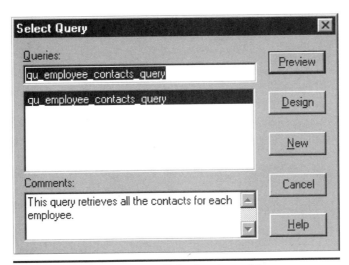

Figure 9.26 The Select Query dialog box is used to access an existing query for modification or to create a new query.

2. Choose the New button.

3. Choose the tables to add to the Query from the Select Tables dialog box.

4. Choose Open. The Select painter displays.

5. Choose the columns.

6. Set any sort and selection criteria.

7. Select Preview to run the form or report. InfoMaker displays the results of the query in a Grid format, as shown in Fig. 9.27.

8. Choose the Preview button on the Query painter bar to return to the Select painter.

9. Choose the Save button on the Select painter bar.

10. When you have finished, the Save Query dialog box will look similar to Fig. 9.28.

11. Choose OK.

12. Exit the Select painter.

Contact Id	Employee Id	Last Name	First Name	Work Phone	Last Name	First Name
JONE-9634	Mary Carter	Jones	Claudia	206 555-857	Carter	Mary

Query - (Untitled)

Figure 9.27 This is an example of query results.

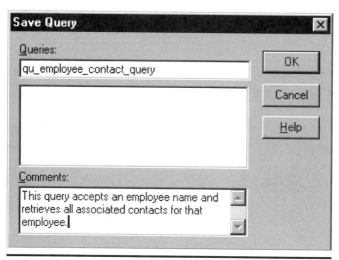

Figure 9.28 Saving a query for reuse at a later time.

External data source

Choose an external data source to report on data that doesn't reside in a database. When selecting an external data source, InfoMaker prompts for the columns to pull from either a .dbf or tab-separated text file and then builds the report. When using the external data source, you must know your data. You must know the columns and what the data contains.

To build a report based on an external data source, do the following:

1. Select the Report painter from the PowerBar.
2. When the Select Report dialog box displays, choose New. Choose the External data source and the Grid presentation style, as shown in Fig. 9.29.
3. Choose the OK button. The Result Set Description dialog box displays, as shown in Fig. 9.30.
4. Enter a column name, data type, and length. These attributes must match the external file. When you have finished, the Result Set Description dialog box should look similar to Fig. 9.31.
5. Choose OK. InfoMaker creates the report that will contain the data.
6. Choose Preview from the Report painter bar. InfoMaker displays a preview of the report, but it doesn't contain any data.
7. Choose Rows | Import... from the Report painter menu. When the Select Import File dialog box displays, choose the file that contains the data, as shown in Fig. 9.32.
8. Choose the Open button. InfoMaker retrieves the data from the file and displays it in the Report Preview workspace, as shown in Fig. 9.33.

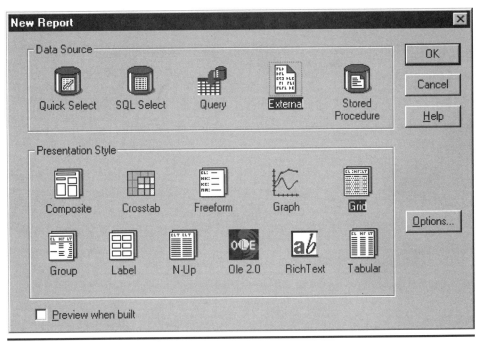

Figure 9.29   Selecting an External data source with a grid format for a new report.

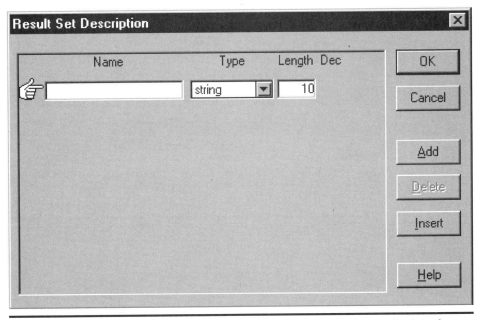

Figure 9.30   The Result Set Description dialog box is used to define the data coming into the report.

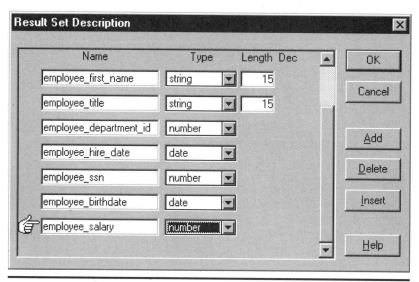

Figure 9.31 The Result Set Description dialog box with columns defined.

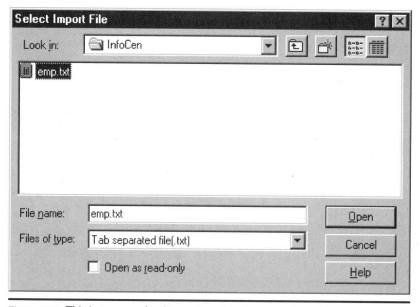

Figure 9.32 This is an example of importing data from an external file.

Stored procedure data source

If your DBMS supports stored procedures, a stored procedure can be specified as the data source for a report or data pipeline. A stored procedure is nothing more than a set of precompiled SQL statements that perform a database operation. Stored procedures reside in the database and can be accessed to build

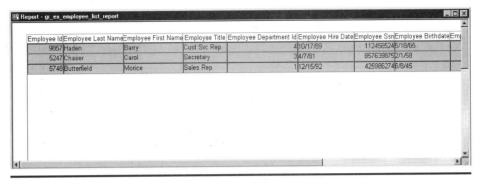

Figure 9.33 Displaying data from an external data source.

reports and pipelines. SQL Anywhere is capable of using stored procedures. The icon for the Stored Procedure data source displays in the New Report and New Data Pipeline dialog boxes only if the database to which you are connected supports stored procedures. Otherwise it does not display.

A stored procedure can have any combination of SQL SELECT, UPDATE, DELETE, decision branching, return results, etc. For more information about stored procedures, read your DBMS documentation.

To build a report based on a stored procedure, do the following:

1. Enter the Report or Pipeline painter from the PowerBar or PowerPanel.

2. Choose the New button on the Select Report dialog box.

3. Choose the Stored Procedure data source and the Grid presentation style, as shown in Fig. 9.34.

4. Choose the OK button. The Select Stored Procedure dialog box displays.

5. Select a stored procedure from the list, as shown in Fig. 9.35.

6. To view system procedures, check the System Procedure check box.

7. InfoMaker automatically creates a result set. However, you can build it yourself. Choose the Manual Result Set check box. The Result Set Description dialog box displays to enter the result set parameters.

8. When you have finished, select OK.

9. To view the stored procedures, choose the More ≫ button. The stored procedure displays, as shown in Fig. 9.36.

Putting It All Together

In this section you will learn how to build a form from a Quick Select data source. Additionally, you'll learn how to create a query with retrieval arguments and build a report based on the query. By the end of this tutorial, you will be very comfortable accessing some of the more advanced features available in InfoMaker.

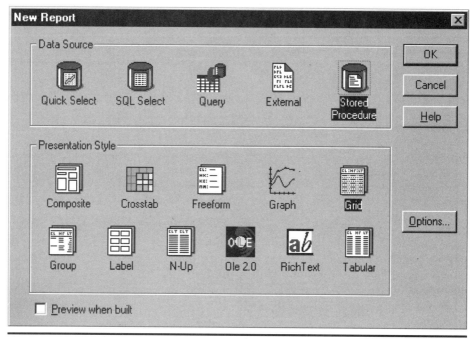

Figure 9.34 Creating a report based on a Stored Procedure data source.

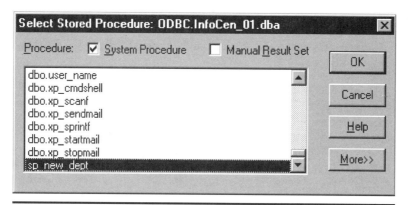

Figure 9.35 Selecting a stored procedure from the Select Stored Procedure dialog box.

Creating a form based on a Quick Select data source

Let's build a Quick Select form now. We want a form to update the Contact table in the InfoCenter application.

1. Choose the Form painter from either the PowerBar or the PowerPanel. The Select Form dialog box displays, similar to Fig. 9.37.

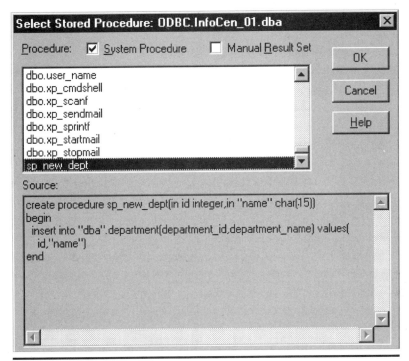

Figure 9.36 Viewing a stored procedure.

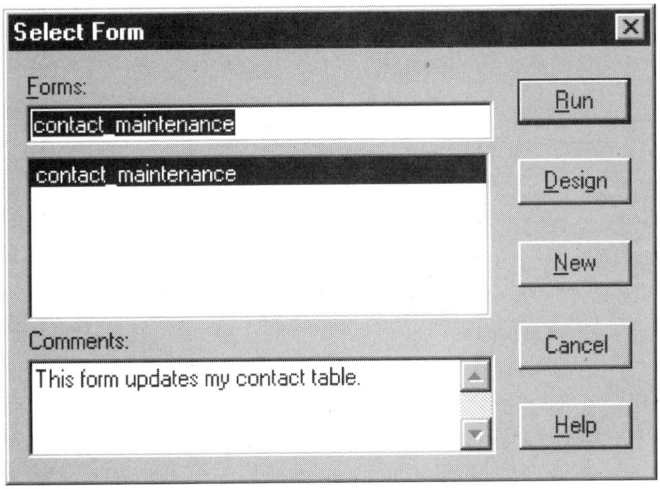

Figure 9.37 The Select Form dialog box displays to change an existing form or to create a new one.

2. Click on the New button on the Select dialog box. The New Form dialog displays.

3. Choose the Quick Select Data Source.

4. Choose the FreeForm presentation style. When you have finished, your screen should look like Fig. 9.38.

5. Click OK on the New Form dialog box. The Quick Select dialog box displays, as shown in Fig. 9.39.

6. Right-click on the Contact table in the Tables list box. You'll notice that in the middle of the Quick Select dialog box the table comments appear, telling you about the table.

7. Click on the Contact table in the Tables area to select it.

8. Then click on the Add All button. This adds all the columns in the Contact table to the form. The first few columns in the table are displayed horizontally at the bottom of the dialog box. There are also areas to sort and set selection criteria. The Quick Select dialog box should look like Fig. 9.40.

9. Now right-click on the contact_title in the Columns list box. You'll notice that any comments associated with a column display in the Comments area.

10. Move the cursor to the contact_work_state column by clicking on the column name and dragging the column after the contact_work_city column. This changes the order of the columns.

11. Now click on OK. InfoMaker goes on to create a new form.

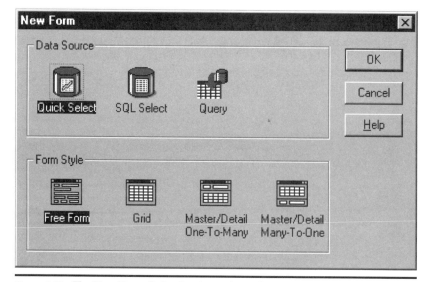

Figure 9.38 The New Form dialog box is used to select a data source and form style.

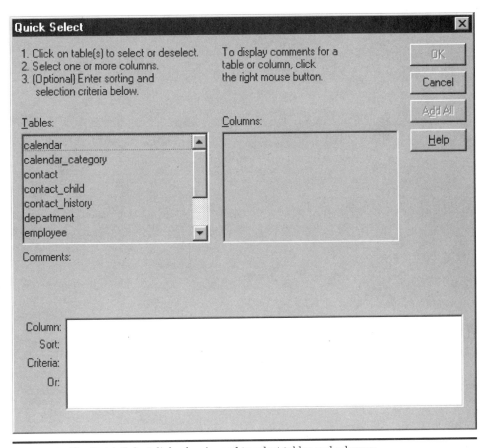

Figure 9.39   The Quick Select dialog box is used to select tables and columns.

12. For now, let's just close the form by selecting the Close button from the painter bar. When you are prompted to save changes, select No.

Creating a query

To create a query, do the following:

1. Open the Query painter from the PowerBar. The Select Query dialog box displays.

2. Choose the New button.

3. Select the `Contact` and the `Employee_View` tables from the Select Tables dialog box, and choose Open. The Select painter displays.

4. In the Contact table, choose the `contact_id`, `employee_id`, `contact_last_name`, `contact_first_name`, and the `contact_work_phone`.

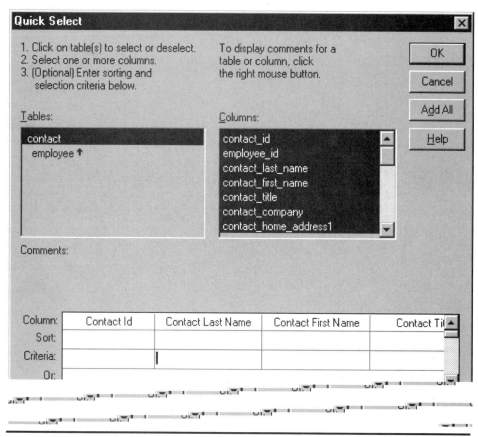

Figure 9.40 Selecting the columns for a new form.

5. In the `Employee_View`, choose the `employee_last_name` and the employee_first_name. When you have finished, your screen should look similar to Fig. 9.41.

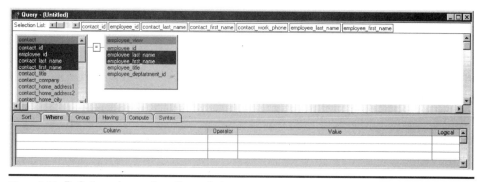

Figure 9.41 Defining columns for a Query data source.

6. Now let's define retrieval arguments. We often need reports that retrieve all the contacts for a particular employee. So we want to prompt for a specific employee. Choose Design | Retrieval Arguments... from the Select painter menu. The Specify Retrieval Arguments dialog box displays.

7. In position 1, enter `employee_last_name`. Make sure the data type is String.

8. Click on the Add button.

9. In position 2, enter `employee_first_name`. The data type should be String again. When you have finished, the Specify Retrieval Arguments dialog box should look like Fig. 9.42.

10. Click on OK.

11. Now we need to reference the retrieval arguments in our SELECT statement. Choose the Where tab in the SQL toolbox.

12. In the first column, select the `employee_last_name` column.

13. The operator should be equals (=).

14. Set the Value column to the argument `employee_last_name`.

15. Now on the second line, select the `employee_first_name` column.

16. The operator is equals (=).

17. The Value column should have the argument `employee_last_name`. You'll notice that InfoMaker automatically puts the Logical connector AND in the first row. This tells the database to retrieve those rows which have a specific last name AND a specific first name. When finished, the SQL toolbox should appear as in Fig. 9.43.

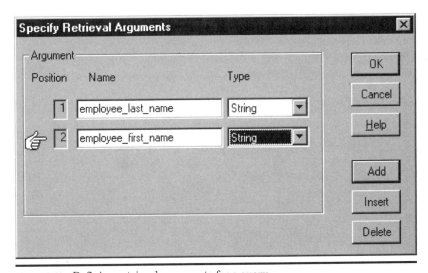

Figure 9.42 Defining retrieval arguments for a query.

Figure 9.43 Setting the retrieval arguments for a query.

18. Select Preview from the Select painter bar. The Specify Retrieval Arguments dialog box displays.

19. Enter an employee you've entered into your Contact table. For example, we can enter Mary Carter. When you have finished, the dialog box should look like Fig. 9.44.

20. Choose OK. As you can see, InfoMaker displays the results of the query we've defined in a grid format, as shown in Fig. 9.45.

21. Choose the Preview button on the Query painter bar to return to the Select painter.

22. Choose the Save button on the Select painter bar.

23. Save the Query as `qu_employee_contact_query`, and enter a descriptive comment in the Comments box. When you have finished, the Save Query dialog box will look similar to Fig. 9.46.

24. Choose OK and exit the Select painter.

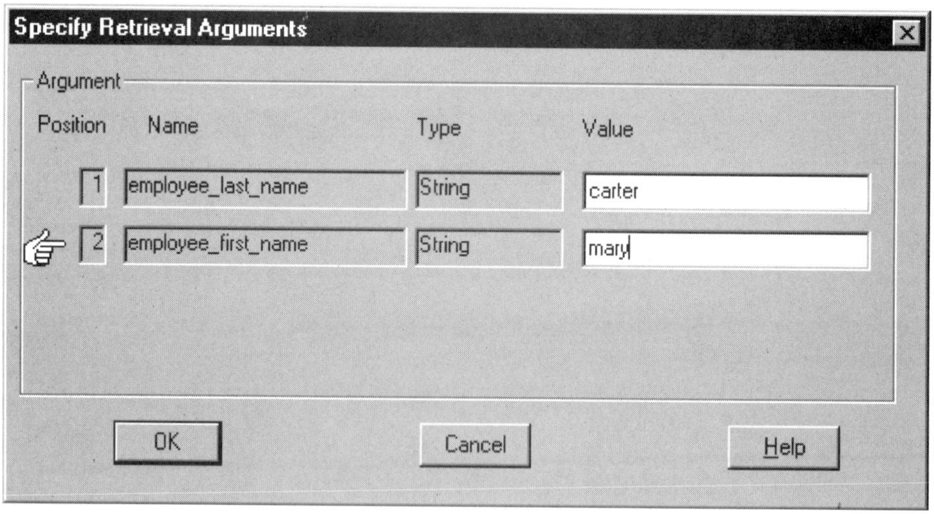

Figure 9.44 Entering retrieval criteria for a query.

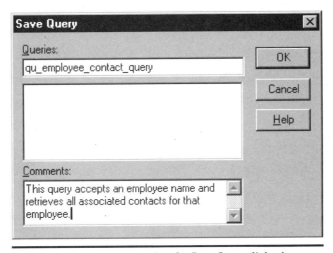

Contact Id	Employee Id	Last Name	First Name	Work Phone	Last Name	First Name
JONE-9634	Mary Carter	Jones	Claudia	206 555-857	Carter	Mary

Figure 9.45   Displaying the results of a query with retrieval criteria specified.

Save Query

Queries:

qu_employee_contact_query

Comments:

This query accepts an employee name and retrieves all associated contacts for that employee.

OK

Cancel

Help

Figure 9.46   Saving a query using the Save Query dialog box.

Now, let's create a report based on our query.

1.   Open the Report painter.

2.   Choose New in the Select Report dialog box.

3.   Select a Query data source and the Grid presentation style, as shown in Fig. 9.47.

4.   Choose the OK button on the New Report dialog box. The Select Query dialog box displays.

5.   Choose `qu_employee_contacts_query`, as shown in Fig. 9.48.

6.   Choose the OK button. InfoMaker creates the report as specified by the predefined query and displays the report in the Report painter's Design mode.

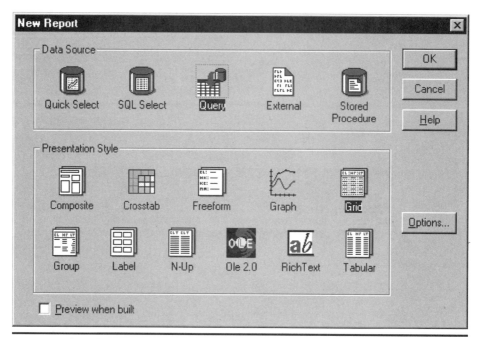

Figure 9.47 Specifying a Query data source to access a predefined query.

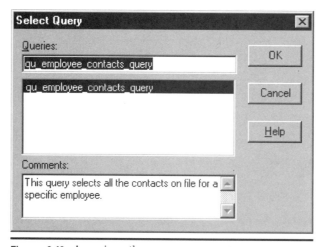

Figure 9.48 Accessing the query qu_employee_con-
tacts_query to retrieve data for a report.

Summary

We've covered all the data sources available in InfoMaker in this chapter. You now know which data sources are accessible when you are building forms, reports, queries, and pipelines. You also learned how to select tables and columns, create sort and selection criteria, and build retrieval arguments for reports.

Building Forms

What You Will Learn

Chapter 10 explains what a form is and in what situations to use the different presentation styles. We'll discuss in detail all the different form styles available in the Form painter—what they are and how to create them. By the end of this chapter, you will have a basic understanding of forms and can begin to create your own.

About Forms

A form is a type of InfoMaker object which allows you to view, update, delete, and create information in a database. A form displays the data in an organized format, making it easy to work with.

The Data Manipulation painter, which we discussed in Chap. 8, Working with Data in InfoMaker, has the same type of functionality as a form. Both the Data Manipulation painter and the Form painter create objects that permit viewing, updating, etc., of data held in tables. However, the Data Manipulation painter is more difficult to work with if there are frequent changes to the database. Forms make data entry easier and faster.

As a comparison, let's take a look at the Database Manipulation painter in contrast to the Form painter. Figure 10.1 shows a table in grid style in the

Data Manipulation for calendar						Calendar D
Calendar Id	Employee Id	Date	Start Time	End Time		
10	Mary Carter	5/15/96	08:00:00	10:00:00	Meeting for project 40	
11	Mary Carter	5/15/96	01:00:00	03:00:00	Meeting with vice-pres for new computers for office.	
12	Mary Carter	5/16/96	07:00:00	11:00:00	Introduction to new vendors for scanning project	
13	Cal Harden	5/18/96	07:00:00	05:00:00	Vacation today	
14	Harry Alban	5/15/96	10:00:00	11:00:00	Meet with product dev. group	

Figure 10.1 An example of a table displayed in the Data Manipulation painter.

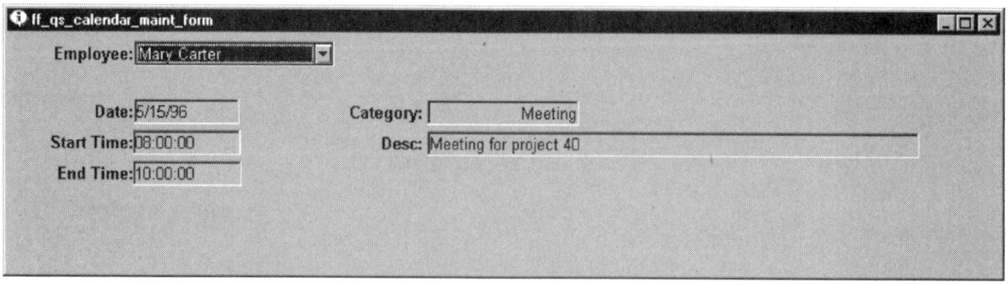

Figure 10.2   An example of a table in a freeform style form.

Database Manipulation painter. Notice that not all the columns are visible on the screen. You have to tab to the right to view additional information.

Now let's contrast the Data Manipulation view with a form showing the same table (see Fig. 10.2).

Looking at the form in Fig. 10.2, you'll notice that only one entry for an employee is shown at a time and in a pleasant-looking manner, so all columns are shown at once. This type of form makes it much easier to work with the data. Also with a form, you can create edit styles and display formats which make entering data much faster.

Creating forms

The data source and form style must be selected whenever a new form is created. Then the data appearing on the form is defined, which entails choosing columns to appear on the form. Once these tasks are completed, InfoMaker creates a basic form that can be modified in any number of ways to make the data easier to read and manipulate.

InfoMaker has four different form styles to choose from—Freeform, Grid, Master/Detail One-to-Many, and Master/Detail Many-to-One. We discuss each of these presentation styles in this chapter.

Selecting the form style

InfoMaker forms have four different styles, each with its own unique uses. We go through each of the presentation styles next and tell you when is a good time to use them and how to optimize their use in an InfoMaker application. Additionally, PowerBuilder developers in an organization can create custom-made form styles for specific use in InfoMaker applications. We discuss this further in Chap. 17, InfoMaker and the PowerBuilder Connection.

The freeform form style.   When you are viewing information from a database one row at a time, use a free-form presentation style. You can arrange columns anywhere on the form. Additionally, the Form painter has the functionality to add boxes to group-related information, add buttons with predefined actions, etc. There are many options available to enhance reports, which we cover in

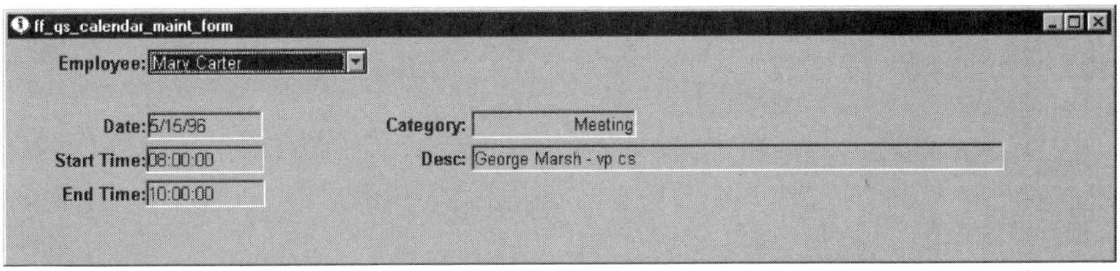

Figure 10.3   This is an example of a free-form form style.

detail in Chap. 11, Enhancing Forms. Figure 10.3 shows an example of a freeform form.

To create a form:

1. Select the Form painter button from the PowerBar or PowerPanel. The Select Form dialog box displays, as shown in Fig. 10.4.

2. Select the New button on the Select Form dialog box to create a new form. The New Form dialog box displays, as shown in Fig. 10.5.

3. Select a data source.

4. Next select the FreeForm form style.

5. Choose the OK button.

Grid form style.   A grid style form displays data in a spreadsheetlike view, showing all rows in a table at once. The grid style allows you to reorder and resize the columns on the form. The grid style is useful to view and update sev-

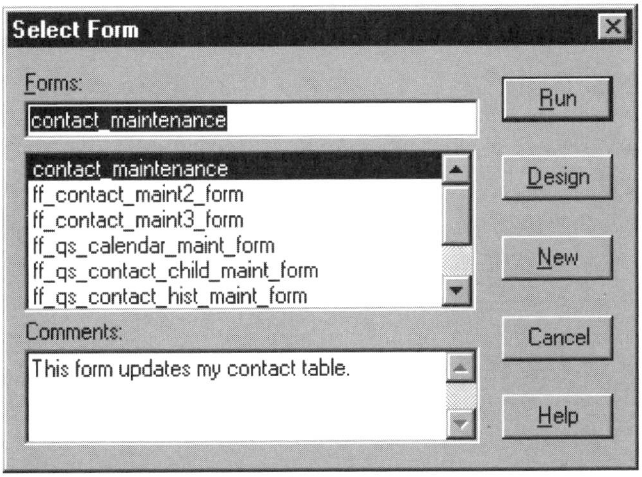

Figure 10.4   The Select Form dialog box is used either to access an existing form or to create a new form.

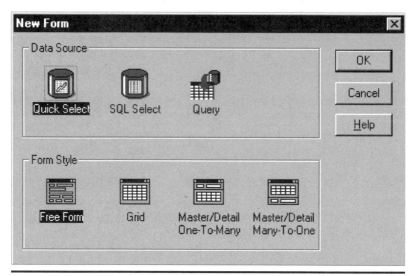

Figure 10.5 When you create a new form, the data source and presentation style must be selected.

eral rows of data at once. Figure 10.6 shows an example of a form built with the grid presentation style.

To create a grid-style form:

1. Select the Form painter button from the PowerBar or PowerPanel. The Select Form dialog box displays, as shown in Fig. 10.7.

2. Select the New button to create a new form. The New Form dialog box displays, as shown in Fig. 10.8.

3. Select the data source.

4. Select the Grid form style.

5. Choose the OK button.

Employee Schedule

Employee	Date	Start Time	End Time	Category	Desc
Mary Carter	5/15/96	01:00:00	03:00:00	Meeting	George Marsh - vp cs
Mary Carter	5/15/96	08:00:00	10:00:00	Meeting	George Marsh - vp cs
Harry Alban	5/15/96	10:00:00	11:00:00	Meeting	Sunspot Inc. offices
Mary Carter	5/16/96	07:00:00	11:00:00	Meeting	George Marsh - vp cs
Cal Harden	5/18/96	07:00:00	05:00:00	Vacation	

Figure 10.6 This is an example of a grid style form.

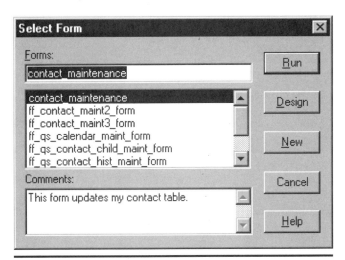

Figure 10.7 The Select Form dialog box is used either to access an existing form or to create a new form.

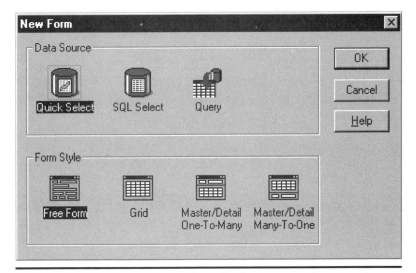

Figure 10.8 When you create a new form, the data source and presentation style must be selected.

The Master/Detail One-to-Many form style. The Master/Detail One-to-Many form style is used in those situations where data from two or more tables is related in a one-to-many relationship. For instance, in our InfoCenter application, each person in the contact table has many items related to her or him from the contact_history table. This means we only have to store the information about the contact, such as address, phone, etc., once. But we can store multiple lines of history information in the contact_history table. Each time a contact calls or writes to us, we can add another line in the history table without

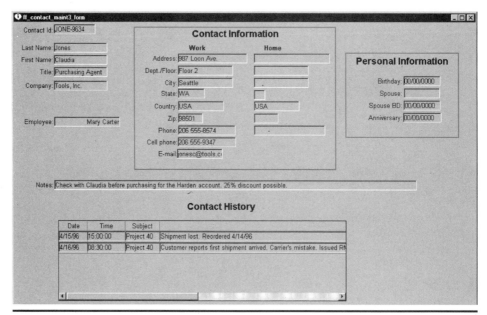

Figure 10.9 This is an example of a form using a one-to-many presentation style.

having to re-add address information. We use a Master/Detail One-to-Many form style to depict this type of relationship, as shown in Fig. 10.9.

Notice that the master table, `contact`, contains information about the contact. At the bottom of the screen is the Contact History table, showing a line for each time the contact has called. When you create a Master/Detail One-to-Many form, remember that the linked tables must have a primary key–foreign key relationship. In Fig. 10.10, we see the relationship between the `contact`

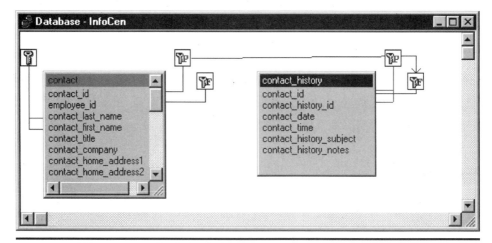

Figure 10.10 This is an example of table linkage with primary and foreign keys necessary for a one-to-many presentation style.

and the `contact_history` tables. Notice that the `contact_id` in the contact_history table is a foreign key to the `contact_id` in the `contact` table.

To create a Master/Detail One-to-Many form:

1. Select the Form painter button from the PowerBar or PowerPanel. The Select Form dialog box displays, as shown in Fig. 10.11.

2. Select the New button to create a new form. The New Form dialog box displays, as shown in Fig. 10.12.

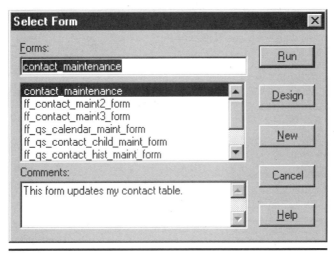

Figure 10.11 The Select Form dialog box is used either to access an existing form or to create a new form.

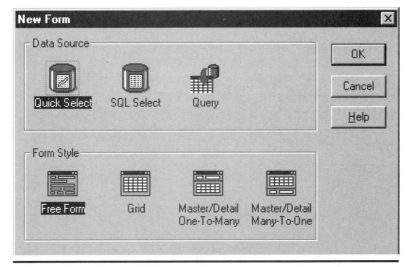

Figure 10.12 When you create a new form, the data source and presentation style must be selected.

3. Select the Quick Select data source. This is the only data source that will work properly with a one-to-many form.

4. Choose the Master/Detail One-to-Many presentation style.

5. Choose the OK button. The Select Master Table dialog box displays, as shown in Fig. 10.13. This dialog box accepts information about the table and columns to place in the master table on the form. Remember that the master table in a one-to-many relationship refers to the table that displays only one row at a time. Only one table may be selected for the master table. Once the form has been completely defined, you can edit the data source and add another table if necessary.

6. Click on the table in the Tables list box. All the columns in the table display in the Columns list box on the right side of the dialog box.

7. Select the columns to appear on the form by clicking on them with the mouse, or choose the Add All button to add all the columns. The screen should look similar to Fig. 10.14.

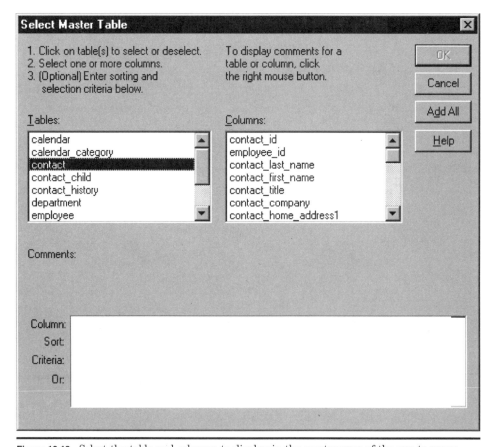

Figure 10.13 Select the table and columns to display in the master area of the one-to-many form, using the Select Master Table dialog box.

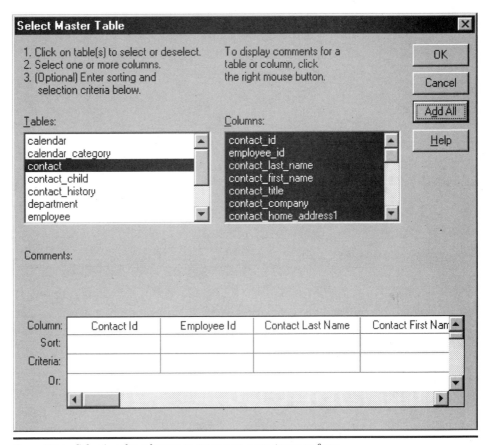

Figure 10.14   Selecting the columns to appear on a one-to-many form.

8. Specify sort criteria. See Chap. 9, Data Sources, for information on setting sort criteria.

9. Specify selection criteria. See Chap. 9 for information on setting selection criteria.

10. Choose the OK button. The next dialog box, Select Detail Table, displays, as shown in Fig. 10.15.

11. In the Select Detail Table dialog box, choose the detail table. Only one table may be selected. Once the form is designed, you can edit the data source and add another table if necessary.

12. When the columns appear, select the columns for the detail table by clicking on them with the mouse or selecting the Add All button to add all the columns to the form. When you have finished, your screen should look similar to Fig. 10.16.

13. Specify the sort order. See Chap. 9 for information on defining sort orders.

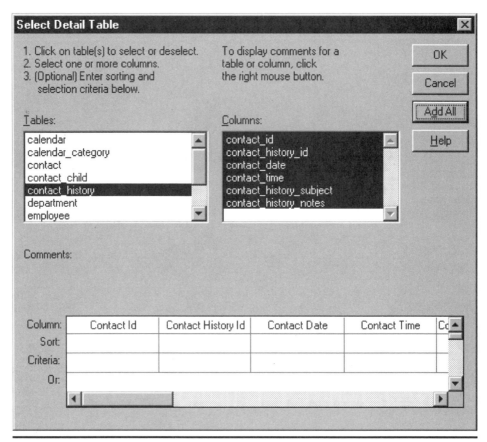

Figure 10.15 The Select Detail Table dialog box is used to select a detail table for a one-to-many presentation style form.

14. Specify any selection criteria. See Chap. 9 for information on defining selection criteria.

15. Choose OK when you have finished. InfoMaker then displays the Select Master/Detail Relationship dialog box, as shown in Fig. 10.17. This dialog box is used to verify the relationship between the two tables added to the master/detail form. If the relationship was not correct, we could choose the More ≫ button, select the master key, and match it to the detail key to create a link between the tables.

16. Now choose OK, and InfoMaker creates the form shown in Fig. 10.18.

Master/Detail Many-to-One form style. Master/detail many-to-one forms work in reverse of the one-to-many forms. Instead of having one contact related to a contact history, as in our previous example, in a many-to-one form, you could have a list of contacts to scroll through and view information on the assigned employee for one of them. It is in this type of situation where a many-to-one form style is useful.

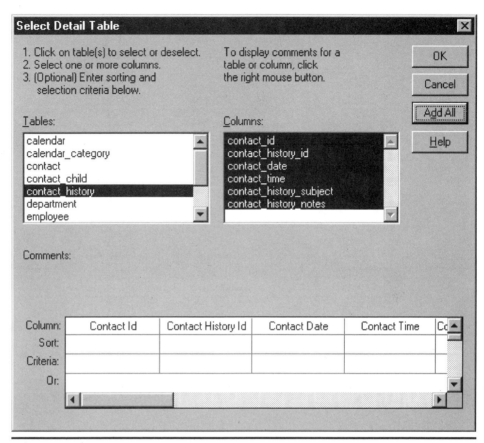

Figure 10.16   This is an example of selecting the detail information to display on a one-to-many form.

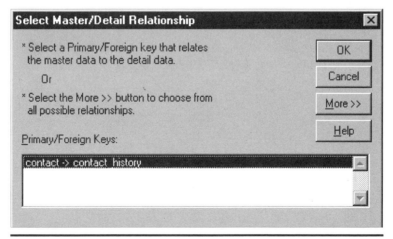

Figure 10.17   Define the relationship between the tables in the Select Master/Detail Relationship dialog box.

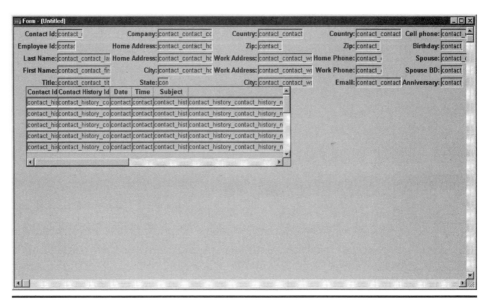

Figure 10.18 An example of a one-to-many form in Design mode.

Normally, in the list view of the form, display only enough information from a table to identify the row. Usually one or two columns are enough for this purpose. Then the detail area has many columns and data is updatable there. The data from the list view is normally updated from another form. This is demonstrated in Fig. 10.19.

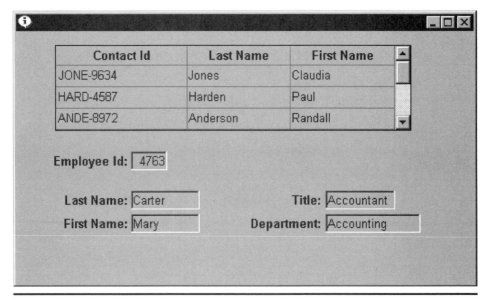

Figure 10.19 This is an example of a many-to-one form.

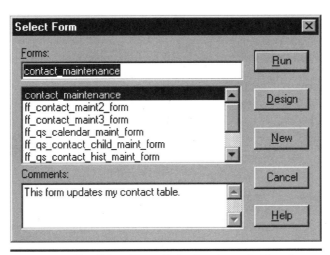

Figure 10.20 The Select Form dialog box is used either to access an existing form or to create a new form.

To create a master/detail many-to-one form:

1. Select the Form painter button from the PowerBar or PowerPanel. The Select Form dialog box displays, as shown in Fig. 10.20.

2. Select the New button to create a new form. The New Form dialog box displays, as shown in Fig. 10.21.

3. Choose the Quick Select data source. This is the only data source which will work properly with a many-to-one form style.

4. Choose the Master/Detail Many-to-One presentation style.

5. Choose the OK button. The Select Master Table dialog box displays, as shown in Fig. 10.22. This dialog box accepts information about the table and columns to place in the master table on the form. Remember the master table in this case is the table that shows several rows of information at a time.

6. Click on the table in the Tables list box. All the columns in the table display in the Column list box on the right side of the dialog box. Only one table may be chosen for a many-to-one form. Once the form is designed, you can edit the data source and add another table if necessary.

7. Select the columns to appear on the form by clicking on them with the mouse, or choose the Add All button to add all the columns. The screen should look similar to Fig. 10.23.

8. Specify sort criteria. See Chap. 9, Data Sources, for information on setting sort criteria.

9. Specify selection criteria. See Chap. 9 for information on setting selection criteria.

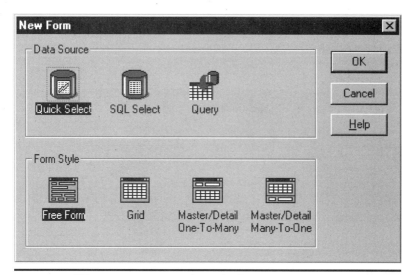

Figure 10.21 When you create a new form, the data source and presentation style must be selected.

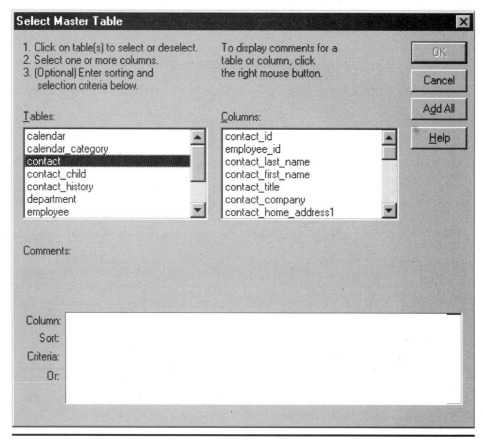

Figure 10.22 Select the table and columns to display in the master area of the many-to-one form, using the Select Master Table dialog box.

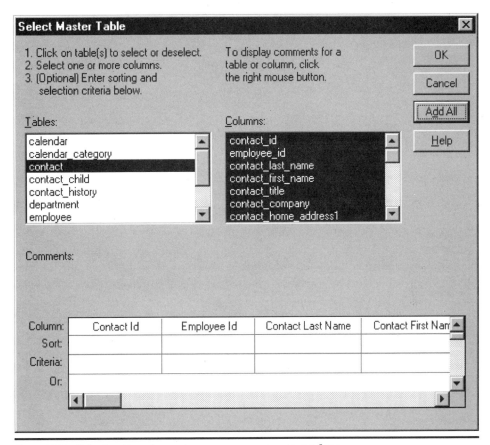

Figure 10.23 Selecting the columns to appear on a many-to-one form.

10. Choose the OK button. The next dialog box, Select Detail Table, displays as shown in Fig. 10.24.

11. In the Select Detail Table dialog box, choose the detail table. Only one table may be chosen. Once the form is designed, you can edit the data source and add another table if necessary.

12. When the columns display, select the columns to appear on the detail table by clicking on them with the mouse or selecting the Add All button to add all the columns to the form. When you have finished, the screen should look similar to Fig. 10.25.

13. Specify the sort order. See Chap. 9, Data Sources, for information on defining sort orders.

14. Specify any selection criteria. See Chap. 9 for information on defining selection criteria.

15. Choose OK when you have finished. InfoMaker then displays the Select Master/Detail Relationship dialog box, as shown in Fig. 10.26. This dialog

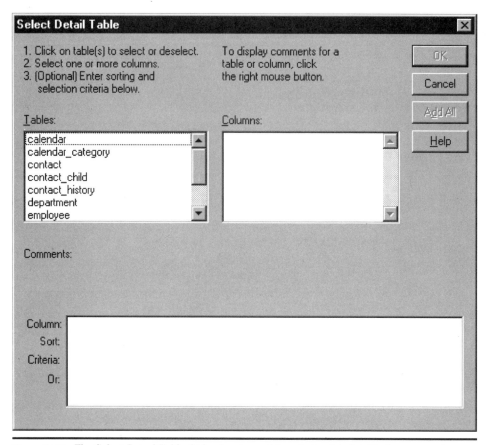

Figure 10.24 The Select Detail Table dialog box is used to select a detail table for a many-to-one presentation style form.

box is used to verify the relationship between the two tables you've added to the master/detail form. If the relationship was not correct, we could choose the More ≫ button on this dialog box, select the master key, and match it to the detail key to create a link between the tables.

16. Now choose OK. InfoMaker creates the form shown in Fig. 10.27.

Summary

There are four types of forms: free-form, grid, master/detail one-to-many, and master/detail many-to-one. The free-form type allows you to view data one row at a time. The grid form shows you data in a spreadsheet style. Master/detail one-to-many shows an item such as a customer in a free-form type area, and then it has a grid area with information such as all the orders for that particular customer. The master/detail many-to-one form displays many items in a

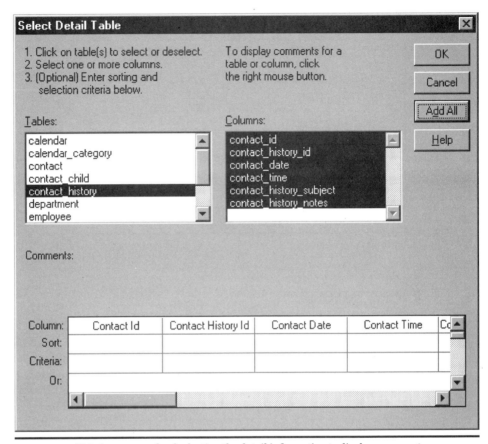

Figure 10.25 This is an example of selecting the detail information to display on a one-to-many form.

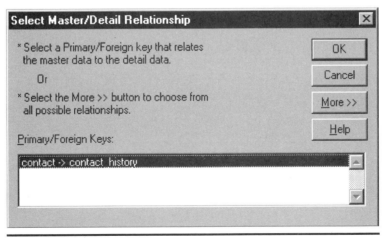

Figure 10.26 The Select Master/Detail Relationship dialog box verifies the relationship between database tables.

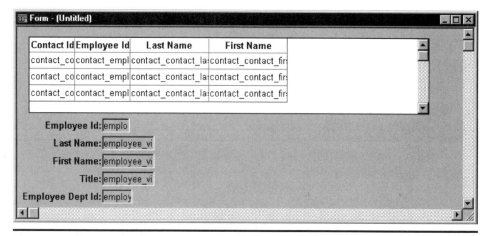

Figure 10.27   An example of a one-to-many form in Design mode.

grid area of the form, such as all the customers in a database, and allows you to scroll through and choose one. The information about the customer is then displayed in another area.

If you need to add data to or change data in a database frequently, a form is a better method to do this and provides validation and error checking. Forms are easier to read. Another advantage of using a form is that it can be packaged into an application by using the Environment painter and distributed to others. You now have the information you need to begin building reports on your own.

Enhancing Forms

What You Will Learn

Up to this point you have learned how to create a basic form in InfoMaker by defining a data source and form style. You have also learned how to select columns and specify the sort order and selection criteria. However, the Form painter has many tools to make forms more visually appealing and useful. Within the Form painter you can move columns, set fonts, add controls, and emphasize areas of the form by using group boxes. By the end of this chapter, you will be building your own forms and using them as a foundation for your InfoMaker applications.

Creating a New Form

Creating a new form in the Form painter is just like creating a form from the PowerBar. The data source and presentation style are selected. But be careful. If there is a form currently in the workspace, you must save the changes to the form before continuing, or else all the changes will be lost. InfoMaker prompts before closing the original form.

To create a new form in the Form painter, select the New button in the Form painter bar or File | New from the menu. InfoMaker displays the New Form dialog box, as shown in Fig. 11.1. Continue to define data just as you would normally.

Editing an Existing Form

To open an existing form while working in the Form painter, choose the Open button on the Form painter bar or choose File | Open from the menu. InfoMaker asks you to save changes in the current form. Then the Select Form dialog box opens, as shown in Fig. 11.2. Select the form and choose Run to preview the form or Design to make changes to the form.

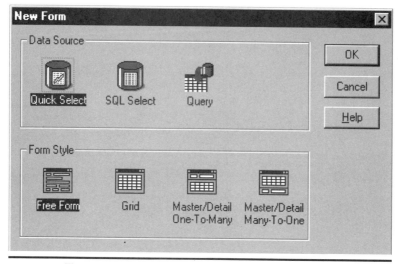

Figure 11.1 The New Form dialog box displays when you create a new form. The data source and form style must be selected before you can continue.

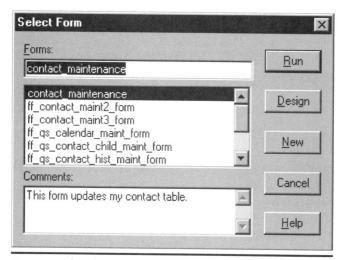

Figure 11.2 Opening an existing form inside the Form painter opens the Select Form dialog box.

Saving a Form

To save a form, choose the Save button on the Form painter bar or choose File | Save on the menu. InfoMaker displays the Save Form dialog box to enter the new form's name and a comment associated with the form.

Deleting a Form

It is possible to delete a form that is open in the Form painter. InfoMaker will not close the form when it's deleted. But when the form is closed, it's gone. The only way to retrieve it is to do so before closing it; make sure it's saved under a different name.

To delete a form, choose File | Delete... from the Form painter menu. The Delete Form dialog box appears, as shown in Fig. 11.3. Choose the form to delete and press OK. InfoMaker verifies the delete before taking any action.

Form Properties

General properties for a specific form are set by right-clicking anywhere on a form and selecting properties from the pop-up menu. On the Form property sheet, specify the form's title, which displays at the top of the form. Additionally, the color and the type of scrolling are set on this property sheet. It is possible to set a different pointer when the mouse passes over the form. Select the pointer from the Pointer tab, and choose OK when you have finished.

Form Objects

There are several different types of objects which can be placed on a form, including columns, group boxes, pictures, and so on. The Object drop-down toolbar contains these objects and a selection tool to select the different objects. The selection tool is used in the situation where another tool is selected, for instance, the Picture Button tool, and you decide you don't want a Picture Button on the form. Choosing the selection tool changes the mouse back to a

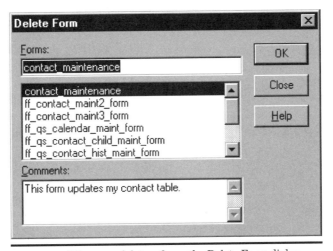

Figure 11.3 When you delete a form, the Delete Form dialog box appears.

pointer, so another object may be selected. To choose the selection tool, choose the Select tool on the Object drop-down toolbar, or select Controls | Select Controls on the menu. Each of the form objects is now discussed in detail.

Placing a column on a form

The Column control places a column from one of the tables included in the form on the Form painter workspace. The Column contains data retrieved from the database.

To place a column on a form, do the following:

1. Choose the Column tool from the drop-down toolbar, or select Controls | Column from the Form painter menu.

2. Click on the form workspace in the area to place the column. InfoMaker displays the Select Column dialog box shown in Fig. 11.4. The list box displays all the columns available in the data source that have not yet been placed on the form.

3. Select one of the columns by clicking on it with the mouse.

4. Choose OK. The column is placed on the form.

Placing a computed column on a form

Another type of control available on a form is a *computed column*. A computed column is not a data column. A computed column is composed of a combination of columns and an expression that equates to a value which displays in the computed column. Data in the computed column cannot be updated. The columns from which the computed column is derived must be changed.

To place a computed column on a form, do the following:

1. Choose the Computed Column button from the toolbar, or choose Controls | Computed Field from the menu.

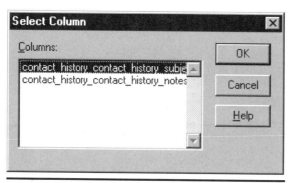

Figure 11.4 The Select Column dialog box appears when you place a column on a form.

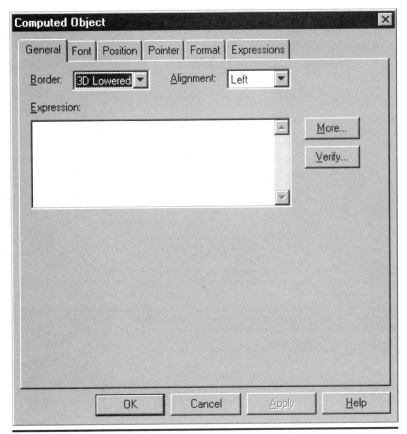

Figure 11.5 Build an expression in the Computed Object dialog box to create a computed column.

2. Click on the area of the screen to place the control. The Computed Object property sheet displays, as shown in Fig. 11.5. The General tab must have a valid expression defined before you access any of the other tabs on the Computed Object property sheet. For more information on creating a valid expression, see the section "Creating an Expression for a Computed Column" in this chapter.

3. Choose OK when you have finished.

Creating an expression for a computed column. When you are creating an expression for a computed column, the General tab on the Computed Column property sheet doesn't offer much assistance. Click the More... button to display the Modify Expression dialog box, as shown in Fig. 11.6. This box contains buttons to insert mathematical symbols in an expression, such as plus and minus. List boxes containing the functions and the columns available from the data source can be selected.

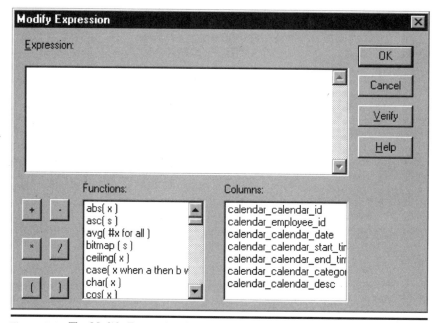

Figure 11.6 The Modify Expression dialog box offers assistance with building an expression by providing columns, functions, and mathematical symbols from which to choose.

The following is a list of some valid expressions:

```
contact_first_name + ' ' + contact_last_name
sum(year(calendar_calendar_date) for all) + 1
sales_amount * .10
```

An expression is validated by choosing the Verify button on the Modify Expression dialog box. InfoMaker displays a message letting you know if the expression is valid. To exit, choose the OK button.

Placing buttons on a form

Buttons are available to add to an InfoMaker form. These buttons initiate some type of activity necessary to complete a task on a form, such as deleting or saving a row or importing a file.

To add a button to a form, do the following:

1. Choose the button from the Form painter bar.

2. Then click on the area of the form where you want to place the button. A button appears with a label *None*. Notice that *None* is displayed in the Form's style bar in the upper right.

3. Enter the title to display on the button.

4. Define an action for the button by right-clicking on the button in the Form painter workspace. The button's pop-up menu displays.

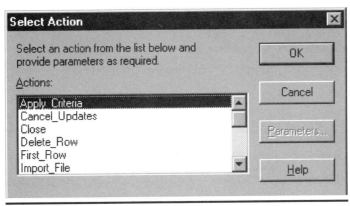

Figure 11.7 The Select Action dialog box displays a list of predefined actions available for a command button on the Form painter.

5. Choose Action. The Select Action dialog box displays, as shown in Fig. 11.7.

6. Select an action. For more information on button actions, see the section on Form button actions in this chapter.

7. Select OK on the dialog box.

Form button actions. Depending on the type of form style selected, different button actions are available. Table 11.1 summarizes each of the buttons, in which form presentation style they are available, and what they do.

TABLE 11.1   Summary of the Action Buttons Available in the Form Painter

Action	Form style	Purpose	Painter bar button	Menu item
Apply_Criteria	Free-form Grid One-to-many Many-to-one	Validates the selection criteria and then re-retrieves the rows based on the criteria	Apply	Rows | Apply Criteria
Cancel_Updates	Free-form Grid One-to-many Many-to-one	Ignores updates made since last update	None	Rows | Cancel Changes
Close	Free-form Grid One-to-many Many-to-one	Closes the form	Design	File | Close
Delete_Row	Free-form Grid One-to-many Many-to-one	Deletes the current row in the form from the table	Delete	Rows | Delete
First_Row	Free-form	Moves the cursor to the first row in the form	First	Rows | First
	One-to-many	Moves the cursor to the first row in the master form	First	Rows | Get First

TABLE 11.1   Summary of the Action Buttons Available in the Form Painter

Action	Form style	Purpose	Painter bar button	Menu item
Import_File	Free-form Grid	Imports data to the underlying form's table	None	Rows | Import
Insert_Row	Free-form Grid	Inserts a row into the form's table	Insert	Rows | Insert
	One-to-many Many-to-one	Inserts a row in the area that has focus	Insert	Rows | Insert
Last_Row	Free-form	Moves the cursor to the last row in the form	Last	Rows | Last
	One-to-many	Moves the cursor to the last row in the master area	Last	Rows | Get Last
Next_Row	Free-form	Moves the cursor to the next row in the form	Next	Rows | Next
	One-to-many	Moves the cursor to the next row in the master area	Next	Rows | Get Next
Print	Free-form Grid One-to-many Many-to-one	Prints the retrieved data in the form	None	File | Print
Print_Setup	Free-form Grid One-to-many Many-to-one	Allows you to change your printer's settings	None	File | Print Setup
Prior_Row	Free-form	Moves the cursor to the previous row	Prior	Rows | Prior
	One-to-many	Moves the cursor to the previous row in the master area	Prior	Rows | Get Prior
Retrieve	Free-form Grid One-to-many Many-to-one	Retrieves rows from the form's table(s)	Retrieve	Rows | Retrieve
Save_As	Free-form Grid	Saves rows of data to a specified file format	None	File | Save Rows As
Specify_ Criteria	Free-form Grid One-to-many Many-to-one	Saves any changes made to the form's table(s) and allows you to specify selection criteria	Criteria	Rows | Specify Criteria
Update_Rows	Free-form Grid One-to-many Many-to-one	Updates the current row in the database Updates all modified rows in the database	Update	Rows | Update

Placing a picture button on a form

A picture button is basically the same thing as a regular command button except that it displays a picture instead of text. The picture can be a bitmap (`.bmp`) file, a Windows metafile (`.wmf`) or a run-length-encoded (RLE) file. This is useful for placing pictures, such as company logos, on a form.

To place a picture button on the workspace, do the following:

1. Choose the picture button from the toolbar, or choose Controls | Picture Button from the menu.

2. Click on the area of the workspace where you want to place the button.

3. Then to add a picture, right-click on the button to bring up the object pop-up menu.

4. Choose the Properties... option. The PictureButton property sheet displays, as shown in Fig. 11.8.

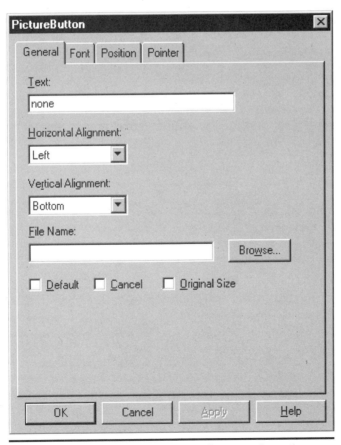

Figure 11.8 The PictureButton property sheet contains options to set the graphic alignment and default functionality.

5. Set the horizontal and vertical alignment for the picture by choosing the appropriate justification from the drop-down list boxes.

6. In the File Name box, specify the filename. Click on the Browse... button to display the Open File dialog box. Choose the appropriate file and choose Open. The filename displays in the File Name box.

7. To set the button as the default, set the Default check box.

8. To set the button to a Cancel action, choose the Cancel check box.

9. To set the graphic to display at its original size instead of increasing to fit within the size of the picture button itself, select the Original Size check box.

10. Choose OK to return to the Form painter workspace.

11. Right-click on the button to display the object's pop-up menu.

12. Choose the Action option.

13. In the Select Action dialog box, select an appropriate action.

14. Choose OK.

Placing text on a form

Text can be placed anywhere on the workspace. Text is convenient for grouping and labeling information.

To place text on the workspace, do the following:

1. Choose the Text button from the Control drop-down toolbar, or choose Controls | Static Text.

2. Click on the workspace where you want to place the text.

3. Type the text to display on the form.

4. Click elsewhere on the workspace to deselect the text item. The text item is on the screen.

Placing pictures on a form

You can also add pictures to your forms. Pictures are useful in a realty application to display houses or in a human resources application to display employee photographs, for instance.

To place a picture on a form, do the following:

1. Choose the Picture control from the Control drop-down toolbar or choose Controls | Picture.

2. Click on the area of the workspace where you want to place the picture. The Picture Object property sheet displays, as shown in Fig. 11.9.

3. First select a file. Choose the Browse... button and select the file to display. Pictures can be in bitmap (.bmp) format, Windows metafile (.wmf), or a run-length-encoded (.rle) file.

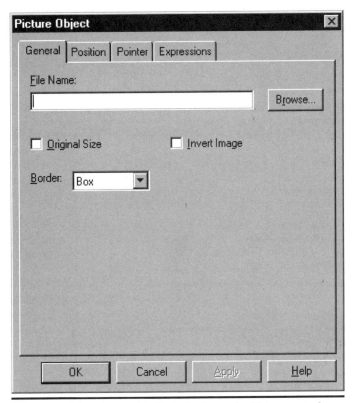

Figure 11.9   Select the graphic file to display on the Picture control using the Picture Object property sheet.

4. To have the picture display its original size on the form, choose the Original Size check box.

5. The Invert Image check box inverts the colors on the graphic.

6. In the border drop-down list box are several different borders to place around the picture.

7. When you have finished, choose OK to return to the Form painter workspace.

Placing drawing objects on a form

The Form painter has four different drawing objects which can be added to a form. The drawing objects are used to focus attention or to group certain logical sets of columns. The drawing objects create lines, rectangles, ovals, and round rectangles.

To place one of these objects on a form, do the following:

1. Choose one of the drawing objects from the Control drop-down toolbar or from the Controls menu.

2. Click the mouse button on the Form workspace to place the object. When the object appears, it is selected.

3. Make the object larger or smaller, or move it elsewhere on the workspace.

To change the way the drawing object appears:

1. Right-click on the object to display the object's pop-up menu.

2. Choose Properties from the menu. The Rectangle Object dialog box displays, as shown in Fig. 11.10.

3. Change the drawing object's visual appearance.

4. Choose OK when you have finished.

Adding reports to a form

It is possible to add a prebuilt report to a form. The report can contain any information, including a graph.

To add a report to the form, do the following:

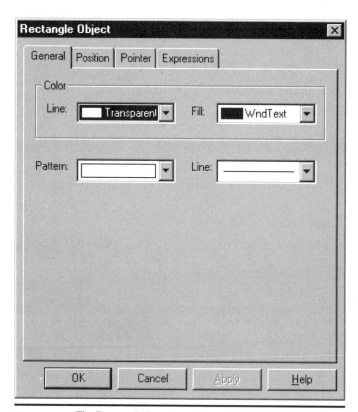

Figure 11.10 The Rectangle Drawing Object dialog box is used to modify the appearance of a drawing object.

1. Select the Report button from the Control toolbar or Controls | Report from the menu.
2. Click on the area of the workspace where you want to place the report. The report appears as a box.
3. Right-click on the report.
4. Select Properties from the pop-up menu. The Report dialog box displays, as shown in Fig. 11.11.
5. Specify the report control window's visual attributes, including scrolling and borders.
6. Choose the Browse... button. The Select Report dialog box displays, listing all the reports in the current library, as shown in Fig. 11.12.
7. Choose the report to display on the form.
8. Choose OK.
9. Then enter a title for the report on the Report property sheet.
10. Choose OK when you have finished.

Modifying Object Attributes

Each object on a form (headings, boxes, columns, etc.) has an associated pop-up menu. Right-clicking on an object displays a pop-up menu. Choosing the

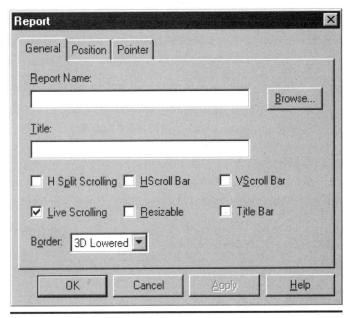

Figure 11.11 The Report dialog box contains options to set report control attributes.

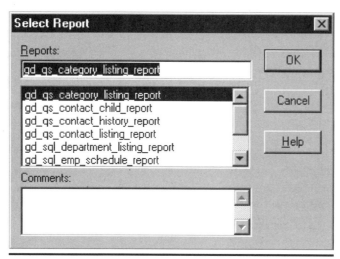

Figure 11.12 Use the Select Report dialog box to select a prede-fined report to place on a form.

Properties... option on this menu, or selecting Edit | Properties from the Form painter menu, displays a relevant property sheet with the different attributes available for that control. Many of the attributes are unique for each object and contain options to customize forms. Figure 11.13 shows an example of a property sheet for a column object on a form.

Forcing retrieval criteria

If retrieval criteria are defined for a form, it is optional to enter selection criteria when the report is run. However, it is possible to force the user to enter information before the form runs. This is accomplished by selecting the Equality Required check box on the General tab of the Form property sheet. This sets the entry of retrieval criteria to required instead of optional.

Overriding editing

If a column uses a code table on a radio button, check box, or drop-down list box edit style, to prevent data values from displaying in the Specify Retrieval Criteria dialog box, select the Override Editing option on the General tab of the Form property sheet.

Changing fonts

There are a couple of different ways to change fonts on a form object. One way to change fonts for an object is to access the object's property sheet and select the Font tab. Both the font and color are modified here.

The Form painter also has a Style bar in which text labels are modified; objects are made bold, italicized, and underlined; fonts and font sizes are

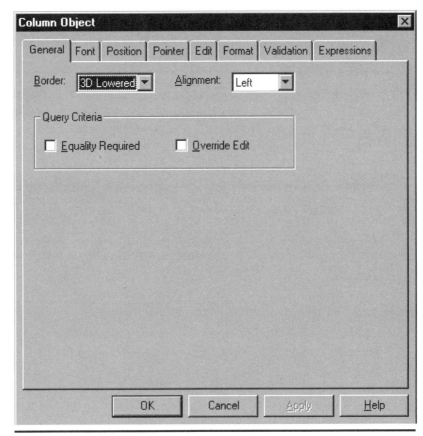

Figure 11.13   This is a property sheet displaying all the available tabs with the attributes which can be modified for a form.

changed; and justification is set. If the style bar doesn't appear in the Form painter, right-click on the Painterbar and click on the Style Bar option on the pop-up menu. The style bar is shown in Fig. 11.14.

Setting borders

Both the border on a form and object borders can be changed. To change the border on all forms, choose the Design | Options menu item. This opens the Form property sheet. On the Generation tab are options to specify borders. These settings can be overridden in individual forms.

Additionally, InfoMaker has several different types of borders available to enhance an object's visibility on the form. By selecting the object(s) and click-

Figure 11.14   This is an example of the style bar in the Form painter.

ing on the Border drop-down toolbox on the Form painter bar, an object can be set to have no border, can be underlined, can have a box, can be shadowed, can be resizable, etc.

Changing an object's position

To move an object, select it with the mouse and move it to a new location. To specify exact positions, access the object's property sheet and select the Position tab. Then enter the x and y coordinates in the spaces provided. Another way to move an object on the Form painter workspace is to select it and then use the cursor keys to move the object in small increments.

Modifying edit styles

To override or create edit styles for an object on a form, select the Edit tab on the Object property sheet. For a complete discussion of creating edit styles, see Chap. 7, Working with Databases.

Display formats

To modify display formats, select the Format tab on a property sheet. For a complete discussion of creating display formats, see Chap. 7.

Validation rules

To modify or create validation rules, access the Validation tab on the property sheet. For a complete discussion of creating validation rules, see Chap. 7.

Expressions

By depending on the data retrieved into a column, it is possible to build an expression that acts under certain circumstances. For instance, it is possible to turn the text color to red when a negative number displays in a column. To create or edit an expression, access the Expressions tab on the Form property sheet. Double-click on the property to affect, such as the color. The Modify Expression dialog box opens. Enter the expression. When you have finished, choose the OK button. For more information on building expressions, see Chap. 8, Working with Data in InfoMaker, or the section "Creating an Expression for a Computed Column" in this chapter.

Reversing Actions on a Form

To reverse the last change made on a form, choose the Undo button on the Form painter bar or the Edit | Undo item on the menu. The Undo item toggles between undo and redo, which reverses the undo.

Removing Items from a Form

An option is available to remove objects from the form. One way to delete an item is to select the object(s) and press the Delete key on the keyboard. Another useful method is Clear. The Clear option is accessed either from the Clear button on the Form painter bar or from the Edit | Clear item on the Form painter menu.

Reordering Columns in a Form

When you create a grid form, it is possible to reorder columns. To reorder a column, do the following:

1. Place the mouse cursor on a column heading. The column is highlighted and displays a line representing the column border, as shown in Fig. 11.15.

2. Then drag the mouse in the direction where you want to move the column. When the mouse button is released, the column is placed in the new position.

Aligning Objects

To make a form appear neater and to make it easier to read, the objects on the form should be aligned and sized uniformly. InfoMaker includes several tools to accomplish these tasks quickly. One way to align objects is to access the General tab on the Form property sheet by choosing Design | Options from the Form painter menu. The General tab includes options to set objects placed on the Form to snap to a grid and to set the size of the grid.

In addition, there are several very useful tools to help align objects in the Form painter itself. These alignment tools are located on the painter bar and are also accessible from the Edit item on the menu.

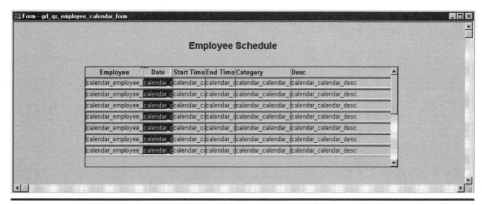

Figure 11.15 The Form painter running a grid presentation style form. In this example, the date column is selected in preparation for moving.

Left, right, top, and bottom alignment

Objects can be aligned on either the left, right, top, or bottom edge. For instance, let's begin with the objects shown in Fig. 11.16.

The objects in Fig. 11.16 need some serious realigning to make the form more visually appealing. The first object selected is the one InfoMaker uses to align all the objects.

To align objects, do the following:

1. First, place the top column in the location where you want to align all the objects.

2. Then select the other objects to align in that position by holding down the Control button on the keyboard and clicking on them with the mouse. The screen should look similar to Fig. 11.17.

3. Now select one of the alignment tools from the Alignment drop-down toolbar, or choose Edit | Align Controls from the Form painter menu. In this example, we chose the left alignment tool. All the columns line up on the left side, as shown in Fig. 11.18.

Center alignment

The align center horizontal option aligns objects by using the center of the object as a focal point, instead of the edge. See Fig. 11.19 for an example.

The align center vertical option aligns objects by using the center of the object as a focal point, instead of the edge. See Fig. 11.20 for an example.

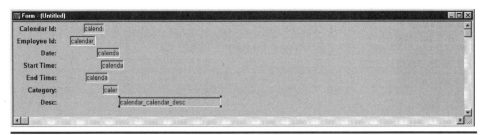

Figure 11.16 This is an example of objects which must be aligned.

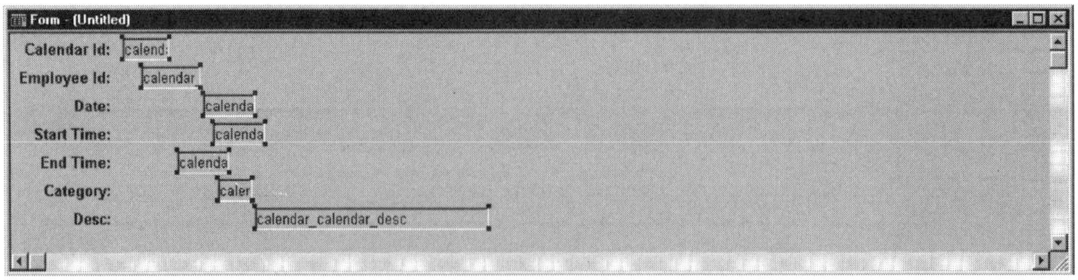

Figure 11.17 Selecting objects in preparation for aligning.

Figure 11.18   An example of aligning objects on the left edge.

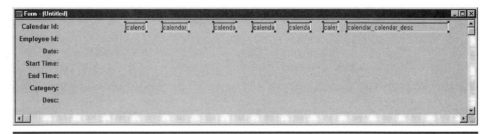

Figure 11.19   The align center horizontal tool uses the center of an object as the focal point and aligns objects horizontally on the form.

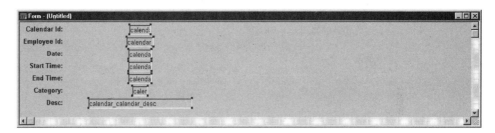

Figure 11.20   The align center vertical tool uses the center of an object as the focal point and aligns objects vertically on the form.

Spacing objects

There are two tools to set the spacing between objects. They're called Space Horizontal and Space Vertical. The Space Horizontal tool spaces the objects the same distance apart horizontally across the form. The Space Vertical tool spaces objects the same distance apart vertically down the form. The spacing tools are accessed from the Alignment drop-down toolbar on the Form painter or from the Edit | Space Controls item on the menu. Fig. 11.21 demonstrates how the Space Horizontal tool spaces the four objects on the lower part of the form.

In the next example (see Fig. 11.22), the first two columns are spaced correctly, but the third is not. Select the columns and choose the Space Vertical tool. The columns are then spaced the same distance apart, as shown in Fig. 11.23.

Figure 11.21 TheSpacing Horizontal tool places the lower four objects on the form an equal distance apart horizontally across the form.

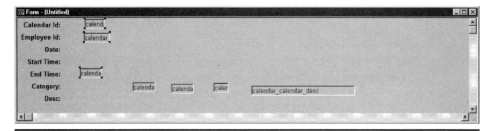

Figure 11.22 The three selected objects on the form are not spaced correctly.

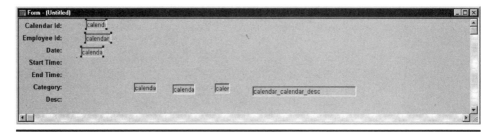

Figure 11.23 Selecting the Space Vertical tool spaces all three objects the same distance apart vertically on the form.

Sizing controls

Two options are also available to make selected controls the same size. These tools are called Size Width and Size Height. The sizing tools are available from the Alignment toolbar on the Form painter bar or from the Edit | Size Controls menu item. Figure 11.24 demonstrates the results of sizing objects the same width. Figures 11.25 and 11.26 display an example of the results of the Size Height tool.

Changing Form Colors

Colors for both the form and each of the objects can be changed in the Form painter. Tools are available to set the background and foreground colors and to set the entire color of a form. To set default colors for all forms, select the

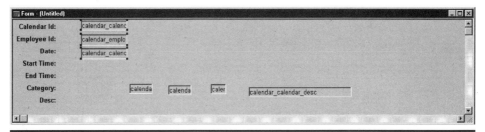

Figure 11.24 The Size Width tool changes all selected objects to the same width.

Figure 11.25 This is an example of objects which must all be the same height.

Figure 11.26 These are the same objects from the previous example after the Size Height tool was applied.

Generation tab from the Design | Options menu item. Even though colors are specified for all forms, the settings can be overridden in each individual form.

Setting the form color

The color of a form can be changed by right-clicking on an empty place on the form and choosing the Properties item from the pop-up menu. The Form property sheet appears, as shown in Fig. 11.27.

Select the desired color from the Color drop-down list box, and choose OK to change the form's color.

Background colors

The Form painter bar has a button to control the background color of objects. To change an object's background color, do the following:

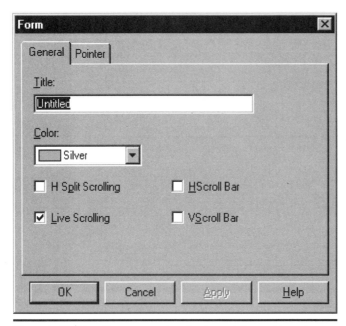

Figure 11.27 The Form property sheet contains options to change the colors on a form.

1. Select the object(s), using the mouse.
2. Click on the Background button on the toolbar, and a drop-down box opens with all the different colors to choose from.
3. Choose the color. The background color of the object is modified.

Foreground colors

It is possible to change the foreground color of an object. To change an object's foreground color, do the following:

1. Select the object(s), using the mouse.
2. Click on the Foreground button on the toolbar, and a drop-down box opens with all the different colors to choose from.
3. Choose the color. The foreground color of the object is modified.

Defining custom colors

If none of the default colors are to your liking, it is possible to define a custom color. This is accomplished by selecting Design | Custom Colors… on the Form painter's menu. The Color dialog box displays as shown in Fig. 11.28.

To read more about how to define custom colors, refer to your Microsoft Windows documentation.

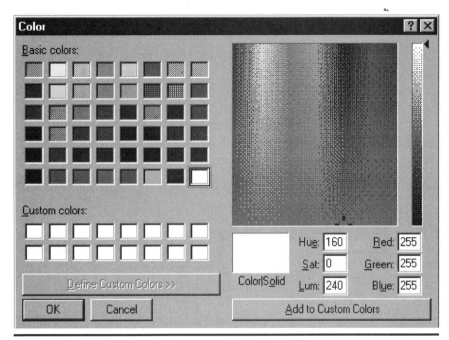

Figure 11.28 To define custom colors, choose Design | Custom Colors from the menu.

Autosizing

A column or other object on a form can be set to autoheight. This means that the column's height will change depending on the data that is retrieved into the column. Notice that in Fig. 11.29 the `calendar_date` column has been increased in height. Now notice what happens when we run the form with auto-size height turned off (see Fig. 11.30).

Now let's set autosize height on and run the report again. Notice this time that the date column shrank to fit the data that was retrieved into that column (see Fig. 11.31).

Figure 11.29 The third object in this example shows an object set to a specific height.

Figure 11.30 When autosize height is turned off, the object remains the same size as it was in Design mode.

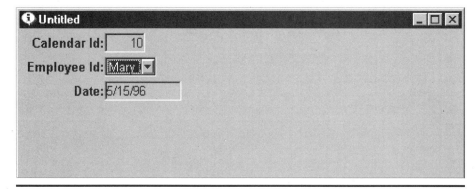

Figure 11.31 This is an example of running the same form with autosize height on. The third column is reduced in size automatically when information is retrieved.

Setting the Tab Order

When InfoMaker creates a form, it creates a default order in which users access the columns when entering information into the form. This order is reset by using the Tab Order functionality available in the Form painter. The tab order is composed of a sequential numbering scheme. A column with a lower numbered tab order is accessed before a column with a higher numbered tab order. A column with a tab order of 0 is not accessible and can not be updated.

To change the tab order, do the following:

1. Choose the Tab Order button on the Form painter bar, or choose Design | Tab Order from the menu. Numbers appear on each of the columns on the form, as shown in Fig. 11.32.

2. To change the order in which the columns are accessed, click on the number of the column to change. The number is highlighted, as shown in Fig. 11.33.

3. Now type in the order in which to access the column. For instance, in the previous example, we want to access the employee id after we enter the description. So we would change the number to 70. (Anything higher than

Figure 11.32   This is an example of the tab order for a form.

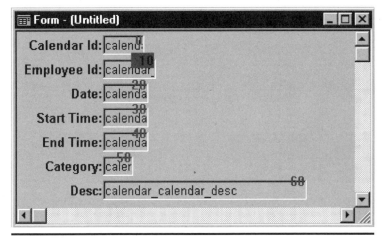

Figure 11.33   This is an example of selecting an object's tab order in preparation for changing it.

60 will work, but it's always a good idea to leave room in case you add more columns to the form later.)

4.   Now choose the Tab Order button again, and InfoMaker accepts the changes.

Editing the Data Source

There are many reasons why you may decide to modify the data source. You may need to add or remove columns or add tables, and so on. To modify the data source, choose the SQL Select button on the painter bar or Design | Edit Data Source from the menu. When this option is selected, the Select painter related to the data source is started. For a master/detail form, InfoMaker first prompts for either the master or the detail form data source, as demonstrated in Fig. 11.34.

Closing a Form

When you have finished working on a form, there are several ways to close it. To close a form, select the Close button on the Form painter bar, or choose the Close option on the Form Window menu, as shown in Fig. 11.35.

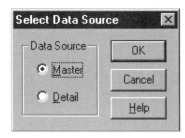

Figure 11.34 When you edit the data source on a master/detail form, the Select Data Source dialog box opens.

Figure 11.35 To access this menu, choose the Window Control Menu box in the upper left corner of the form.

Another way to close a form is by pressing the Control + F4 key combination or by selecting the File | Close menu item from the Form painter menu. Regardless of how a form is closed, InfoMaker will verify the close action if changes have been made, as shown in Fig. 11.36.

If you choose Yes when InfoMaker prompts to save the form but the form hasn't been named, then the Save Form dialog box is opened, as shown in Fig. 11.37. Enter the name of the new form and save it. If No is chosen, changes are

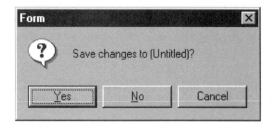

Figure 11.36 When changes have been made to a form without being saved, InfoMaker prompts for saving, discarding changes, or canceling the action.

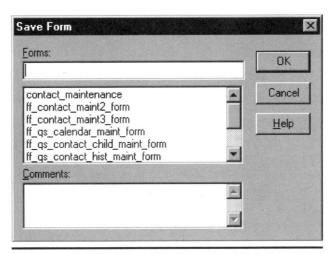

Figure 11.37 The Save Form dialog box opens when you save a form that hasn't been named.

discarded and the form is closed. Choosing the Cancel button returns to the Form painter.

Specifying Retrieval Criteria

To set up the form so a user can enter a name or other type of information to retrieve information from the form's underlying tables, specify retrieval criteria.

To set up a form to prompt for retrieval criteria, do the following:

1. Choose Design | Prompt for Criteria from the painter menu. The Prompt For Criteria dialog box displays, as shown in Fig. 11.38.

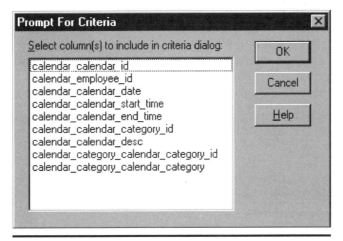

Figure 11.38 The Prompt For Criteria dialog box specifies the columns from a table in which users enter information to retrieve data.

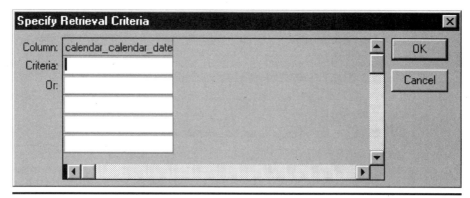

Figure 11.39 Before running a form with retrieval criteria specified, InfoMaker displays the Specify Retrieval Criteria dialog box to accept values.

2. Select the column(s) for which the users have the option of entering selection criteria, and press OK.

3. Now run the form. Before the form displays, the Specify Retrieval Criteria dialog box displays, as shown in Fig. 11.39.

4. Enter the information to use to retrieve the data from the database.

5. Press OK. InfoMaker displays only those rows that meet the criteria.

Setting Update Properties

InfoMaker's update properties specify how to update the form's table(s). By default, if a form contains one table with the key columns, InfoMaker sets all the columns to updatable. A form can be updatable only if all the primary keys and all the columns that are not allowed to be null are included on the form. But if the form contains columns from two or more tables or from a view, InfoMaker sets the form as not being updatable. If the default behavior isn't acceptable, it can be changed by using the Update Properties functionality. In a master/detail form, the data sources for both the master and detail tables can be updated.

To set update properties, do the following:

1. Choose Design | Update Properties from the painter menu. The Specify Update Properties dialog box displays, as shown in Fig. 11.40.

2. Set the form's update properties. For more information on update properties, see the section on specifying update property attributes in this chapter.

3. When you have finished, choose OK.

Specifying Update Property Attributes

The Specify Update Properties dialog box contains several options to select tables, columns, keys, and the update method to use when updating a form. Each of the options is explained in the following sections.

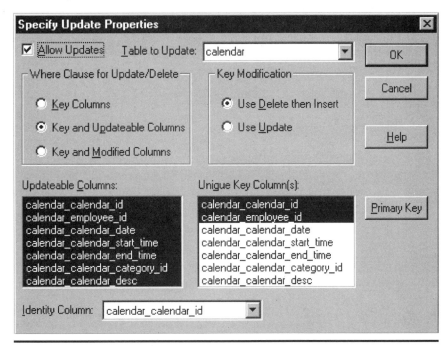

Figure 11.40 The Specify Update Properties dialog box specifies how InfoMaker should modify the columns included in the form.

Allowing updates

To set the form to updatable, select the Allow Updates box. To make the form display only, uncheck this box.

Table to update

Each form can only update one table. The exception to this is a master/detail form where one table in both the master and detail areas can be set to updatable. The Table to Update drop-down list box displays the available tables to update. If a form contains several tables, you can set separate update properties for each.

Where clause for key columns

When you are using a single-user database or database locking mechanisms are in place, select this option. Existing columns are updated in the database as long as the key columns in the database and form match.

Where clause for key and updatable columns

This option specifies that an update to the database fails if the key and columns updatable in the database have changed since the data was retrieved into the form.

Where clause for key and modified column

The values in the key and modified columns are compared in the database and the form. If any columns in the database have changed since the data was retrieved into the form, the update fails.

Modifying keys

The Modify Keys setting has two options: Use Delete then Insert and Use Update. When Delete then Insert is selected, if a row is being changed, the row residing in the file is deleted and then the new row is inserted. This is useful if multiple rows are being updated. However, if you are modifying one row at a time before the database is updated, select Update. It overwrites the existing row, resulting in faster performance.

Updatable columns

In the Updatable Columns area, the specific columns to update on the form are selected.

Unique key columns

The Unique Key Columns area specifies the column InfoMaker uses to identify a row. The key columns must uniquely identify a row. To use the primary key as a unique identifier, click on the Primary Key button.

Identity column

The Identity Column list box lists all the columns that can be used as an alternate identity column if necessary.

Running a Form

While you are developing a form, it is possible to switch between designing the form and seeing how the form looks with data. The Run Form option allows you to view the form as it would appear to a user. You can see changes that must be made to the form more readily, such as moving and resizing objects, viewing data, and testing display formats. To run the form, choose the Run button on the painter bar. To return to Design mode, choose the Design button from the painter bar.

When you are running a form, the painter bar changes to accommodate the different tools available when running a form. InfoMaker automatically includes functionality that in another environment would require extensive programming.

Searching in the form table

When it's unclear which row you want to view, InfoMaker includes an option called Criteria. Accessed either from the Criteria button on the painter bar or

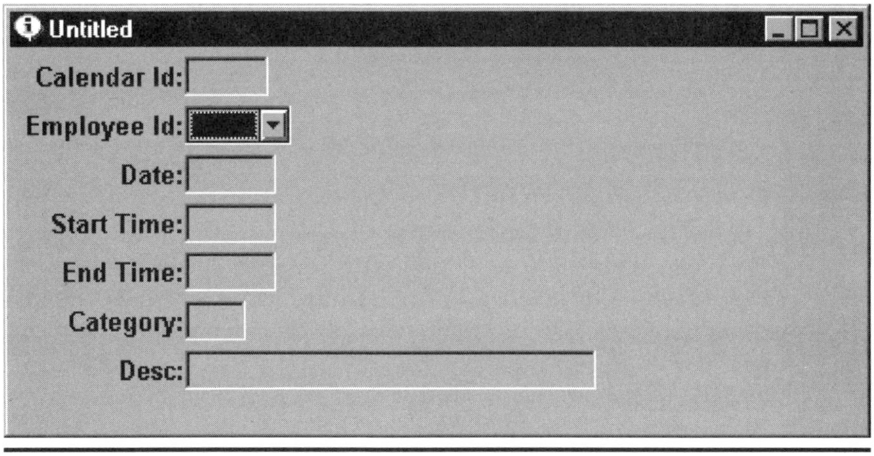

Figure 11.41 Pressing the Criteria button on the painter bar clears any data from entry objects and accepts information to search the table.

from the Rows | Specify Criteria item on the menu, this button clears all the data in the form and allows you to specify which data to pull from the table.

To enter selection criteria, do the following:

1. Press the Criteria button. The columns on the form are cleared of data, as shown in Fig. 11.41.

2. Now move the cursor to one of the columns. For instance, to view only those entries for 5/16/96, enter the date in the date column.

3. Then press the Apply button. InfoMaker retrieves the data from the table and displays those rows.

Maneuvering in the table

When you are viewing data, it is possible to go to the first row in the retrieved set of data, the last, and so on. These buttons are labeled First, Prior, Next, and Last. These tools are also accessed from the Rows | First, Prior, Next, and Last menu items. When these buttons are selected, the form displays the first row in the retrieved set of information for the form, the previous, the next and the last row in the retrieved set respectively. Using this tool enables you to move to specific rows of information quickly.

Deleting a row

To delete a row from a table, press the Delete button on the painter bar or choose the Rows | Delete menu option. The row is removed from the form. However, the row isn't actually removed from the database. To actually delete it from the database, choose the Update button to save the changes, return to the form design mode and choose to save changes, or exit the form and save changes.

Adding a row

To add a new row to a form, press the Insert button or select Rows | Insert from the menu. A new row is created, and you can enter a new set of information on the form.

Saving data

When you are making changes to data on a form, the information must be saved before changes are made to the database. This is accomplished by choosing the Update button on the Form painter bar or selecting the Rows | Update item on the menu.

Saving rows to an external file

When running a form, you can choose to save the information in another format. This extends InfoMaker's power by exporting data to spreadsheets, text files, HTML forms, etc., in which the data may be further manipulated and modified.
   To save rows to an external file, do the following:

1. Select the File | Save Rows As option on the Form painter menu. The Save As dialog box displays, as shown in Fig. 11.42.

2. Select the file type from the Save as type drop-down list box. You'll notice from the Save as type drop-down list box that there are many different file formats in which to save the data in the table, as shown in Fig. 11.43. File formats available include saving the data in an Excel spreadsheet, in SQL, in a Powersoft Report, or in HTML.

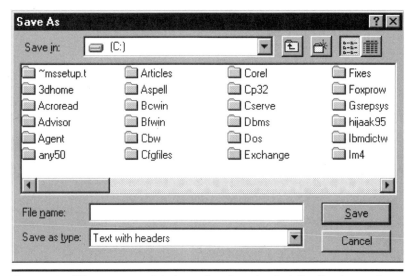

Figure 11.42 When you save data in another format, select the directory and the filename in which to save it.

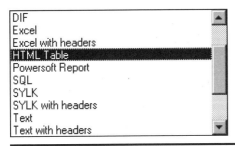

Figure 11.43 When you save data, it is possible to save it in many formats, including HTML or a Powersoft Report.

3. Enter the filename.

4. Choose Save when you have finished.

Saving to spreadsheets.   InfoMaker can save the data from a table on which a form is based to an Excel or Lotus spreadsheet. Each column and each row are extracted and placed in columns and rows in the spreadsheet. InfoMaker cannot save rows from a master/detail table.

Saving to text.   To export data contained in a form to a text file, select the text file type. Each row in the form is sent to a separate row in a text file.

Saving to HTML.   When you are saving rows which have been retrieved into a form, it is possible to save the information to an HTML document. The form can then be further modified in HTML. The results you receive depend on the type of presentation style used in the form. With a free-form style, all rows are displayed haphazardly on the HTML document. In contrast, the grid presentation style displays the data within a table, as shown in Fig. 11.44. It is not possible to use a form with a master/detail presentation style in an HTML format.

Saving to a Powersoft Report.   A form can be saved as a Powersoft Report. A Powersoft Report file contains the form with the underlying source code, so the form can be modified by another InfoMaker or PowerBuilder user. Additionally, the underlying data selected in the form is also extracted and stored in the Powersoft Report. The Powersoft Report can be opened in File Manager or Explorer, within a mail message as a file attachment, and from InfoMaker's File Menu. When the Powersoft Report is started, an instance of InfoMaker is initiated and the form is opened in the Report painter. It is not possible to save master/detail forms to a Powersoft Report.

Saving forms as SQL.   Saving a form to SQL translates the current form to the SQL commands necessary to create a table and insert the values selected in the form as rows. These commands can then be executed independently to create a new database table.

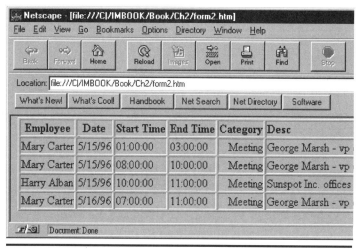

Figure 11.44 This is an example of saving a form to HTML file format and opened in The Netscape Navigator browser.

Retrieving data

The Retrieve button is used to retrieve a fresh copy of the data from the database into a form. This is useful when several people are sharing the same database and it is possible for data to change in the database while information is being viewed in a form. To retrieve data from the database, press the Retrieve button or choose Rows | Retrieve from the menu.

Importing data

InfoMaker has the ability to import data from another text or .dbf file format into a table. Having the ability to import data from other files makes loading new InfoMaker tables much easier and faster. When you import data, the file columns must match all the columns specified in the form's SQL Select command. Otherwise, InfoMaker will display an error message.

To import data, do the following:

1. From within the Form painter, select Rows | Import... from the menu. The Select Import File dialog box displays.

2. Enter the import filename, and set the file type: .txt or .dbf.

3. Now click on the Open button. The data is loaded into the open form. The data must be saved before it is added to the database.

Canceling changes

If changes are made to a database and you wish to discard them but want to remain in the form to continue viewing or modifying data, choose Rows |

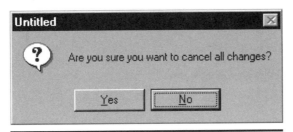

Figure 11.45 Canceling changes made to data invoked this message box.

Cancel from the menu. InfoMaker will verify the cancel action, as shown in Fig. 11.45.

If the Yes button is selected, all changes are discarded. If the No button is chosen, InfoMaker returns to the Form painter with all changes intact.

Putting It All Together

Now that we've covered all the options available in the Form painter, we're going to design a complete form for our InfoCenter application. I will show you how the form appears when it is finished and the type of edit and validation, etc., that you should add to build it. I will go through the entire process step-by-step so you can see how to create it.

Figure 11.46 shows what the form should look like when finished.

1. Select the Form painter button from the InfoMaker workspace. The Select Form dialog box displays, as shown in Fig. 11.46.

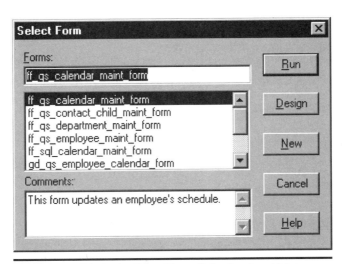

Figure 11.46 This is the Select Form dialog box in which we can either edit or preview an existing form or create a new form.

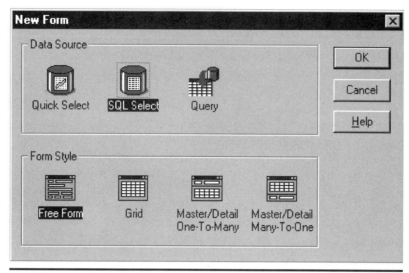

Figure 11.47   This is the New Form dialog box with the SQL Select and Free-form form style selected.

2. Choose the New button. The New Form dialog box displays.

3. Choose the SQL Select data source.

4. Select the FreeForm form style. The dialog box should look like Fig. 11.47.

5. Choose OK. The Select Tables dialog box displays in the Select painter workspace.

6. Choose the `contact` table, and click on the Open button, as shown in Fig. 11.48.

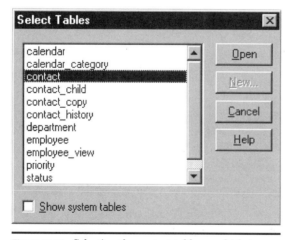

Figure 11.48   Selecting the contact table on which to base our form in the Select Tables dialog box.

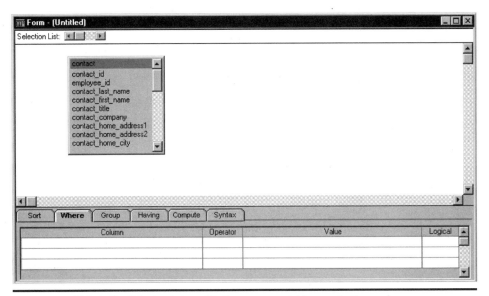

Figure 11.49 This is the Select painter with the `contact` table open in the workspace.

7. The Select painter opens, as shown in Fig. 11.49.

8. We want the ability to update all the columns in the table, so we right-click on the `contact` table title bar and choose Select All from the pop-up menu. All the columns in the table are highlighted.

9. We aren't interested in setting any selection criteria in this instance because we want the ability to update all contacts in the table. At this point we can choose the SQL Select button to proceed to the Form painter. The Form painter looks similar to Fig. 11.50.

   At this point our basic form is created. Notice that although the form has all the columns we want and it is possible to use it this way, the form has a crowded look. We can make this more aesthetically pleasing and easier to work on with a few modifications. First let's save the form.

10. Choose the Save button on the Form painter bar. The Save Form dialog box appears.

11. Enter the form name according to the naming conventions we discussed in Chap. 4, Standards and Guidelines. In this case, enter the name `ff_sql_contact_maint_form`.

12. Enter the comments describing the form: "This form updates the contact table." The Save Form dialog box should look like Fig. 11.51 when completed.

13. Choose the OK button, and InfoMaker saves the form.

14. First we want to create group boxes to group related information. This will make the form easier to work on. Using the mouse, place the pointer to the right of the `contact_home_address1` column.

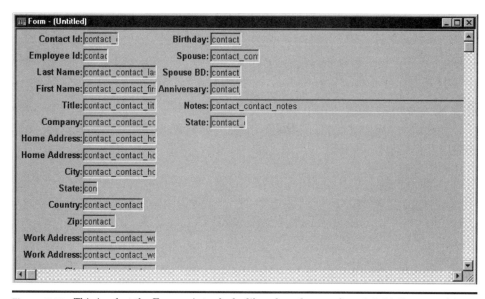

Figure 11.50 This is what the Form painter looks like when the new form is initially created.

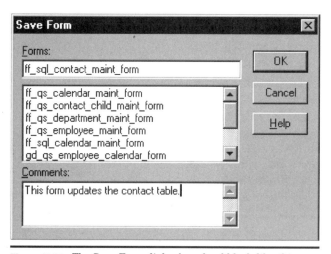

Figure 11.51 The Save Form dialog box should look like this when you're ready to save the new form.

15. Press the left mouse button, and drag the group selection tool that appears until it encloses or touches all the columns related to the contact's home address. All these columns should be selected.

16. Once selected, click on one of the columns with the mouse, and drag the group of columns off to the side, as shown in Fig. 11.52.

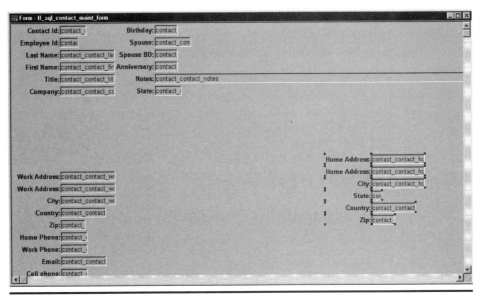

Figure 11.52 Moving the columns related to the contact's home address.

17. Now do the same thing for the group of columns related to the contact's work address.

18. We can also group a contact's personal information. Select all columns related to the contact's birthday, anniversary, and so on, and place them to the side. When you have finished, your screen should look similar to Fig. 11.53.

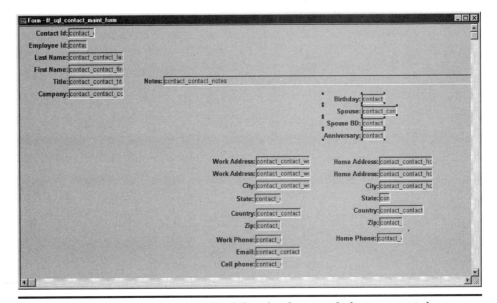

Figure 11.53 This is the Form painter with all the related groups of columns separated.

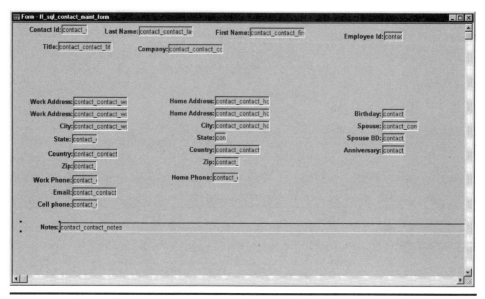

Figure 11.54 Placing all the columns in their approximate positions.

19. Now arrange all the columns in the approximate positions where you want them on the form (see Fig. 11.54).

20. This is a good place to save the form, so do so now.

21. Now let's add the titles for the group box information. Select the Text tool from the Control drop-down toolbox in the Form painter bar.

22. Click on the area above the work and home address column groupings.

23. Type "Contact Information." Notice that the text in the style bar also changes as you type.

24. Change the font to 16 and bold, using options on the style bar.

25. You'll notice that the text object is not large enough to display the entire text. Move the mouse to the right edge of the text object, click the left mouse button, and drag the column to the right, until all the text displays.

26. Now above the work address grouping, place the text "Work." Make it a 12-point font and bold.

27. Put another text object above the home address "Home." Use the same font as you used for the work columns.

28. Change the label for the `contact_work_address1` and `contact_home_address1` columns to read as "Address". This is accomplished by selecting the text label with the mouse. Notice the text appears on the style bar. Change the text in the text area of the style bar.

29. Remove the label entirely for the `contact_work_address2` and `contact_home_address2` columns.

30. Now let's ensure that all the objects are aligned the way we want. Position the first text label for the work address where you want. Then select all the text objects in the work address column by clicking on the other labels and pressing the Control key.

31. Select the right alignment tool from the Alignment drop-down toolbar on the painter bar. This aligns all the text objects.

32. Deselect the address text label by holding the Control key and clicking on it with the mouse. This will leave the other text objects selected.

33. Choose the Space Vertical tool from the Alignment drop-down toolbar to space all the objects evenly.

34. Now do the same thing for the column objects for work, and both the text and column objects for home.

35. You will also want to use the Align Top tool to make sure all objects align across.

36. Let's place a group box around the home and work address information. Choose the rectangle group box from the Controls drop-down toolbar on the painter bar.

37. Click in the upper right-hand corner of where the box starts. A small black box appears.

38. Using the mouse, grab the lower right corner of the box and drag it until it covers all the work and home columns.

39. The group box resides on top of the text labels and column objects. To display the objects beneath, right-click on the group box and select Send to back from the pop-up menu.

40. You'll notice that only the column objects display. This is because the group box has a black background, which is the same as all the text labels. To fix this, right-click on the group box again and select Properties... from the pop-up menu. The Rectangle Object property sheet appears.

41. Choose a line color of WndText, a fill color of ButtonFace, and a thicker line. The Rectangle Object property sheet should look similar to Fig. 11.55.

42. Choose OK when you have finished. Your form should now look similar to Fig. 11.56.

43. We still have a ways to go. Put the contact's personal information in a group box just as we did with the contact information group box.

44. Save the report.

45. Press the Run button on the Form painter bar to see how the form appears with data.

46. The first thing we notice is the contact id column needs to be made larger.

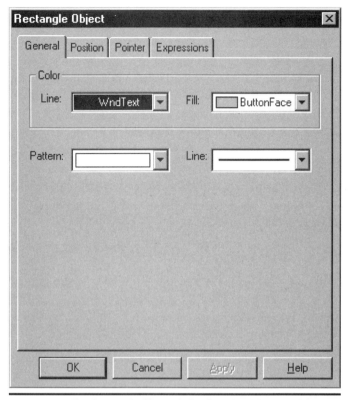

Figure 11.55 The Rectangle Object dialog box should appear like this when all options have been selected.

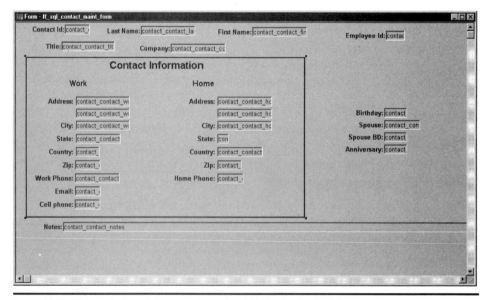

Figure 11.56 The contact maintenance form should look similar to this now.

Choose the Design button on the painter bar to return to Design mode and enlarge the column.

47. Now run the form again. Notice that the contact's first and last names look out of place. Instead of having the name appear as two separate columns, let's create a computed column. Return to Design mode.

48. Delete the last name and first name text labels and columns from the form by selecting them and pressing the Delete key on the keyboard.

49. Place a text object in their place that reads "Name:".

50. Select the Compute object from the Control drop-down toolbar on the Form painter bar.

51. Using the mouse, click to the right of the Name text label you just created. The Computed Object property sheet appears.

52. Choose the More... button. The Modify Expression dialog box displays.

53. In the Columns list, choose the `contact_first_name` column by clicking on it with the mouse. Notice the name appears in the Expression box.

54. Press the plus sign symbol on the lower left corner of the Modify Expression dialog box. Notice it also appears in the Expression box.

55. After the plus sign in the Expression box type, ' ' .

56. Add another plus sign to the expression.

57. Then in the Columns list, choose the `contact_last_name` column. The Modify Expression dialog box should look like Fig. 11.57.

58. Now select the Verify button. InfoMaker will display a message box letting you know the expression is valid.

59. Choose OK on the Modify Expression dialog box.

60. Choose OK on the Computed Object dialog box.

61. Enlarge the name computed column so both the first and last names won't be truncated.

62. Save the form.

63. Run the form.

64. Notice the columns that must still be adjusted. Return to Design mode and fix them.

65. Let's change the tab order. Choose the Tab Order button on the Form painter bar. Numbers appear at each column.

66. Change the tab order by selecting a number and entering a new number. When you tab through the form, columns are accessed in sequential order.

67. Save the form.

68. Run the form. It should now appear similar to Fig. 11.58.

You can continue to modify and enhance the form to fit your needs.

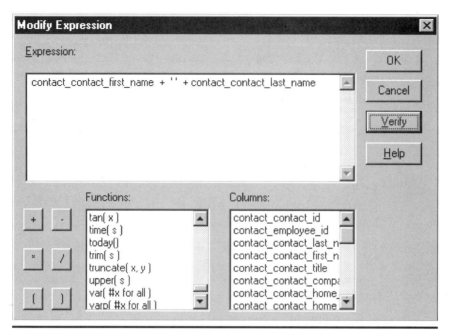

Figure 11.57 Build an expression to join the contact's first and last names in the Modify Expression dialog box.

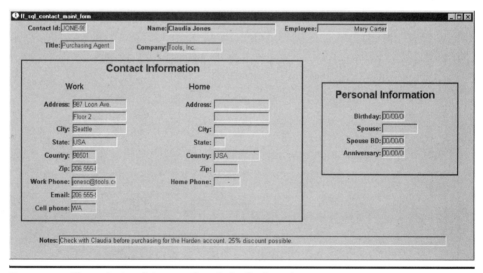

Figure 11.58 The contact maintenance form in its final version.

Summary

In this chapter we discussed all the available options in the Form painter we can use to enhance the visual appearance of a form and how we can change the form's functionality. You now know how to toggle between Design and Preview modes in the Form painter and all the options available in each. Using the Form painter is a quick and painless way to create forms to retrieve information from the database.

Building Reports

What You Will Learn

Chapter 12 is a high-level discussion of reports and how to create and access them. You will learn about each of the report types available in the Report painter and when and how to access them. By the end of this chapter, you will have a clear understanding of reports and will be on your way to creating your own.

About Reports

Reports display data residing in a database. Data is not modified in a report. InfoMaker leaves that work up to the Form painter and the Data Manipulation painter. There are several different presentation styles in which to display data. An InfoMaker report can be a customer invoice, mailing labels, an inventory report, a sales graph, or a number of other report types.

Report Data Sources

The New Report dialog box, shown in Fig. 12.1, is where the data source and report presentation style for reports are selected. Reports can have Quick Select, SQL Select, and Query data sources, just as a form does. But, in addition, a report can have an External or a Stored Procedure data source. For a complete discussion of the data sources, see Chap. 9, Data Sources.

Report Generation Options

Report generation options are used in all styles using a banded workspace. These presentation styles are Freeform, Grid, Label, N-Up, Tabular, Group, and Crosstab. Specific types of reports can be set with certain attributes such

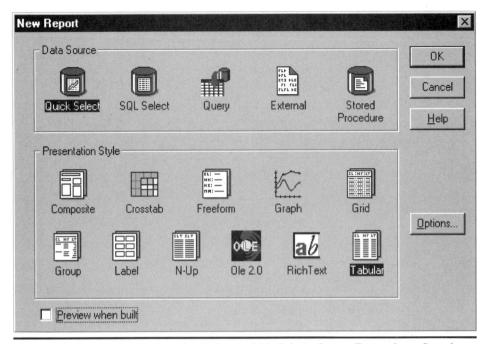

Figure 12.1 Reports can have a Quick Select, SQL Select, Query, External, or Stored Procedure data source.

as background colors, text and column borders and colors, and zooming characteristics.

To change the report generation options, do the following:

1. When you are creating a new report, click on the Option... button on the New Report dialog box. The Report Options property sheet displays, as shown in Fig. 12.2.

2. Select the Report Options. For more information about report options, see the sections "Setting Default Colors and Borders," "Setting Wrap Height on a Free-Form Form," and "Zooming" in this chapter.

3. Choose OK when you have finished.

Setting default colors and borders

It is possible to set the default colors and borders for each of the banded workspace report presentation styles and the objects on the report. Tools to accomplish this reside on the Generation tab on the Report Options dialog box. Each type of report can have a specific color scheme. Instead of changing the options individually on each report, they can be set for all the reports here. This functionality saves time when you are building forms. But the nice thing about it is that if one of the reports must appear differently, the options can be overridden in an individual report.

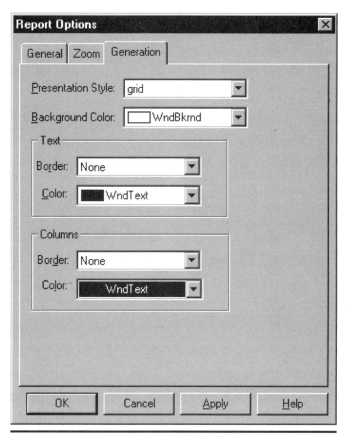

Figure 12.2 The Report Options dialog box contains options to set general properties for each report presentation style.

Setting wrap height on a free-form report

In addition to setting the colors and borders, the wrap height can be set on a free-form report. The *wrap height* refers to the height of the detail band. When the wrap height is set to none, the number of columns in the report determines the height of the detail band, with the columns displaying in a single vertical line. But if the wrap height is set to a specific value, the detail band height is set to that number and the columns wrap within the detail band. See Figs. 12.3 and 12.4 for an example of setting the wrap height.

Zooming

It is possible to view a report at a specific zoom percentage. This is accomplished by selecting the Zoom tab on the Report Options dialog box. Simply choose one of the percentages and choose OK. The reports are modified to display larger or smaller depending on the percentage set.

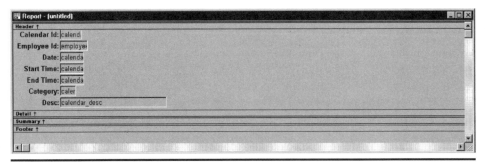

Figure 12.3 Setting the wrap height to none sets a free-form report detail band to the height necessary to accommodate all the columns in a report.

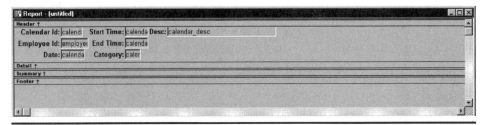

Figure 12.4 Setting the wrap height to 3, as in this example, sets the detail band to only contain three data columns before wrapping.

Preview a Report

On the New Report dialog box, there is a check box titled Preview when built. If this box is checked, as soon as the data is defined for the report, InfoMaker goes directly to Preview mode instead of Design mode. When this box is unchecked, InfoMaker goes to Design mode first where modifications are made.

Creating New Reports

When you create a new report, the data source and a presentation style must be specified. Once that is done, the columns appearing on the report are defined and InfoMaker builds the basic report. This report can be further enhanced by moving columns, adding display formats, and many other types of actions. Chapter 13, Enhancing Reports, covers the tools available in the Report painter which can modify a report to appear as you want it.

To create a new report, do the following:

1. Start the Report painter from the PowerBar or PowerPanel.

2. Choose New from the Select Report dialog box, as shown in Fig. 12.5.

3. When the New Report dialog box displays, choose the data source.

4. Choose the presentation style.

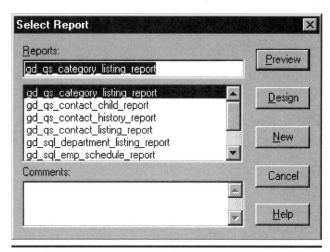

Figure 12.5 In the Select Report dialog box, it is possible to create a new report or view or edit an existing report.

5. Choose OK. What happens next depends on the data source selected. For more information about data sources, see Chap. 9, Data Sources.

Accessing an Existing Report

Once created, reports can be opened at any time for further modifications or viewing in the Report painter.

To open an existing report, do the following:

1. Start the Report painter from the PowerBar or PowerPanel. The Select Report dialog displays, as shown in Fig. 12.6.

2. Select the report from the current library by clicking on it with the mouse.

3. To run the report, choose the Preview button.

3. To make modifications to the report, choose the Design button.

The Repository

The repository contains information about database tables and columns which were set in the Database painter. When defining a report, InfoMaker pulls information from the repository about column labels, headings, display formats, edit styles, and so on. However, repository information may be overwritten in individual reports by changing the attributes. Using the repository saves development time and ensures consistency throughout an application or across several applications.

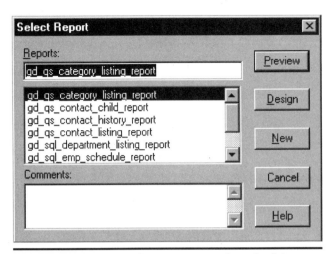

Figure 12.6 Select a specific report to open from the Select Report dialog box.

Report Presentation Styles

Once a data source is defined, the presentation style must be selected. The presentation style determines how the basic report appears. Since the report has the basics necessary for the type of report needed, it is possible to build sophisticated reports faster and easier. In this section we'll take a look at each of the different report styles and discuss what they're best used for and in what situations.

Composite reports

A composite report is simply a report consisting of one or more reports. The composite report does not have a data source. Since the composite report doesn't have a data source and is only a container for other reports to view information in one place, reports cannot be linked. This means one report cannot send information to another report. To do something like that, you must create a nested report. For information on nested reports, see Chap. 13, Enhancing Reports. Figure 12.7 shows an example of a composite report.

To create a composite report, do the following:

1. Start the Report painter from the PowerBar or PowerPanel. The Select Report dialog box displays.

2. Choose New. The New Report dialog box displays.

3. Select the Composite presentation style. Note that since a composite report doesn't have a data source, all the data sources in the dialog box are disabled, as shown in Fig. 12.8.

4. Choose OK. The Select Reports dialog box displays, as shown in Fig. 12.9.

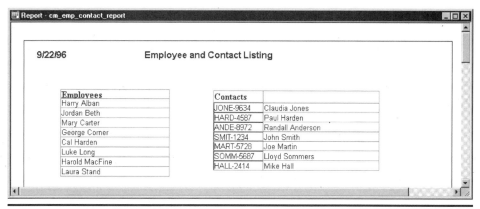

Figure 12.7   This is an example of a composite report.

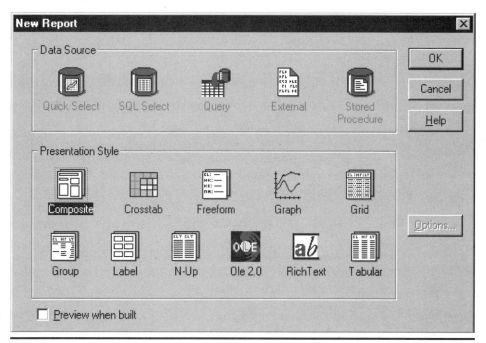

Figure 12.8   Since a composite report doesn't have a data source, the data sources in the New Report dialog box are disabled.

5. Select the report(s) to include in the composite report by clicking on it (them) with a mouse.

6. Choose OK when you have finished.

7. The Report painter opens with each report selected in a box in the detail area.

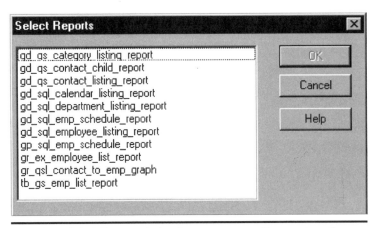

Figure 12.9 Select the reports to place on a composite report on the Select Reports dialog box.

For more information on modifying the composite report, see Chap. 13, Enhancing Reports.

Crosstab reports

Crosstabs are useful for analyzing data. A crosstab report displays summaries of data in a spreadsheet-like grid. So, to view information such as how may customers accessed customer service by phone, e-mail, or letter, broken down by months, the crosstab breaks the information into the categories and displays the information. An example of a crosstab report is shown in Fig. 12.10.

There are two different types of crosstab reports: a dynamic crosstab and a static crosstab. Each has its own advantages and disadvantages.

Dynamic crosstabs.   In a dynamic crosstab, InfoMaker builds the columns and rows for the crosstab each time the report is run. As the data in the database changes, the information in the crosstab changes. By default, crosstabs are dynamic.

Report - cr_contact_count_per_emp_report

Count Of Contact Employee	Contact HALL2414	HARD4587	JONE9634	MART5728	SMIT1234	SOMM5687	Grand Total
Cal Harden					1		1
Luke Long				1			1
Mary Carter			1				1
George Corner		1					1
Jordan Beth	1					1	2
Grand Total	1	1	1	1	1	1	6

Figure 12.10 This is a simple example of a crosstab report.

Static crosstab. In a static crosstab report, the rows and columns displayed in the report are defined when the report is created. Each time the report runs, the data rows and columns remain the same. For instance, in our example of contact method in each month, there may be four employees defined as rows when the report is built: Mary, Paul, George, and Henry. If George quits, his name will still remain as a row on the crosstab. However, as the data changes, the data displayed in the crosstab changes.

In most cases the dynamic crosstab is a better solution to a problem than a static report. Dynamic crosstabs are defined quickly because there is no need for database access. They use current data from a database, and they're very easy to modify.

To create a crosstab report, do the following:

1. Click on the Report painter button in the PowerBar or PowerPanel. The Select Report dialog box displays.

2. Choose the New button. The New Report dialog box displays.

3. Choose the data source.

4. Choose the Crosstab presentation style.

5. Choose OK. What happens next depends on the data source selected. For more information about data sources, see Chap. 9.

6. Once the Report painter opens, the Crosstab Definition dialog box displays, as shown in Fig. 12.11.

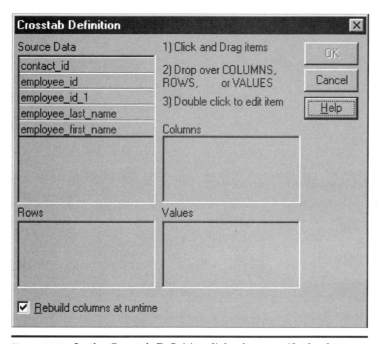

Figure 12.11 In the Crosstab Definition dialog box, specify the data columns to display in the rows and columns on the crosstab.

7. Drag the data columns to display across the top of the crosstab to the Columns box.

8. Drag the data columns to display down the crosstab to the Rows box.

9. Drag the data column on which the count is performed into the Values box.

10. When you have finished, choose OK. InfoMaker builds the report and displays the Report painter workspace.

Free-form reports

A free-form report is used when data is displayed one row at a time. Columns are placed anywhere on the report in the detail area. Figure 12.12 shows an example of a free-form report.

To create a free-form report, do the following:

1. Start the Report painter from the PowerBar or the PowerPanel. The Select Report dialog box displays.

2. Choose the New button on the Select Report dialog box. The New Report dialog box displays.

3. Choose the data source.

4. Then choose the Freeform presentation style.

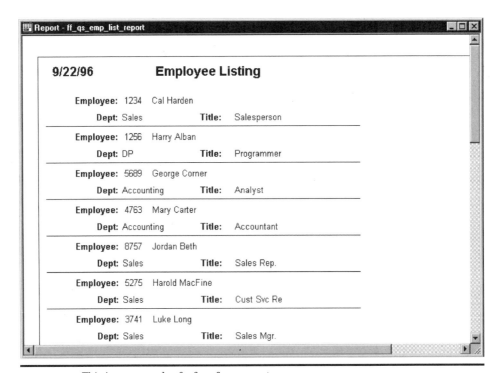

Figure 12.12 This is an example of a free-form report.

5. Choose OK. The data source selected determines what happens next. For more information about selecting a data source, see Chap. 9.

Graph reports

In the Report painter it is possible to have two different types of reports: a report with an added graph or a stand-alone graph. In this chapter we will cover stand-alone graphs. A stand-alone graph does not depend on a report to extract the information needed to build the graph. The underlying data doesn't display.

Graphs display data retrieved from the database in a graphical format. Graphs make it easy to see at a glance what a report with long lists of numbers may express. There are many types of graphs to choose from including bar, pie, scatter, and line. Figure 12.13 shows an example of a graph.

To create a stand-alone graph, do the following:

1. Start the Report painter from the PowerBar or PowerPanel. The

Select Report dialog box displays.

2. Choose the New button. The New Report dialog box displays.

3. Choose the data source.

4. Then choose the Graph presentation style.

5. Choose OK. The data source selected determines what happens next. For more information about selecting a data source, see Chap. 9.

6. When the Report painter opens, the Graph Object property sheet displays, as shown in Fig. 12.14.

7. Set the properties for the graph. For more information about setting graph properties, see Chap. 14, Building Graphs.

8. Choose OK when you have finished.

9. The graph object appears in the Report painter workspace.

For more information about placing graphs inside a report, see Chap. 13, Enhancing Reports. For more information about graph properties, see Chap. 14.

Grid reports

The grid presentation style is useful for displaying all retrieved rows in a spreadsheetlike format. Grid lines separate the rows and columns and thus make the data easier to read. When previewing a grid report, a user can reorder and resize columns to her or his liking. Figure 12.15 shows an example of a grid report.

To create a grid report, do the following:

1. Start the Report painter from the PowerBar or PowerPanel. The Select Report dialog box displays.

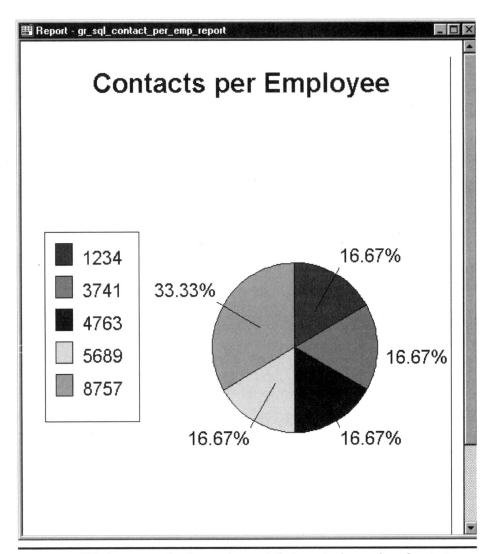

Figure 12.13 This is an example of a graph report that counts the number of contacts assigned to each employee.

2. Choose the New button. The New Report dialog box displays.

3. Choose the data source.

4. Then choose the Grid presentation style.

5. Choose OK. The data source chosen determines what happens next. For more information about selecting a data source, see Chap. 9.

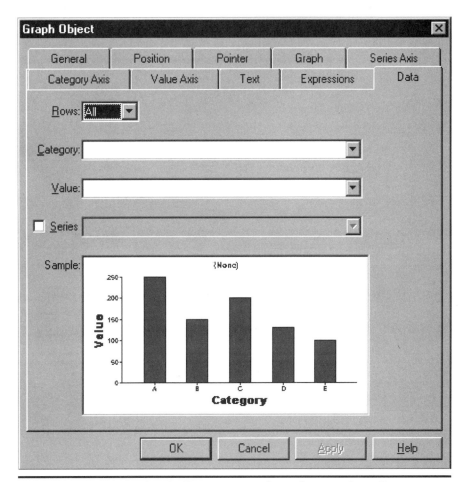

Figure 12.14 This is the Graph Object property sheet where graph attributes are defined.

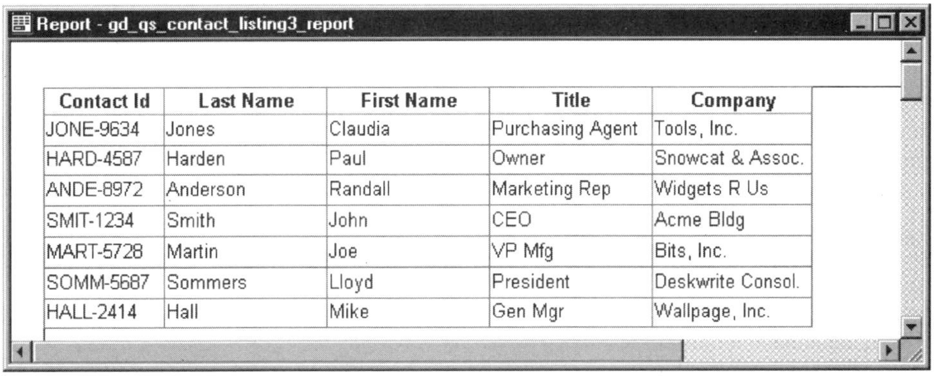

Contact Id	Last Name	First Name	Title	Company
JONE-9634	Jones	Claudia	Purchasing Agent	Tools, Inc.
HARD-4587	Harden	Paul	Owner	Snowcat & Assoc.
ANDE-8972	Anderson	Randall	Marketing Rep	Widgets R Us
SMIT-1234	Smith	John	CEO	Acme Bldg
MART-5728	Martin	Joe	VP Mfg	Bits, Inc.
SOMM-5687	Sommers	Lloyd	President	Deskwrite Consol.
HALL-2414	Hall	Mike	Gen Mgr	Wallpage, Inc.

Report - gd_qs_contact_listing3_report

Figure 12.15 This is an example of a grid report.

Grouped reports

A grouped report is simply a tabular report within a group level and other grouping properties. This is useful when you want to group data. The grouped report provides a shortcut to building this type of report because InfoMaker does all the grouping automatically. Figure 12.16 shows an example of a grouped report.

To create a grouped report, do the following:

1. Start the Report painter in the PowerBar or PowerPanel. The Select Report dialog box displays.

2. Choose the New button. The New Report dialog box displays.

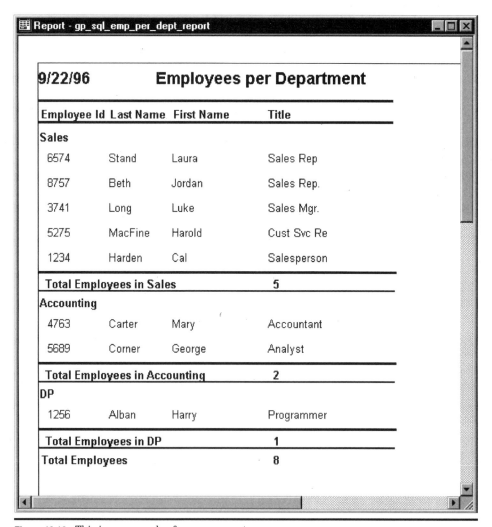

Figure 12.16 This is an example of a group report.

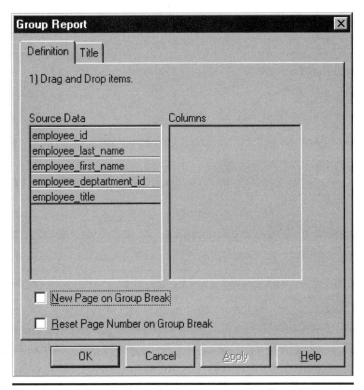

Figure 12.17   Select the data columns to group in the Group Report dialog box.

3. Choose the data source.

4. Choose the Group presentation style.

5. Choose OK. What happens next depends on the data source selected. For more information about data sources, see Chap. 9.

6. When the Report painter starts, the Group Report dialog box displays, as shown in Fig. 12.17.

7. Select the column(s) to group in the report.

8. When you have finished, choose OK.

Label reports

The label presentation style creates a report for building mailing labels. The labels contain information such as customer name and address details. The labels can be set to work with many types of predefined label sheets, including those for file folders, cassettes, videotapes, etc. Figure 12.18 shows an example of mailing labels in Preview mode.

To create a label report, do the following:

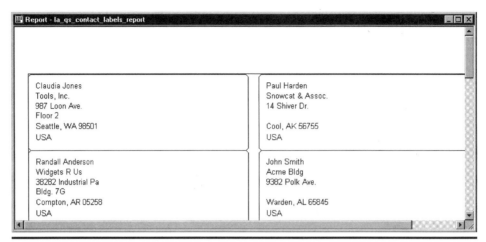

Figure 12.18 This is an example of mailing labels created in the Report painter.

1. Start the Report painter from the PowerBar or PowerPanel. The Select Report dialog box displays.

2. Choose the New button. The New Report dialog box displays.

3. Choose the data source.

4. Then choose the Label presentation style.

5. Choose OK. The data source chosen determines what happens next. For more information about selecting a data source, see Chap. 9.

N-Up reports

N-Up reports display two or more data rows next to one another. An N-Up report is similar to a free-form report in that the data columns can be placed anywhere in the detail area. Figure 12.19 shows an example of an N-Up report.
   To create an N-Up report, do the following:

1. Start the Report painter from the PowerBar or PowerPanel. The Select Report dialog box displays.

2. Choose the New button. The New Report dialog box displays.

3. Choose the data source.

4. Then choose the N-Up presentation style.

5. Choose OK. The data source chosen determines what happens next. For more information about selecting a data source, see Chap. 9.

6. When the Report painter opens, the Specify Rows in Detail dialog box appears, as shown in Fig. 12.20. Enter the number of columns to display horizontally on the report.

7. Choose OK. InfoMaker builds the report and displays it in the Report painter workspace.

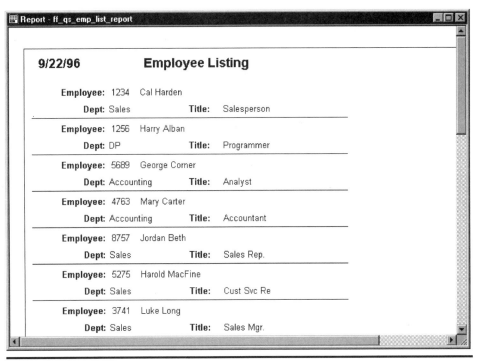

Figure 12.19 This is an example of an N-Up Report.

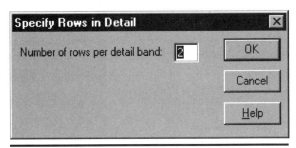

Figure 12.20 Specify the number of rows to display horizontally in an N-Up report on the Specify Rows in Detail dialog box.

Tabular reports

A tabular report shows data in a row and column format similar to a spreadsheet. This is useful when you want to see many rows in a table. Figure 12.21 shows an example of a tabular report.

To create a tabular report, do the following:

1. Start the Report painter from either the PowerBar or the PowerPanel. The Select Report dialog box displays.

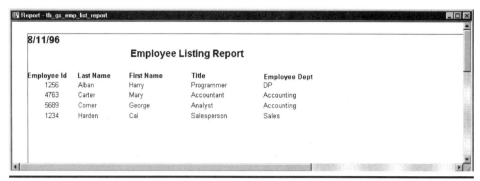

Figure 12.21   This is an example of a tabular report.

2. Choose the New button. The New Report dialog box displays.

3. Choose the data source.

4. Then choose the Tabular presentation style.

5. Choose OK. The data source chosen determines what happens next. For more information about selecting a data source, see Chap. 9.

OLE 2.0 reports

There are three instances where OLE objects can be used within InfoMaker. The first is the OLE report, in which an OLE object fills an entire report. The second occurs by placing an OLE object in a report. (See Chap. 13, Enhancing Reports, on adding OLE objects to a report.) And in the third instance, an OLE object can be contained in a blob column in a database and placed in a column on a report. (See Chap. 7, Working with Databases, for more information.) In this chapter, we will discuss how to create an OLE report. Figure 12.22 shows an example of a report using the OLE presentation style.

To create a report based on an OLE object, do the following:

🔳 Report - ol_sql_equip_report	_□☒
Computer Equipment Inventory	
Equipment Type	**Count**
PCs	105
Workstations	28
Terminals	15
Printers	10

Figure 12.22   This is an example of an OLE report that contains an Excel spreadsheet.

1. Open the Report painter by choosing the Report painter button from the PowerBar or PowerPanel.

2. Select New in the Select Report dialog box.

3. Select the data source.

4. Select the OLE presentation style.

5. Choose OK.

6. Specify the data to retrieve into the report. For more information on data source types, see Chap. 9.

7. Continue to report Design mode.

8. When the Report painter workspace opens, the Insert Object dialog box appears, as shown in Fig. 12.23.

9. Set the object properties. For more information on setting object properties, see the section "Defining OLE Object Properties" in this chapter.

10. Choose OK when you have finished. The OLE object fills the Report painter workspace.

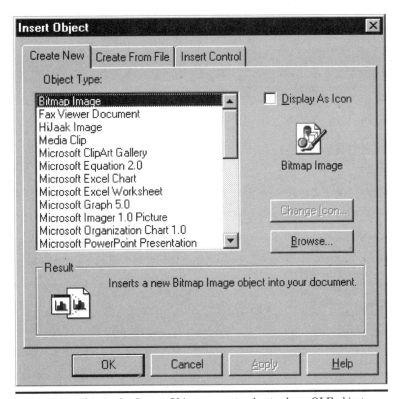

Figure 12.23 This is the Insert Object property sheet where OLE object attributes are set.

RichText reports

A RichText report consists of static text with column values which are retrieved from the database. This is useful for creating form letters or other types of documents in which the information changes in each instance of the report.

To create a RichText report, do the following:

1. Choose the Report painter button from the PowerBar or PowerPanel. The Select Report dialog box displays.

2. Choose the New button. The New Report dialog box displays.

3. Choose the data source.

4. Then choose the RichText presentation style.

5. Choose OK. The data source chosen determines what happens next. For more information about selecting a data source, see Chap. 9.

6. When you have finished defining the data, continue to the Report painter workspace. The RichText Definition dialog box displays, as shown in Fig. 12.24.

7. Define the RichText report.

8. Choose OK when you have finished. The Report painter workspace appears with the columns selected from the data source in the detail area of the report.

9. Add the text to the report either by typing it in or by importing it from a RichText file. Do not make changes in Preview mode. Any changes made are lost.

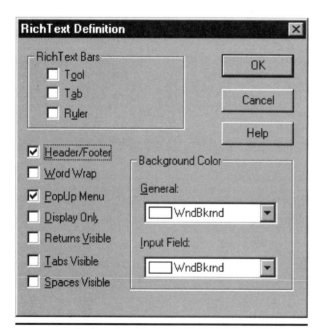

Figure 12.24 Define the RichText report properties in the RichText Definition dialog box.

Defining OLE Object Properties

When you create an OLE report, there are several object properties to define before you can actually run the report. These properties are selected on the Insert Object property sheet.

Creating a new OLE object

When defining an OLE report, you can place an entirely new OLE object on the report. This is accomplished by selecting the New Object tab on the Insert Object property sheet.

To create a new OLE object, do the following:

1. Select the Object type from the list box. Several file types are available including bitmap, Microsoft PowerPoint, and Microsoft Excel.
2. Choose OK on the property sheet when you have finished.
3. The painter for the type of object selected opens, allowing you to create the new object.
4. When you've created the new object, choose Close from the menu.
5. Save the report. When the report is run, the object is displayed in the workspace.

Create from file

Another way to define an OLE object to place on the report is to select the Create from file tab on the Insert Object property sheet when creating a new report. This option uses an existing object and places it on the report.

To create an OLE report from an existing file, do the following:

1. Select the Create from file tab on the Insert Object property sheet.
2. Click on the Browse... button, and select the file to define as the OLE object.
3. To link the object to its application, so that any changes made in the object are also transferred to the original object, choose the Link check box.
4. Choose OK when you have finished. The object displays in the report workspace.

Inserting OCX controls

An OCX control is a predefined control that performs a specific task. InfoMaker includes several OCX controls which can be included on a report, such as a gauge or meter. OCX controls are useful to define specific types of functionality for a report.

To place an OCX control on a report as an OLE object, do the following:

1. Choose the Insert control tab on the Insert Object property sheet.
2. Select the OCX control to place on the report.

3. To register a new OCX control with InfoMaker, choose the Register... button and select the control.

4. To remove a control from the InfoMaker list, select the control by clicking on it with the mouse and selecting the Unregister button.

5. When you have finished, choose the OK button.

6. The control's property sheet displays where you define specific functionalities.

Importing Text into a RichText Report

When you build a RichText report, it is possible to import a file in RichText format. You may find this method more convenient than typing text directly into the Report painter. Text can be inserted into the header, detail area, and footer area of a RichText report.

To import text into a RichText report, do the following:

1. Place the insertion point in the desired location of the RichText report, by clicking on it with the mouse.

2. Right-click in the workspace and select Insert File from the pop-up menu.

3. Select the file containing the text you want to import, using the Select a File Name dialog box. You can choose either a RichText file format or text file. If the document has a header or footer, it is not used.

Summary

In this chapter you learned what each of the report presentation styles were, the types of data sources available in a report, and how to create a basic report in each of the presentation styles. You learned about OLE objects and OCX controls and how to insert them in reports. You are now well on your way to creating basic reports.

13

Enhancing Reports

What You Will Learn

Up to this point you have learned how to create a basic report in InfoMaker by defining a data source and report presentation style. You have also learned how to select columns and specify the sort order and selection criteria. However, the Report painter has many tools to make reports more visually appealing and useful. Within the Report painter you can move columns, set fonts, and add controls. By the end of this chapter, you will be building your own reports and extracting data from the database in a variety of ways.

Creating a New Report

Creating a new report in the Report painter is just like creating a report from the PowerBar. The data source and presentation style are selected, etc. But be careful. If there is a report currently in the workspace, you must save the changes to the report before continuing, or else all the changes are lost. InfoMaker prompts before closing the original report.

To create a new report in the Report painter, select the New button in the Report painter bar or File | New from the menu. InfoMaker displays the New Report dialog box, as shown in Fig. 13.1. Continue to define data just as you would normally.

Editing an Existing Report

To open an existing report while working in the Report painter, choose the Open button on the Report painter bar or choose File | Open from the menu. InfoMaker asks you to save changes in the current report. Then the Select Report dialog box opens, as shown in Fig. 13.2.

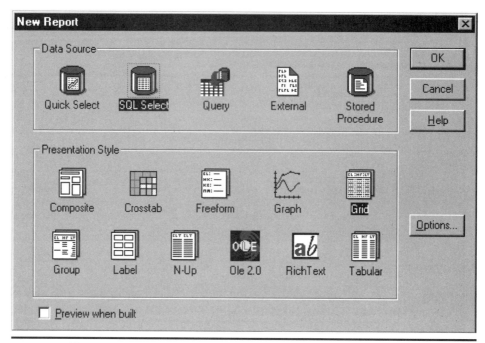

Figure 13.1 The New Report dialog box displays when you create a new report. The data source and report style must be selected before you continue.

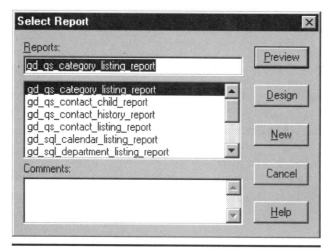

Figure 13.2 Opening an existing report inside the Report painter opens the Select Report dialog box.

Saving a Report

To save a report, choose the Save button on the Report painter bar or choose File | Save on the menu. InfoMaker displays the Save Report dialog box to enter the new report's name and a comment associated with the report.

Deleting a Report

To delete a report, choose File | Delete... from the Report painter menu. The Delete Report dialog box appears, as shown in Fig. 13.3. Choose the report to delete and press OK. InfoMaker verifies the delete before taking any action.

It is possible to delete a report that is open in the Report painter. InfoMaker will not close the report when it's deleted. But when the report is closed, it's gone. You can only retrieve it before you close it; make sure it's saved under a different name.

Closing a Report

When you have finished working with a report in Design mode, it can be closed by clicking on the Close button on the Report painter bar or choosing File | Close from the menu. Yet another way to close a report is from the Window menu on the report, by choosing Close.

If you choose Yes when InfoMaker prompts to save the report but the report hasn't been named, then the Save Report dialog box is opened. Enter the name of the new report, and save it as shown in Fig. 13.4.

If you choose No when closing a report, changes are discarded and the report is closed. Choosing the Cancel button returns you to the Report painter.

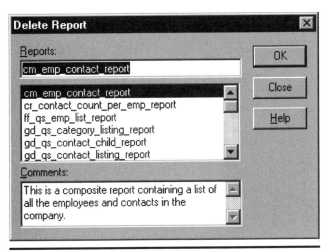

Figure 13.3 When you delete a report, the Delete Report dialog box appears.

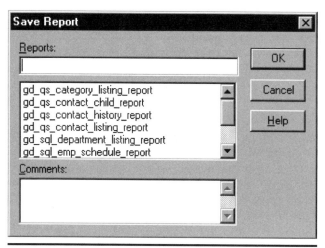

Figure 13.4 The Save Report dialog box opens when you save
a report that hasn't been named.

Storing Data in a Report

Normally, when information is retrieved from the database into a report, the
data is dynamic. This means that as the data changes in the database, the data
displayed in the report also changes. However, at times it may be necessary to
store the data directly in a report. The data displaying in the report doesn't
change, i.e., it becomes static. When the report is run in this instance, it
doesn't go out to the database to retrieve the information; data is stored in the
report itself.

To store data in a report, do the following:

1. In the Report painter, choose Rows | Data from the menu. The Data
    Retained On Save dialog box displays, as shown in Fig. 13.5.

2. To add your own data to the report, choose the Add button.

3. To retrieve all the rows in the database, choose the Retrieve button.

4. To delete specific rows, select a row with the mouse and choose Delete.

5. When you have finished, click on OK. The rows are saved in the report. The
    next time the report is run, only the data specified here will appear.
    However, changes made to the data are not saved to the database; they
    affect only the report.

Retrieving Rows as Needed

When InfoMaker retrieves information from the database, the default setting
is used to retrieve all rows before displaying the information in a report. If a
large database is retrieved, this will result in long wait times before you can

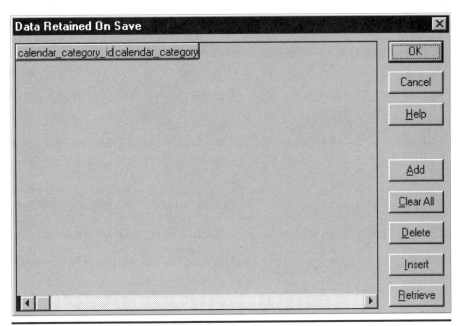

Figure 13.5 This box displays all the columns included in the data source of the report.

view the report. However, it is possible to tell InfoMaker to only retrieve enough rows to display on the current page and to continue to retrieve while the user is viewing the data. However, there are a couple of things to keep in mind when you use this option. If several users are accessing the same database, they may be locked out of the table(s) while the report runs. If the report sorts data or uses aggregate functions, such as Average, the Retrieve Rows option is overridden.

To retrieve only as many rows as are needed into a report, do the following:

1. Select Rows | Retrieve | Rows as needed from the menu.
2. To return to the default of retrieve all rows, choose Rows | Retrieve | Rows as needed again and deselect the option.

Saving Retrieved Rows to Disk

In the Windows 95/NT environment, it's possible to maximize the amount of memory available on a system. InfoMaker can be set to save retrieved data on the hard disk instead of holding the data in memory. To enable this option, choose Rows | Retrieve | Rows to Disk from the menu.

Selecting Objects in a Report

Use the mouse to select objects in the Report painter. If another tool is selected, for instance, the Picture Button tool, and you decide you don't want a picture button on the report, choosing the Selection tool changes the mouse back to a pointer so that another object may be selected. To choose the Selection tool, choose Select on the Object drop-down toolbar, or select Objects | Select Object on the menu.

Placing a column on a report

The Column control places a column from one of the tables included in the data source on the Report painter workspace. Columns contain data directly from the database.

To place a column, do the following:

1. Choose the Column tool from the Objects drop-down toolbar, or select Objects | Column from the Report painter menu.
2. Then click on the report workspace in the area where you want to place the column. InfoMaker displays the Select Column dialog box, as shown in Fig. 13.6. The list box displays all the columns available in the data source that have not yet been placed in the report.
3. Select one of the columns.
4. Choose OK. The column is placed in the report.

Placing a computed column in a report

Another type of control available on a report is a *computed column*. A computed column is not a data column. A computed column is composed of a combination of columns and an expression that equates to a value which displays in the computed column.

To place a computed column in a report, do the following:

1. Choose the Compute button from the toolbar, or choose Objects | Computed Field from the menu.

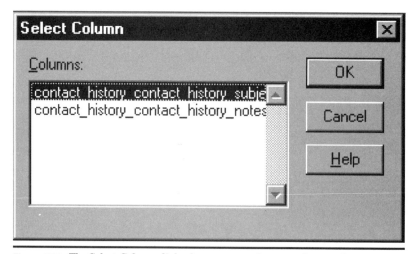

Figure 13.6 The Select Column dialog box appears when you place a column on a report.

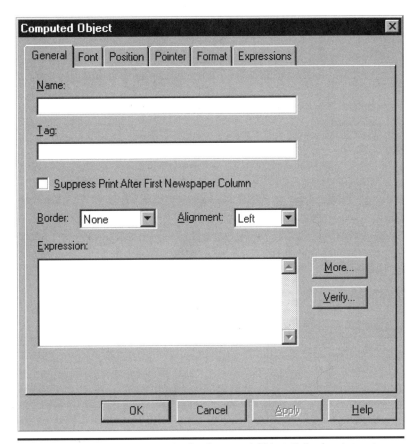

Figure 13.7 Build an expression in the Computed Object dialog box to create a computed column.

2. Click on the area of the screen where you want to place the control. The Computed Object property sheet displays, as shown in Fig. 13.7. The General tab must have a valid expression defined before you can access any of the other tabs on the Computed Object property sheet.

Creating an expression. When you are creating an expression for a computed column, the General tab on the Computed Column property sheet doesn't offer much assistance. Click on the More... button to display the Modify Expression dialog box, as shown in Fig. 13.8. This box contains buttons to insert mathematical symbols in an expression, such as plus and minus. List boxes containing the functions and the columns available from the data source are available for selection.

The following is a list of some valid expressions:

```
contact_first_name+ ' ' + contact_last_name
sum(year(calendar_calendar_date)for all)+ 1
sales_amount*.10
```

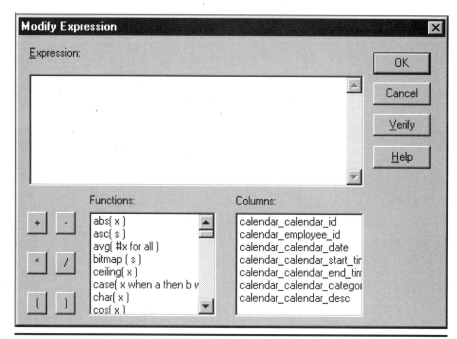

Figure 13.8 The Modify Expression dialog box offers assistance with building an expression by providing columns, functions, and mathematical symbols from which to choose.

An expression is validated by choosing the Verify button on the Modify Expression dialog box. InfoMaker displays a message, letting you know if the expression is valid. To exit, choose the OK button.

Placing text in a report

Text can be placed anywhere on the workspace. Text is convenient for grouping and labeling information.

To place text on the workspace, do the following:

1. Choose the Text button from the Object drop-down toolbar or choose Objects | Text from the menu.
2. Click on the workspace where you want to place the text.
3. Type the text to display on the report.
4. Click elsewhere on the workspace to deselect the text item. The text item is on the screen.

Placing pictures in a report

You can also add pictures to your reports. Pictures are useful in a realty application to display houses or in a human resources application to display employee photographs, for instance.

To place a picture in a report, do the following:

1. Choose the Picture control from the Objects drop-down toolbar, or choose Objects | Picture from the menu.

2. Click on the area of the workspace where you want to place the picture. The Picture Object property sheet displays, as shown in Fig. 13.9.

3. First select a file. Choose the Browse... button, and select the file to display. Pictures can be in bitmap (.bmp) format, Windows metafile (.wmf), or a run-length-encoded (.rle) file.

4. To have the picture display its original size on the report, choose the Original Size check box.

5. The Invert Image check box inverts the colors on the graphic.

6. In the Border drop-down list box are several different borders to place around the picture.

7. When you have finished, choose OK to return to the Report painter workspace.

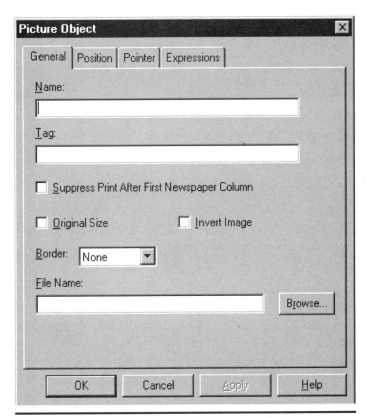

Figure 13.9 Select the graphic file to display on the Picture control, using the Picture Object property sheet.

Placing drawing objects in a report

The Report painter has four different drawing objects to add to reports. The drawing objects are used to bring attention to or group certain logical sets of columns. The drawing objects create lines, rectangles, ovals, and "round" rectangles.

To place one of these objects on a report, do the following:

1. Choose one of the drawing objects from either the Objects drop-down toolbar or from the Objects menu.
2. Click the mouse button on the Report workspace to place the object. When the object appears, it is selected.
3. Make the object larger or smaller, or move it elsewhere on the workspace.

To change the way the drawing object appears:

1. Right-click on the object to display the object's pop-up menu.
2. Choose Properties from the menu. The object's property sheet displays, as shown in Fig. 13.10.

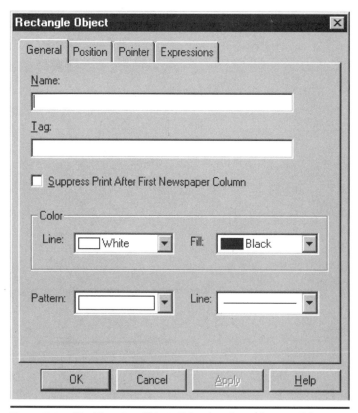

Figure 13.10 The Drawing Object dialog box is used to modify a drawing object's appearance.

3. Change the drawing object's visual appearance.

4. Choose OK when you have finished.

Placing a report object in a report

When a report object is added to an existing report, it is called a *nested report*. The base report can be any type of report other than a crosstab. The nested report can be related or unrelated to the master report. An example of a related nested report in the InfoCenter application is a master report showing employee information. Within that is a detail report containing all the contacts to which the employee is assigned. The common identifier between the two reports is the `employee_id` column. Figure 13.11 shows an example of a nested report.

When you build a nested report, it can be independent of the master report or related to it by a database column. When you place an unrelated nested report within a master report, the entire nested report appears with each row of the master report.

To create a related nested report, do the following:

1. Create the nested report that will be placed in the base report.

2. Define a retrieval argument for the nested report. For information on how to define retrieval arguments, see the section "Defining Retrieval Arguments" in this chapter.

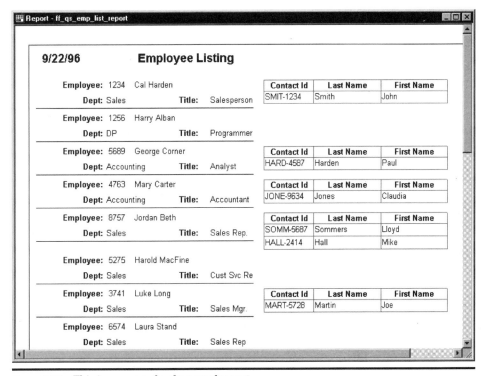

Figure 13.11 This is an example of a nested report.

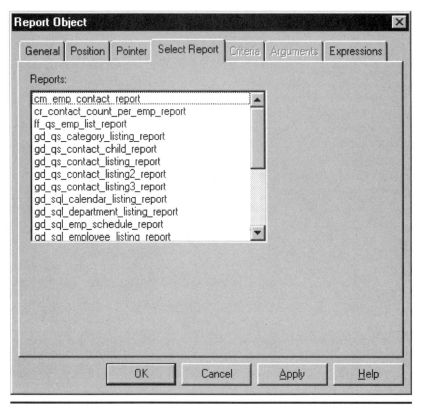

Figure 13.12 Specify the report to add to the base report.

3. Open or create the base report.

4. Select the Report button in the Objects drop-down toolbar, or select Objects | Report from the Report painter menu. The Report Object dialog box displays, as shown in Fig. 13.12.

5. Select the report to add to the base report.

6. When the nested report with retrieval arguments is selected, the Arguments tab is enabled. Choose the Arguments tab, as shown in Fig. 13.13.

7. Select the column from the Expression drop-down list box.

8. Choose OK when you have finished.

To place an unrelated nested report in a base report, do the following:

1. Open the Report painter from either the PowerBar or PowerPanel. The Select Report dialog box displays.

2. Choose the master report.

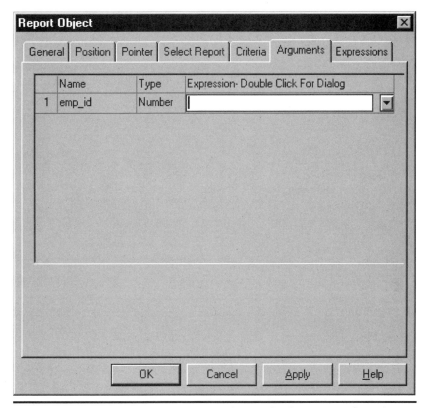

Figure 13.13 Specify the column to retrieve data in the Arguments tab on the Report Object dialog box.

3. Choose the Report button on the Objects drop-down toolbar or from the Objects | Report menu.

4. Click on the area of the master report where you wish to place the nested report.

5. Set the nested report properties. For more information, see the section "Specifying Report Object Properties" in this chapter.

6. Choose OK when you have finished.

Placing a graph object in a report

In the Report painter it is possible to have two different types of reports: a report with an added graph or a stand-alone graph. In this chapter we will cover reports with an added graph. A graph embedded in a report depends on the report to extract the information needed to build the graph. The underlying data is displayed in the report while the graph displays the same information graphically.

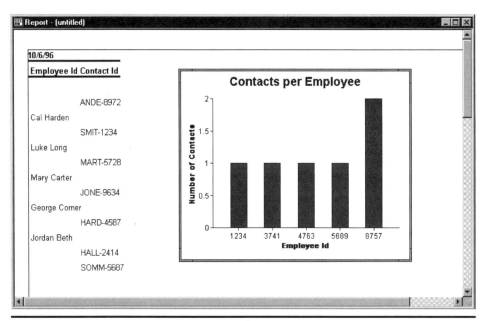

Figure 13.14   This is an example of a graph report that counts the number of contacts assigned to each employee.

Graphs display data retrieved from the database in a graphical format. Graphs make it easy to see at a glance what a report with long lists of numbers may express. There are many types of graphs to choose from including bar, pie, scatter, and line. Figure 13.14 shows an example of a report graph.

For more information about creating stand-alone graphs, see Chap. 12, Building Reports. For more information about graph properties, see Chap. 14, Building Graphs.

To place a graph object on a report, do the following:

1. Choose the Graph button from the Object drop-down toolbar or choose Objects | Graph from the menu.
2. Click on the workspace where you wish to place the graph. The Graph Object property sheet displays, as shown in Fig. 13.15.
3. Set the properties for the graph. For more information about setting graph properties, see Chap. 14.
4. Choose OK when you have finished.
5. The graph object appears in the Report painter workspace.

Placing OLE objects in a report

There are three instances where OLE objects can be used within InfoMaker. The first is the OLE report, in which an OLE object fills an entire report (see Chap. 13). The second involves placing an OLE object in a report. And third, an

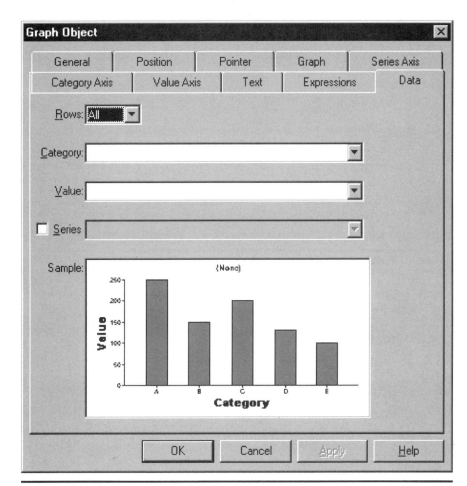

Figure 13.15 Define the data for a graph on the Graph Object property sheet.

OLE object can be contained in a column in a database and placed in a report column. (See Chap. 7, Working with Databases, for more information.) In this chapter, we will discuss how to place an OLE object in a report. Figure 13.16 shows an example of an OLE object in a report.

To place an OLE object in a report, do the following:

1. Choose the OLE button from the Object drop-down toolbar, or choose Objects | OLE from the menu.

2. Click on the workspace where you want to place the graph. The Insert Object property sheet displays, as shown in Fig. 13.17.

3. Set the object properties. For more information on setting object properties, see Chap. 12.

4. Choose OK when you have finished. The OLE object is placed in the Report painter workspace.

Figure 13.16 This is an example of an OLE object on a report:

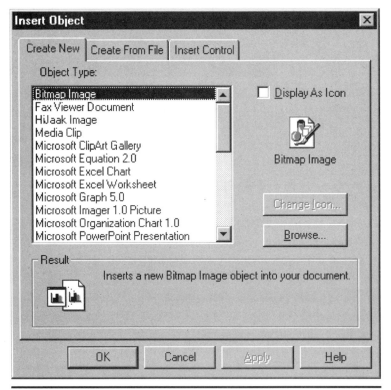

Figure 13.17 Place on object on a report by using the Insert Object property sheet.

Placing a database blob object in a report

A database *blob* is an OLE object which is stored in each row of a database table. By using a blob object in a report, you can access objects residing in the database rather than from another source. Placing the database blob object on the report allows the report to access the OLE object in the database. When you are creating a report that will contain a database blob object, do not add the blob column from the table to the data source.

To place a blob object in a report, do the following,

1. Choose the Blob object from the Objects drop-down toolbar or choose Objects | OLE Database Blob from the menu. The Database Blob Object property sheet displays, as shown in Fig. 13.18.

2. Depending on the OLE server application being used, you may or may not need a class name. The class name tells the server application to create the title for the server window.

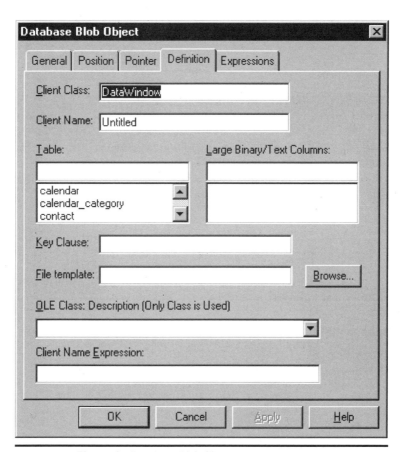

Figure 13.18 This is the Database Blob Object property sheet.

3. Select the table and column that contain the blob data.

4. In the key clause area, enter the clause for the SQL WHERE clause that will retrieve the data, for instance, `contact_id= :contact_id`.

5. Select the file containing the blob object.

6. Enter the client name description. This is the name that will display at the top of the server application.

7. Choose OK when you have finished.

Placing functions in a report

To quickly add a computed column that calculates averages, counts, sums, or adds the page count or today's date to a report, choose one of the aggregate function objects from the drop-down toolbar on the Objects menu.

To place a computed column in a report, do the following:

1. Select the column in the report to do calculations.

2. Choose the object from the Objects drop-down toolbar or Objects from the menu. InfoMaker automatically places the calculation needed to the specified column.

Modifying Object Attributes

Each object in a report (headings, boxes, columns, etc.) has an associated pop-up menu. Right-clicking on an object displays a pop-up menu. Choosing the Properties... option on this menu, or selecting Edit | Properties from the Report painter menu, displays a relevant property sheet with the different attributes available for that control. Many of the attributes are unique for each object and contain options to customize reports. Figure 13.19 shows a property sheet for a column object.

Forcing retrieval criteria

If retrieval criteria have been set on a report, clicking on the Equality Required check box on the General tab of an object property sheet sets the entry of retrieval criteria to required instead of optional. The column must have data specified for it before the report runs.

Overriding editing

To prevent data values from displaying in the Specify Retrieval Criteria dialog box when a column uses a code table on a Radio Button, CheckBox, or DropDown list box edit style, select this option.

Changing fonts

To change fonts for an object, access the object's property sheet and select the Font tab. The font, color, and background color can be modified. The Report

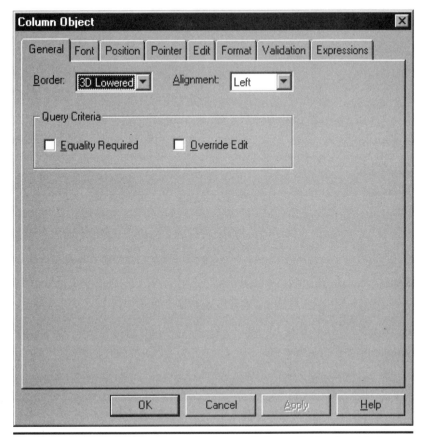

Figure 13.19 This is a property sheet displaying all the available tabs with the attributes which can be modified for a column object.

painter also has a style bar in which text labels are modified; objects are made bold, are italicized, and are underlined; and fonts and font sizes are changed. The style bar also has buttons to set object justification. If the style bar doesn't appear in the Report painter, right-click on the painter bar and click on the Style Bar option on the pop-up menu. The style bar is shown in Fig. 13.20.

Setting an object border

InfoMaker has several different types of borders to enhance both reports and an object's visibility on the report. The Generation tab of the Report Options property sheet has options to specify default borders for all reports. These defaults can be overridden in individual reports. And by selecting the object(s)

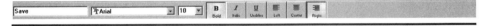

Figure 13.20 This is an example of the style bar in the Report painter.

and clicking on the border drop-down toolbox on the Report painter bar, an object can be set to have no border, can be underlined, can have a box, can be shadowed, can be resizable, etc.

Changing an object's position

To move an object, either select it with the mouse and move it to a new location, or access the object's property sheet and select the Position tab. Once an object is highlighted, the cursor keys can be utilized to move the object in small increments.

Modifying edit styles

To override or create edit styles for an object on a report, select the Edit tab on the Object property sheet. For a complete discussion of creating edit styles, see Chap. 7, Working with Databases.

Display formats

To modify display formats, select the Format tab on a property sheet. For a complete discussion of creating display formats, see Chap. 7.

Expressions

Depending on the data retrieved into a column, it is possible to build an expression that acts under certain circumstances. For instance, it is possible to turn the text color to red when a negative number displays in a column. To create or edit an expression, access the Expressions tab on the object property sheet. Double-click on the property to affect, such as the color. The Modify Expression dialog box opens. Enter the expression. When you have finished, choose the OK button. For more information on building expressions, see Chap. 8, Working with Data in InfoMaker.

Selecting a pointer

It is possible to set a different pointer when the mouse passes over a report or object. Select the pointer from the Pointer tab and choose OK when you have finished.

Setting Currency and Percentage Formats on a Report

It is possible to set numeric data columns on a report to display with either a currency or a percentage format.

To quickly set a column to either currency or percentage format, do the following:

1. Select the column(s) to change by clicking on it (them) with the mouse.

2. Choose the Currency or Percent button in the Report painter bar, or select the Edit | Format | Currency or Percent option on the menu. The column's format is changed and is shown in Preview mode.

Sliding Columns

Sliding columns are used to remove blank spaces between columns and objects. When you are creating mailing labels, sliding columns remove blank spaces. Options available, when you set the sliding attribute are None, All above, or Directly above. To slide the column to the left, check the left check box.

To set a column to slide, do the following:

1. Select the column.
2. Right-click on the column, and select Properties... from the pop-up menu.
3. On the Position tab of the object property sheet, select the type of sliding preferred.
4. Click OK when you have finished.

Newspaper Columns

Newspaper columns are used to specify the number of columns across a page when a report is printed.

To specify newspaper columns, do the following:

1. Choose Edit | Properties from the Report painter menu. The Report Window Options dialog box displays.
2. Choose the Print Specifications tab.
3. Near the bottom of the property sheet is a grouping called Newspaper Columns. Specify the number of columns and the width.
4. Choose OK when you have finished.

Bring to Front/Bring to Rear

When placing objects in a group box, the object either on top or behind must be specified. For instance, when you place a column in a group box, the group box sits on top of the columns so the columns are invisible. But by right-clicking on the group box, you select Send to Back from the menu. The box is placed on the second layer with the columns residing on top—visible.

Viewing Column Specifications

It is possible to view the column attributes for data items in a report. You can see the column name, data type, and the database table from which the column is retrieved. To view the current column specification, choose Rows | Column

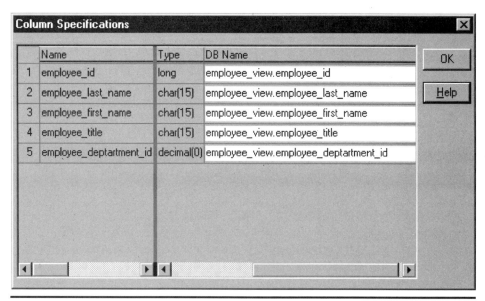

Figure 13.21 This dialog box displays the column name, data type, and database table and columns for a report column.

Specification from the menu. The Column Specifications dialog box displays, as shown in Fig. 13.21.

Suppressing Repeating Values

It is possible to suppress repeating values in a report. This may be necessary when sorting or grouping data and only the first instance of a value should be displayed. To suppress repeating values choose Rows | Suppress Repeating Values... from the menu. The Specify Repeating Values Suppression List displays as shown in Fig. 13.22. Drag the data columns from the source data column to the suppression list column and choose OK.

Layering Objects in a Report

Objects are normally placed in a band on a report. However, there may be an occasion where it's necessary to place an object in the background, band, or foreground of a report.

To change the layer on which an object resides, do the following:

1. Right-click on an object and choose Properties... from the pop-up menu.
2. Choose the Position tab from the property sheet.

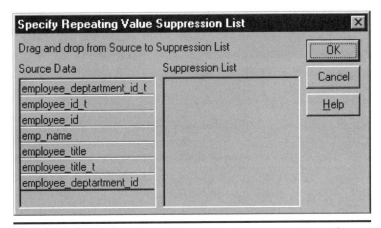

Figure 13.22 To prevent columns from displaying on a report, use the Specify Repeating Value Suppression List dialog box.

3. Select Background, Band, or Foreground from the Layer drop-down list box.

4. Choose OK when you have finished.

Reversing Actions in a Report

To reverse the last change made on a report, choose the Undo button on the painter bar or the Edit | Undo item on the menu. The Undo item toggles between undo and redo, and can also reverse a redo.

Removing Items from a Report

An option is available to remove objects from a report. One way to delete an item is to select the object(s) and press the Delete key on the keyboard. Another useful method provided is Clear. The Clear option is accessed either from the Clear button on the Report painter bar or from the Edit | Clear item on the Report painter menu.

Aligning Text

InfoMaker provides several different tools to help align objects on the Report painter workspace. The General tab on the Report Options property sheet sets objects placed on the report to snap to a grid to align objects. Several other alignment tools are located on the painter bar and are also accessible from the Edit item on the menu.

Left, right, top, and bottom alignment

Objects can be aligned on the left, right, top, or bottom edge. For instance, let's begin with the objects shown on Fig. 13.23. They need some serious realigning to make the report more visually appealing. The first object selected is the one on which InfoMaker will align all the objects.

To align objects, do the following:

1. First, place the top column in the location where you want to align all the objects.

2. Then select the other objects to align in that position by holding down the Control button on the keyboard and clicking on them with the mouse. The screen should look similar to Fig. 13.24.

3. Now select one of the alignment tools from the Alignment drop-down toolbar, or choose Edit | Align Controls from the Report painter menu. In this example, we chose the left alignment tool. All the columns line up on the left side, as shown in Fig. 13.25.

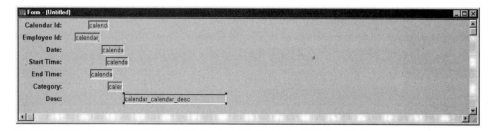

Figure 13.23   This is an example of objects which must be aligned.

Figure 13.24   Selecting objects in preparation for aligning.

Figure 13.25   An example of aligning objects on the left edge.

Center alignment

The align center horizontal option aligns objects by using the center of the object as a focal point, instead of the edge. See Fig. 13.26 for an example of align center horizontal.

The align center vertical option aligns objects by using the center of the object as a focal point, instead of the edge. See Fig. 13.27 for an example.

Spacing objects

There are two tools to set the spacing between objects: Space Horizontal and Space Vertical. The Space Horizontal tool spaces the objects the same distance apart horizontally across the report. The Space Vertical tool spaces the object the same distance apart vertically down the report. The spacing tools are accessed from the Alignment drop-down toolbar on the Report painter or from the Edit | Space Controls item on the menu. Figure 13.28 demonstrates how the Space Horizontal tool spaces the four objects on the lower part of the report.

In the next example (see Fig. 13.29), the first two columns are spaced correctly, but the third is not. Select the columns and choose the Space Vertical tool. The columns are then the same distance apart, as shown in Fig. 13.30.

Sizing controls

Two options are available to make selected controls the same size. These tools are called Size Width and Size Height. The sizing tools are available from the

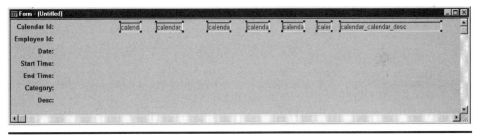

Figure 13.26   The align center horizontal tool uses the center of an object as the focal point and aligns objects horizontally in the report.

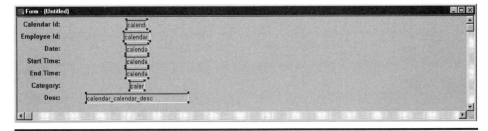

Figure 13.27   The align center vertical tool uses the center of an object as the focal point and aligns objects vertically in the report.

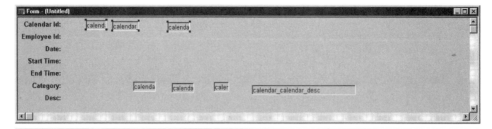

Figure 13.28 The Spacing Horizontal tool places the lower four objects on the report an equal distance apart horizontally across the report.

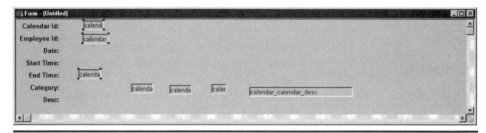

Figure 13.29 The three selected objects on the report are not spaced correctly.

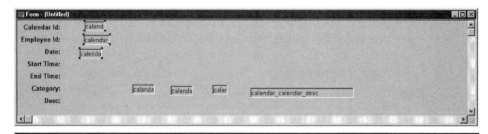

Figure 13.30 Selecting the Space Vertical tool puts all three objects the same distance apart vertically in the report.

Alignment toolbar on the Report painter bar or from the Edit | Size Controls menu item. Figure 13.31 demonstrates the results of making all objects the same width.

Figures 13.32 and 13.33 display an example of the results of using the Size Height tool.

Changing Report Colors

Colors for both the actual report and all the objects residing in the report are completely customizable. Each object can have colors set independent of other objects. To set the same report color for all reports, use the Generation tab on the Report Window Object property sheet. It contains options to specify default colors and borders for all reports. However, these settings can be overridden in

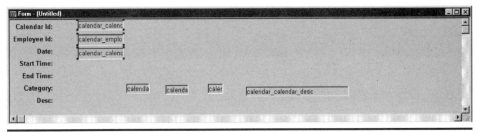

Figure 13.31   The Size Width tool makes all selected objects to the same width.

Figure 13.32   This is an example of objects which must all be the same height.

Figure 13.33   These are the same objects from the previous example after the Size Height tool was applied.

individual reports. To change the color for a particular report, right-click on an empty place on the report and choose the Properties item from the pop-up menu. The Report Window Object property sheet appears, as shown in Fig. 13.34. Select the desired color from the Color drop-down list box, and choose OK to change the report's color.

Background colors

The Report painter bar has a button to control the background color of objects. To change an object's background color, do the following:

1. Select the object(s), using the mouse.
2. Click on the Background button on the toolbar, and a drop-down box opens with all the different colors to choose from.
3. Choose the color. The background color of the object is modified.

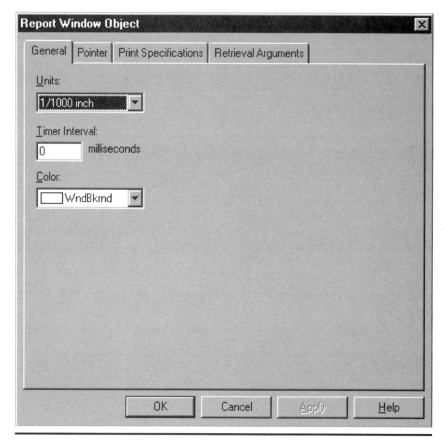

Figure 13.34   The Report Window Object property sheet contains an option to change the color of the report.

Foreground colors

It is possible to change the foreground color of an object. To change an object's foreground color, do the following:

1. Select the object(s), using the mouse.

2. Click on the Foreground button on the toolbar, and a drop-down box opens with all the different colors to choose from.

3. Choose the color. The foreground color of the object is modified.

Defining custom colors

If none of the default colors are to your liking, it is possible to define a custom color. This is accomplished by selecting Design | Custom Colors... on the Report painter menu. The Color dialog box displays, as shown in Fig. 13.35.

To read more about how to define custom colors, refer to your Microsoft Windows documentation.

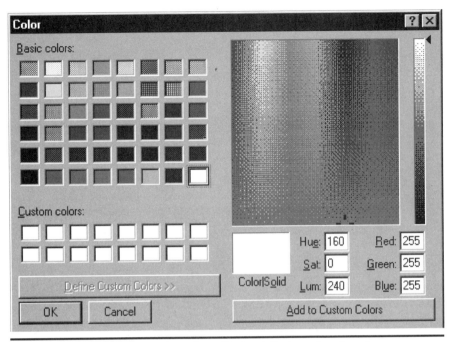

Figure 13.35 To define custom colors, choose Design | Custom colors from the menu.

Autosizing

A column or other object in a report can be set to autoheight. This means that the column's height will change depending on the data that is retrieved into the column. Notice that in Fig. 13.36 the `calendar_date` column has been increased in height.

Now notice what happens when we run the report with autosize height turned off (see Fig. 13.37).

Now let's set autosize height to on and run the report again. Notice this time that the Date column shrank to fit the data that was retrieved into that column (see Fig. 13.38).

Figure 13.36 The third object in this example shows an object set to a specific height.

Figure 13.37   When autosize height is turned off, the object remains the same size as it was in Design mode.

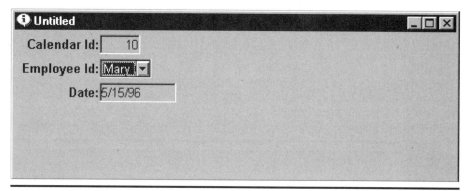

Figure 13.38   This is an example of running the same report with autosize height on. The third column is reduced in size automatically when information is retrieved.

Editing the Data Source

There are many reasons why you may decide to modify the data source. You may need to add or remove columns, tables, and so on. To modify the data source, choose the SQL Data button on the painter bar or Design | Edit Data Source from the menu. When this option is selected, the Select painter related to the data source is started.

Specifying Retrieval Criteria

To set a report so a user can enter a name or other type of information to retrieve information from the report's underlying tables, specify retrieval criteria.

To set a report to prompt for retrieval criteria, do the following:

1. Choose Rows | Prompt for Criteria from the painter menu. The Prompt For Criteria dialog box displays, as shown in Fig. 13.39.

2. Select the column(s) for which users have the option of entering selection criteria, and press OK.

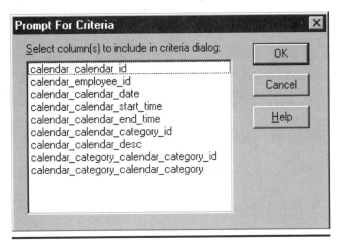

Figure 13.39 The Prompt For Criteria dialog box specifies the column from a table to have users enter information to retrieve data.

3. Now run the report. Before the report runs, the Specify Retrieval Criteria dialog box displays, as shown in Fig. 13.40.

4. Enter the date(s) to retrieve data.

5. Press OK. InfoMaker displays only those rows that meet the criteria.

Sorting Data in a Report

When you run a report, it is possible to sort the data retrieved into the report based on a specific column or set of columns.

To sort data in a report, do the following:

1. Choose Rows | Sort from the menu. The Specify Sort Columns dialog box displays, as shown in Fig. 13.41.

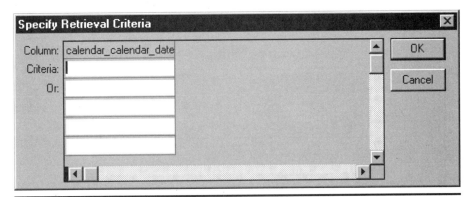

Figure 13.40 Before running a report with retrieval criteria specified, InfoMaker displays the Specify Retrieval Criteria dialog box to accept values.

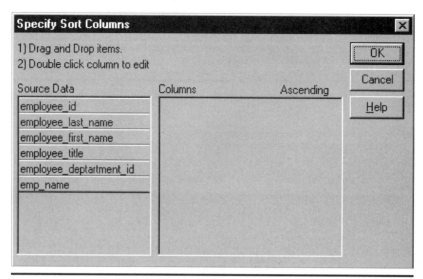

Figure 13.41   Specify sort columns for a report in the Specify Sort Columns dialog box.

2. Drag the column(s) to the right-hand box.

3. Select an ascending or descending sort by checking the box.

4. Choose OK when you have finished.

Filtering Data in a Report

Filtering of data removes data that meets specific criteria from a report. This is useful when there are several thousand rows in a table and you want to view only a small percentage of them.

To only have specific data display on a report, do the following:

1. Choose the Rows | Filter... option on the menu. The Specify Filter dialog box displays, as shown in Fig. 13.42.

2. Create a valid expression in the top portion of the box. For more information on creating expressions, see Chap. 7, Working with Databases.

3. When you have finished, choose OK.

Grouping Data in a Report

Grouping data consists of gathering all related data in one section of a report for easier viewing and manipulation.

To create a group, do the following:

1. Choose Rows | Create Group... from the menu. The Band Object dialog box displays, as shown in Fig. 13.43.

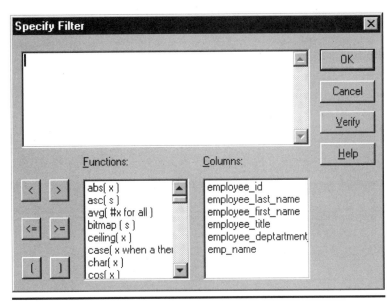

Figure 13.42   Specify a filter expression in the Specify Filter dialog box.

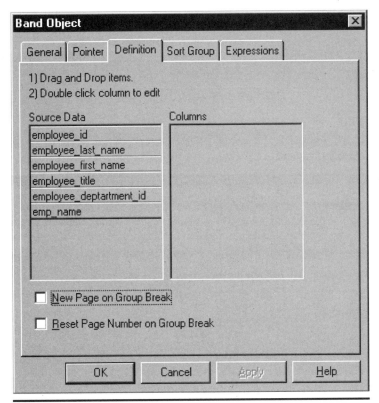

Figure 13.43   Use the Band Object dialog box to group data columns on a report.

2. Drag the column(s) that make up the group.

3. To start a new page when the value in the group changes, check the New Page on Group Break box.

4. To restart numbering when the value in the group changes, choose the Reset Page Number on Group Break box.

5. To sort the group, choose the Sort Group tab on the Band Object dialog box.

6. Drag the data column(s) to be sorted into the right area.

7. When you have finished, choose OK.

To edit a group:

1. Select Rows | Edit Group from the menu, and choose the group to change.

2. The Band Object dialog box displays.

3. Make any changes.

4. Choose OK when you have finished.

To delete a group, do the following: Choose Rows | Delete Group… from the menu, and select the group created in the report to delete. The group is deleted from report.

Reordering Columns in a Report

When you create a grid report, it is possible to reorder columns. To reorder a column, do the following:

1. Place the mouse cursor on a column heading. The column is highlighted and displays a line representing the column border, as shown in Fig. 13.44.

2. Then drag the mouse in the direction in which you wish to move the column. When the mouse button is released, the column is placed in the new position.

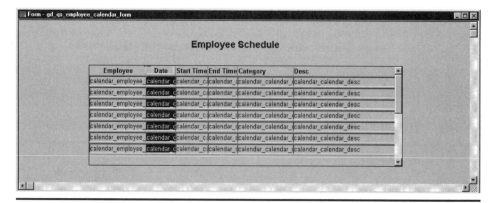

Figure 13.44 The Report painter runs a grid presentation style report. In this example, the date column is selected in preparation for moving.

Running a Report

While you are developing a report, it is possible to switch between designing the report and seeing how the report looks with data. The Preview option allows you to view the report as it would appear to a user. You can see changes that must be made to the report more readily, such as moving and resizing objects, viewing data, and so on. To run the report, choose the Preview button on the painter bar or select Design | Preview from the menu. To return to design mode, choose the Preview button from the painter bar or the Design | Preview option from the menu.

When you run a report, the painter bar changes to accommodate the different tools available. InfoMaker automatically includes functionality that in another environment would require extensive programming.

Maneuvering in the table

When you view data, it is possible to go to the first page in the retrieved set of data, the last page, and so on. These buttons are labeled First, Prior, Next, and Last. When these buttons are selected, the report displays the first page in the retrieved set of information for the report, the previous page, the next page, and the last page in the retrieved set, respectively. Using this tool enables you to move to specific pages of information quickly.

Saving rows to an external file

When running a report, you can choose to save the information in another format. This extends InfoMaker's power by exporting data to spreadsheets, text files, HTML reports, etc., in which the data may be further manipulated and modified.

To save rows to an external file, do the following:

1. Select the File | Save Rows As option on the Report painter menu. The Save As dialog box displays, as shown in Fig. 13.45.

2. You'll notice from the Save as type drop-down list box that there are many different file formats in which to save the data in the table, as shown in Fig. 13.46. File formats available include saving the data in an Excel spreadsheet, as SQL, a Powersoft Report, or HTML. Choose the desired format.

3. Enter the filename.

4. Choose OK when you have finished.

Saving to spreadsheets. InfoMaker can save the data from a table on which a report is based to an Excel or Lotus spreadsheet. Each column and each row are extracted and placed in columns and rows in the spreadsheet.

Saving to text. To export data contained in a report to a text file, select the text file type. Each row in the report is sent to a separate row in a text file.

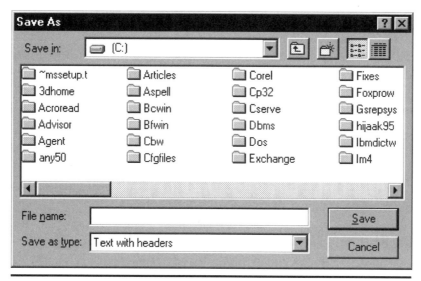

Figure 13.45 When you save data in another format, select the directory and the filename in which to save it.

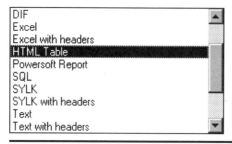

Figure 13.46 When you save data, it is possible to save it in many formats, including HTML or a Powersoft Report.

Saving to HTML. When you are saving rows which have been retrieved into a report, it is possible to save the information to an HTML document. The report can then be further modified in HTML. The results you receive depend on the type of presentation style used in the report. Figure 13.47 shows an example of a report loaded to a Web page.

Saving to a Powersoft Report. A report can be saved as a Powersoft Report. A Powersoft Report file contains the report with the underlying source code, so the report can be modified by another InfoMaker or PowerBuilder user. Additionally, the underlying data selected in the report is extracted and stored in the Powersoft Report. The Powersoft Report can be opened in File Manager or Explorer, within a mail message as a file attachment, and from InfoMaker's File menu. When the Powersoft Report is started, an instance of InfoMaker is initiated and the report is opened in the Report painter.

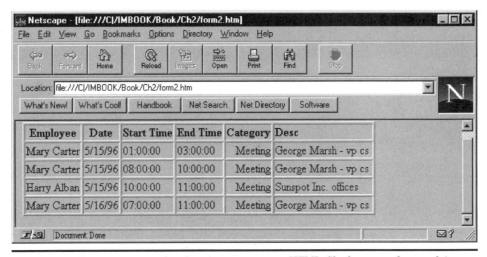

Figure 13.47 This is an example of saving a report to HTML file format and opened in Netscape Navigator.

Saving reports as SQL. Saving a report to SQL translates the current report to the SQL commands necessary to create a table and to insert the values selected in the report as rows. These commands can then be executed independently to create a new database table or execute another type of SQL command.

Mailing reports

Powersoft has added the ability to send a report as a mail message by using a MAPI-compliant mail server such as Microsoft Exchange. The procedure is very easy. Simply preview a report and select Send from the File menu. Fill out to whom you want to send the report, and InfoMaker fires off the report as a .psr file, which includes the actual report with the data and the design. This allows the recipient to redesign the actual report, if necessary.

Retrieving data

The Retrieve button is used to retrieve a fresh copy of the data from the database into a report. This is useful when several people are sharing the same database and it is possible for data to change in the database while information is being viewed in a report. To retrieve data from the database, press the Retrieve button or choose Rows | Retrieve from the menu.

Closing a report in Preview mode

To close a report in Preview mode, select the Exit button on the Report painter bar, or choose the Close option on the Report Window menu.

Another way to close a report is by pressing the Control + F4 key combination or selecting File | Close from the Report painter menu. Regardless of how a report is closed, InfoMaker will verify the close action if changes have been made.

Putting It All Together

Now that we've covered all the options available in the Report painter, we're going to design a report for the InfoCenter application.

1. Start the Report painter from either the PowerBar or PowerPanel. The Select Report dialog box displays.

2. Choose the New button to create a new report.

3. Choose the Quick Select data source.

4. Choose the Tabular presentation style.

5. Click on OK. The Quick Select dialog box displays.

6. Choose the `contact` table from the Tables list box. All the columns for the `contact` table display in the Columns list.

7. Choose the following columns to display in the report: `contact_id`, `contact_last_name`, `contact_first_name`, `contact_title`, and `contact_company`.
   You'll notice that as you select each of the columns, it displays in the toolbox at the bottom of the dialog box.

8. Now let's set sort criteria. In the toolbox, choose the ascending sort order for the `contact_last_name` and `contact_first_name` columns. When we have finished, the Quick Select dialog box should look like Fig. 13.48.

9. Choose OK. InfoMaker builds the basic report and displays it in the Report painter. Notice that since we defined bold for the headings and other attributes for the data columns in the Database painter when the table was built, we don't have to respecify them here in the report. This is where the time we spend defining our tables pays off.

10. Save the report, using the naming conventions discussed in Chap. 4, Standards and Guidelines. In this case, the report could be named `tb_qs_contact_listing_report`.

11. Preview the report by choosing the Preview button on the painter bar.

12. Return to Design mode by choosing the Preview button again.

13. Drag the footer bar down about ½ inch.

14. Add the page number to the bottom center of the report by choosing Object drop-down toolbar and clicking in the footer area under the `contact_first_name` column.

15. Now let's add the date to the top left corner of the report. Select the header bar with the mouse, and drag it down about 1 inch.

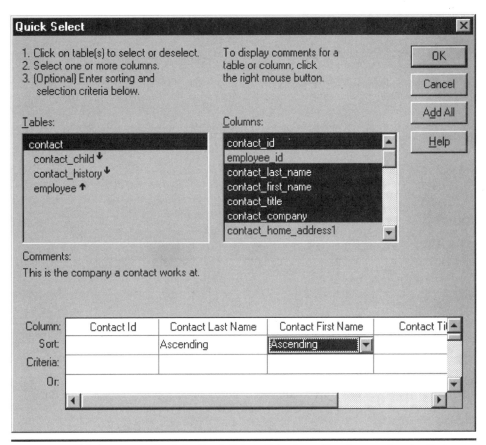

Figure 13.48 This is an example of the Quick Select dialog box with column and sort criteria specified.

16. Move the column headings down until they sit on top of the header bar.

17. Choose the Today object from the Object drop-down toolbar on the painter bar.

18. Click on the upper left corner of the report.

19. Save the report again.

20. Now preview the report. Notice how the current date appears in the upper left corner and the page number displays at the bottom of the report.

21. Return to Design mode.

22. Let's have the report count the number of contacts we've retrieved from the database. Select the `contact_last_name` column.

23. Select the Objects | Count—Computed Field item from the menu.

24. InfoMaker places the calculation needed to count the contacts in the Summary band.

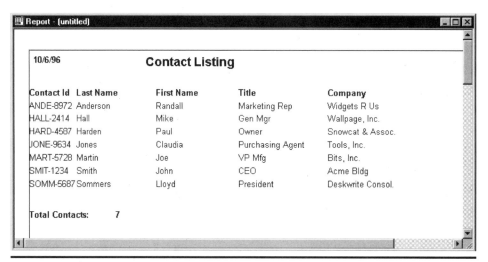

Figure 13.49   This is what the final Contact Listing report looks like. You can continue to make modifications to it.

25. Place a text item to the left of the count in the Summary band to read "Total Contacts:".

26. Both the text item and the count should be bold.

27. Enlarge the Summary band so there is enough room for a blank line after the final contact is printed in the report.

28. Give the report a heading of "Contact Listing."

29. Run the report. It should now look like Fig. 13.49.

Summary

We have covered all the options available for building a report. You have learned how to specify retrieval arguments, create expressions, and place objects in a report. You now have all the information you need to begin building reports on your own.

14

Building Graphs

What You Will Learn

Chapter 14 outlines in detail how to create a graph. You'll learn where to set the graph attributes and what the options do. There is a discussion outlining the parts of a graph you'll need to understand to be most effective in creating a graph. By the end of this chapter, you will be able to build a graph to effectively communicate to others what the information in a database means.

About Graphs

Graphs provide a way to view data in a graphical format. It is very difficult to visualize trends and statistics from a report listing columns of numbers. But graphing that same data shows instantly any troublespots or other areas that need attention.

There are two ways to use graphs in InfoMaker: as stand-alone or embedded in either a form or a report. A graph, whether stand-alone or embedded in a report, is just like any other type of report or object type. Since we've already discussed how to create a stand-alone graph (Chap. 12, Building Reports) and how to embed a graph object in a form and report (see Chaps. 11 and 13), we won't go over it again here. Refer to those chapters if you need help. In this chapter, we will concentrate on how to enhance the graph by adding titles and legends, changing graph types, and so on.

Parts of a Graph

There are several different parts on a graph, and understanding each of these areas is crucial to becoming an effective graph builder. We'll discuss each of these parts in this section. Figure 14.1 labels the parts of a graph.

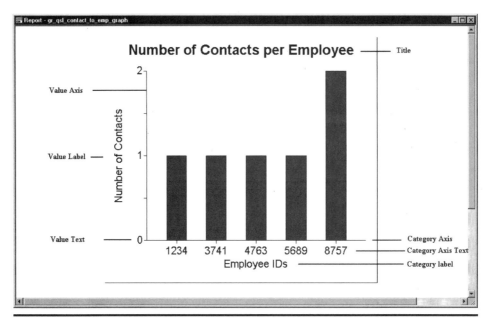

Figure 14.1   A graph with each part labeled.

Title	The title is the name that appears at the top of the graph.
Value axis	The value axis plots the numeric values of the specified data. In Fig. 14.1, the graph is counting the number of contacts.
Value axis label	The value axis label is the title assigned to the value axis, which is Number of Contacts in the graph in Fig. 14.1.
Value axis text	The value axis text is the label assigned to each value interval—0, 1, 2 in Fig. 14.1.
Category axis	The category axis plots the major divisions of the data horizontally on the graph. In Fig. 14.1, it groups the contacts for each employee.
Category axis text	The category axis text is the label assigned to each value.
Category axis label	The category axis label is the name given to the category axis.
Series	Not shown in this graph is a series. A *series* is simply a set of data points or a subgrouping of a category. In a three-dimensional graph there is a series axis, along which the series values are plotted.
Legend	Also not shown in this graph is a legend. A legend is useful when there are subgroupings of data within a category which are color-coded for each subgroup.

Types of Graphs

There are many different types of graphs available in InfoMaker, as the Graph Object property sheet in Fig. 14.2 shows. Each of these graph types serves a specific purpose in presenting data to others.

Area, column, line, and bar graphs

Area, column, line, and bar graphs are much alike, with the only difference being that they use a different type of graphic to represent the data values and use a different orientation. All other properties are the same when you are working with these types of graphs. The area and line graphs are used to dis-

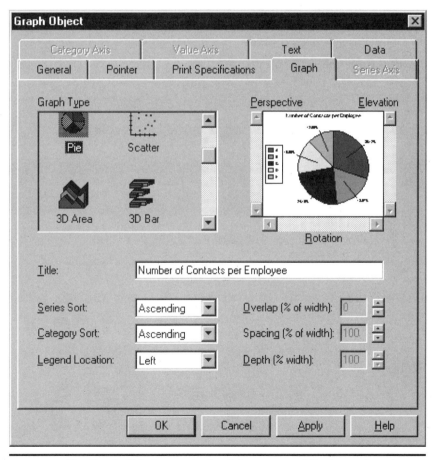

Figure 14.2 The Graph Object property sheet shows some of the types of graphs available.

play continuous data, and the bar and column graphs are used to display non-continuous data. The graphs in Figs. 14.3, 14.4, 14.5, and 14.6 show simple examples of area, column, line, and bar graphs, respectively.

Pie graphs

Pie graphs show one series of data points with each point represented by a slice, which is a percentage of the whole. Figure 14.7 shows an example of a pie graph.

Scatter graphs

A scatter graph shows data points. Scatter graphs are used to view relationships between two sets of numeric values. In scatter graphs, numeric values are plotted along both axes. This is different from other graphs, which have values along one axis and categories along the other axis. See Fig. 14.8.

Three-dimensional graphs

In the three-dimensional graph, the data is plotted in the line, area, bar, and column graphs in just about the same way as in two-dimensional graphs. The difference is that the data is plotted along the series axis instead of along the category axis. Figures 14.9 and 14.10 show the difference between two- and three-dimensional graphs.

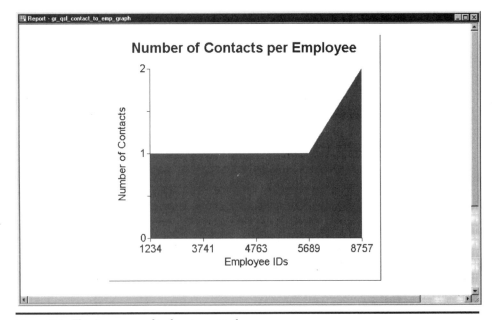

Figure 14.3   This is an example of an area graph.

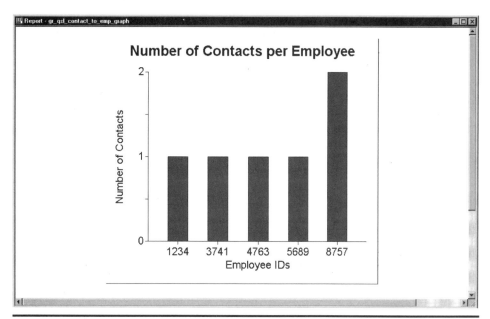

Figure 14.4   This is an example of a column graph.

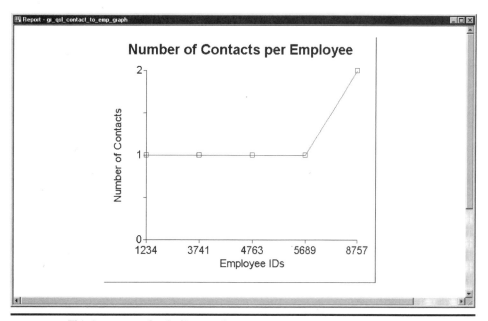

Figure 14.5   This is an example of a line graph.

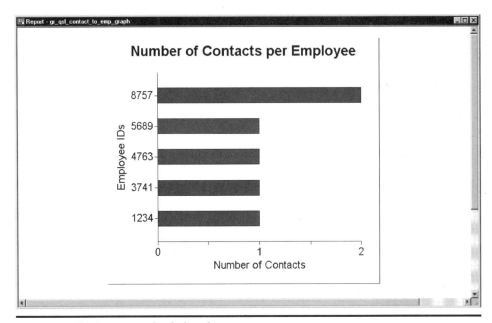

Figure 14.6   This is an example of a bar chart.

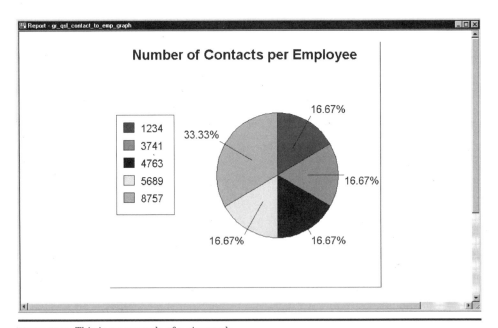

Figure 14.7   This is an example of a pie graph.

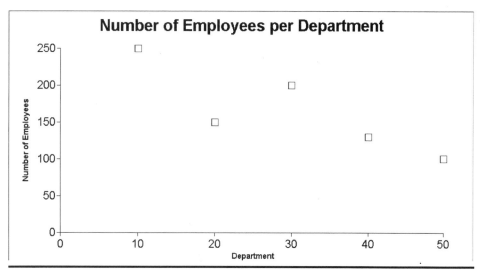

Figure 14.8 This is an example of a scatter graph.

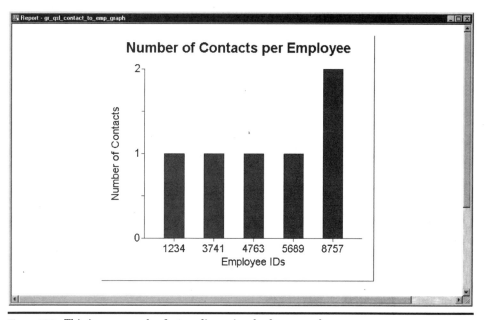

Figure 14.9 This is an example of a two-dimensional column graph.

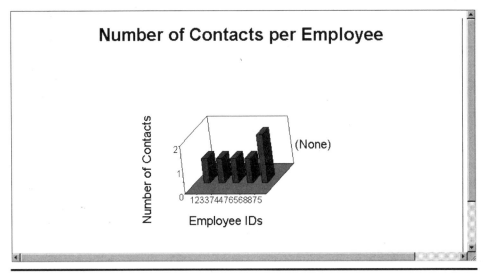

Figure 14.10 This is an example of a three-dimensional column graph.

Stacked graphs

In bar and column stacked graphs, the bars and columns are stacked. In stacked graphs, each category is represented as one bar or column instead of as separate bars or columns for each series. Figure 14.11 shows an example of a stacked graph.

Accessing Graph Attributes

To define or modify the appearance of a stand-alone graph, right-click on an empty area of the report area workspace to display the Report painter's pop-up menu. To modify a graph object, right-click on the object. Choose Properties... from the pop-up menu. The Graph Object property sheet displays, as shown in Fig. 14.12.

Defining Data for a Graph

Before you use a graph, the data must be defined for each of the axes: category, value, and series. If the axes are not defined, the other tabs on the Graph Object property sheet are not accessible.

To define the data for a graph, do the following:

1. Choose the Data tab from the Graph Object property sheet.
2. Select the Category data column.

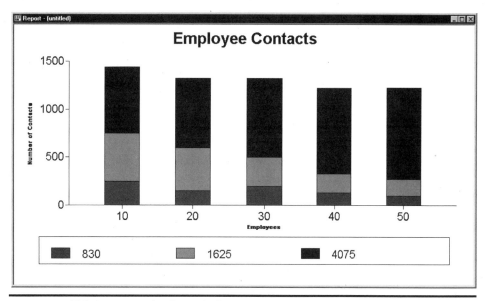

Figure 14.11   This is an example of a stacked graph.

3. Select the Value data column.

4. To define a series, choose the Series check box. This enables the Series drop-down list box. Select a value for the series by choosing a column name from the Series drop-down list box.

5. The Rows box specifies the rows to include in the graph. It is only accessible when you are building a report object. When you are creating a Graph presentation style report, the Rows drop-down list box is disabled and not accessible. When you are using a Graph presentation style, the graph always shows all the rows in the table(s). A page or group of data cannot be specified.

6. Choose OK to accept the changes. InfoMaker creates the graph and displays it in the Report painter workspace.

Selecting a Graph Type

To change the graph type, select the Graph tab on the Graph Object property sheet, as shown in Fig. 14.13. All the different types of graphs available are listed in the Graph Type list box. Choose one. Notice how the example graph to the right of the Graph Type box changes to show how the graph will appear. If one of the three-dimensional graphs is selected, the Perspective, Elevation, and Rotation scroll bars are enabled, allowing the angle the graph displays to be changed.

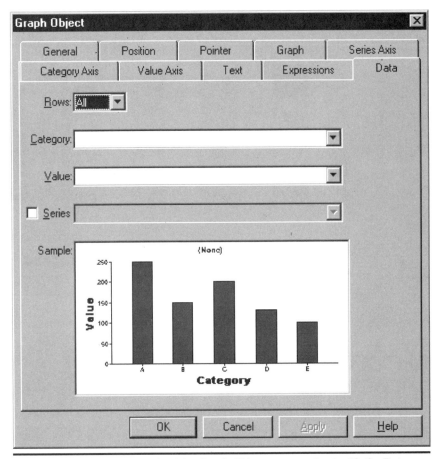

Figure 14.12 This is an example of the Graph Object property sheet with the Data tab on top.

Setting the Graph Title

To give a graph a title, enter the title in the Title box on the Graph tab of the Graph Object property sheet.

Sorting Graph Data

By default, the series and category are sorted in ascending order. This attribute can be changed by choosing the Series Sort and Category Sort drop-down list boxes and changing them to Descending, Ascending, or Unsorted on the Graph tab of the Graph Object property sheet.

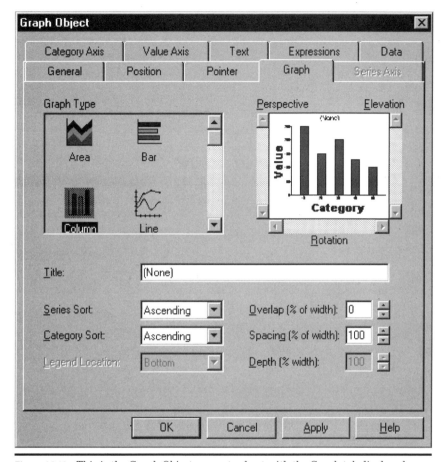

Figure 14.13 This is the Graph Object property sheet with the Graph tab displayed.

Changing the Legend Location

A legend color codes the values in a chart. To change the location of the legend, access the Graph tab on the Graph Object property sheet. Choose the Legend Location drop-down list box and choose from left, bottom, top, right, or no legend. As changes are made to the graph properties, the model graph represents how the graph will appear in the Report painter.

Changing the Overlap

In bar and column graphs, the percentage that the bars or columns overlap can be modified by changing the Overlap (% of width) box on the Graph tab of the Graph Object property sheet. The default is 0, which is no overlap.

Changing the Spacing

The spacing between bars and columns is specified by the Spacing (% of width) box on the Graph tab of the Graph Object property sheet. The default is 100 percent, meaning that the distance between the bars or columns is the width of the bars or columns themselves.

Specifying the Depth

In a three-dimensional graph, the depth of the bars or columns is specified in the Depth (% of width) value on the Graph tab of the Graph Object property sheet. Notice that for any graph other than a three-dimensional one, this box is disabled and not accessible.

Setting Colors

To change the color of a graph, choose the General tab on the Graph Object property sheet, as shown in Fig. 14.14. The background color, the color of the lines, and the shade color in three-dimensional graphs are changed by setting the appropriate box.

Changing the Unit of Measure

When you build a graph, the unit of measure used in the graph can be changed. By default, the unit of measure is set to $\frac{1}{1000}$ of an inch. To deploy applications on many different systems, specify PowerBuilder units (PBUs) to ensure that the application looks the same on all machines. This option is only available in a Graph presentation style and not in a graph object.

Changing the Timer Interval

As data is updated in the database, the graph is automatically updated to reflect the changed data. This is made possible by setting the timer interval to 0. However, depending on the size of the database, this may result in long refresh times. To refresh at longer intervals, change the Timer Interval on the General tab of the Graph Object property sheet. The timer interval option is only available when in a Graph presentation style and not in a graph object.

Changing the Graph Name

The graph name on the General tab of the Graph Object property sheet is the name InfoMaker uses to identify the graphs. Normally, it's not necessary to change the name.

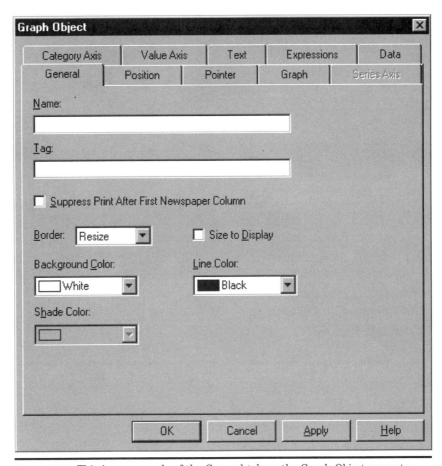

Figure 14.14 This is an example of the General tab on the Graph Object property sheet.

Changing the Graph Border

To change the border of a report object, access the Border drop-down list box on the General tab of the Graph Object property sheet. This option isn't available on a Graph presentation style.

Changing Category, Value, and Series Labels

The labels displayed on the graph are set from the Category, Value, and Series Axis tabs on the Graph Object property sheet, as shown in Fig. 14.15. Simply type the name to display on the label.

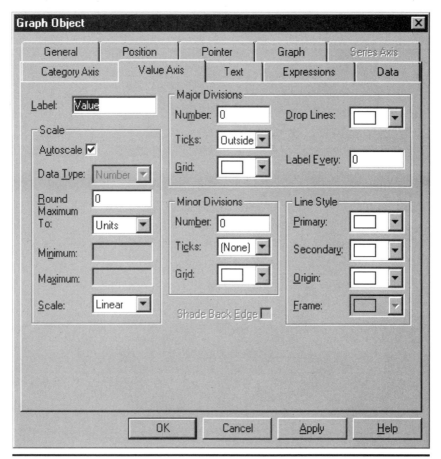

Figure 14.15 To change the value attributes on a graph, select the Value Axis tab on the Graph Object property sheet.

Autoscaling Numbers

To have InfoMaker automatically place numbers along the axes, choose the Autoscale box on the Category, Value, and Series tabs of the Graph Object property sheet.

Changing the Data Type

The data type is based on the axis and the data column selected for the axis. The series axis is always a string data type. However, the other two axes can have Number, Data, DateTime, and Time data types. The data type is changed on the Category, Value, and Series tabs of the Graph Object property sheet.

Rounding the Range of an Axis

The Round Maximum to option is available on the Category, Value, and Series tabs of the Graph Object property sheet. This option sets how to round the range of the endpoint of an axis.

Setting the Minimum and Maximum Numbers on an Axis

The Minimum and Maximum options set the largest and smallest numbers which appear on an axis. These options are disabled if Autoscale is enabled. These options are available on the Category, Value and Series tabs on the Graph Object property sheet.

Scaling the Axes

The Scale option on the Category, Value and series tabs of the Graph Object property sheet specifies the type of scale to use on the axes. The options are linear or logarithmic.

Setting the Major and Minor Divisions

The Major (Minor) Divisions attribute divides an axis into major (minor) divisions of data. Each division gets a tick mark on the axis. InfoMaker automatically divides the axes into major divisions. The major divisions can be set on the Category, Value, and Series tabs of the Graph Object property sheet.

Setting Tick Marks

The Ticks attribute sets the placement of tick marks on an axis to inside, outside, or directly on an axis line. Set the ticks on the Category, Value, and Series tabs of the Graph Object property sheet.

Setting Grids

The Grid attribute controls a line that runs from a tick mark across a graph, which makes the graph easier to read. Set the grids on the Category, Value, and Series tabs of the Graph Object property sheet.

Drop Lines

The Drop Lines attribute controls a line that extends from a data point to an axis. Set the drop lines on the Category, Value, and Series tabs of the Graph Object property sheet.

Label Every Division

The Label Every attribute sets the divisions of the tick marks that should receive a label. Set the Label Every option on the Category, Value, and Series tabs of the Graph Object property sheet.

Setting Line Styles

The Line Style attribute for Primary, Secondary, Origin, and the graph Frame are available on the Category, Value, and Series tabs of the Graph Object property sheet. The Primary line style refers to the axis itself. The Secondary line style refers to the axis parallel to and opposite the primary axis. The Origin line style refers to the grid line representing 0, and the Frame line style is used in three-dimensional graphs and refers to the frame of the graph.

Positioning the Graph

The Position tab on the Graph Object property sheet, as shown in Fig. 14.16, sets attributes relating to the position of a graph object within a form or report. The Position tab is not available for a Graph presentation style.

Setting the Graph Placement

The x and y boxes set the actual placement or location of the graph object on a report. To change the graph's location, choose the x and y boxes from the Placement tab on the Graph Object property sheet.

Setting Graph Width and Height

The width and height boxes on the Placement tab of the Graph Object property sheet refer to the width and height of a graph.

Moving a Graph within a Form or Report

The Placement tab on the Graph Object property sheet contains several options for moving a graph object in a form or report. The Sliding attribute slides a graph left, right, or up and down to remove extra white space when data changes in the report. To make a graph resizable on a report, choose the Resizable option. And finally, to give a graph the capability to move when it's viewed in a report, check the Movable option.

Layering a Graph

When a graph is placed on a report, it is possible to place it on top of data. The Layering options on the Placement tab of the Graph Object property sheet are available to set where the graph should reside in comparison to other objects.

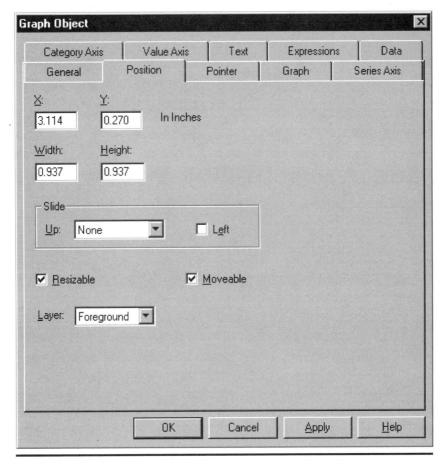

Figure 14.16 This is an example of the Position tab on the Graph Object property sheet.

If Background is selected, the graph will reside behind other objects. If the Foreground option is selected, the graph will always reside on top of any other objects. To have the graph object display in the band, choose the Band option.

Setting Expressions on a Graph

To set certain attributes dynamically while the graph is running, choose the Expressions tab on the Graph Object property sheet, as shown in Fig. 14.17. The Expressions tab contains several attributes which can be modified if necessary to more clearly depict data graphically.

Setting Text Fonts

To set the text font for specific objects on a graph, select the Text tab on the Graph Object property sheet, as shown in Fig. 14.18. Objects for category and

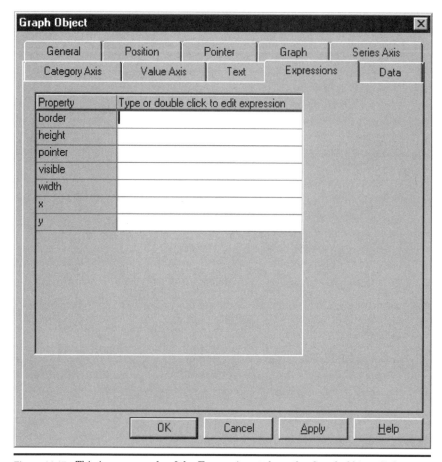

Figure 14.17   This is an example of the Expressions tab on the Graph Object dialog box.

series labels, the legend, and so on can all have different fonts, font sizes, and colors set from this tab.

Putting It All Together

In this section we'll create an embedded graph object in a report. We'll set the titles and data necessary to display when the graph runs.

1. Click on the Report painter button on the PowerBar or PowerPanel. The Select Report dialog box displays.

2. Choose the New button. The New Report dialog box displays.

3. Choose the Quick Select data source.

4. Select the Tabular presentation style.

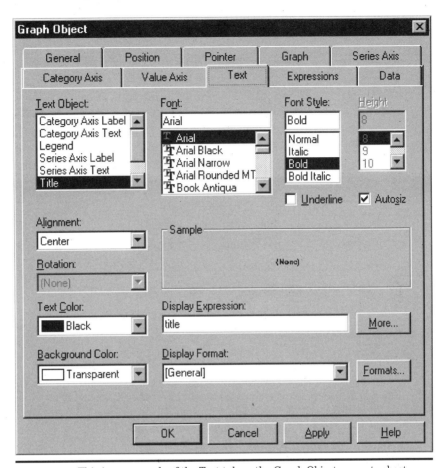

Figure 14.18 This is an example of the Text tab on the Graph Object property sheet.

5. Choose OK.

6. Choose the `contact` table. All the columns in the `contact` table display in the Columns list.

7. Choose the `contact_id` and `employee_id` columns.

8. Choose OK when you have finished. InfoMaker builds the basic report and displays it in the Report painter.

9. Preview the report by pressing the Preview button on the Report painter bar.

10. Take note of any adjustments you'll need to make to display the columns as you prefer.

11. Return to Design mode by clicking on the Preview button in the Report painter bar.

12. Now let's add the graph object to the report. Select the Graph control from the Controls drop-down toolbar on the Report painter bar.

13. Click on the report to the right of the `employee_id` column in the detail band. The Graph Object dialog box displays.

14. What we want to do is to count the number of contacts assigned to each employee in the organization. First, we must define the data. On the Data tab of the Graph Object property sheet, choose Employee in the Category drop-down list box.

15. Choose `count(contact_id` for graph) in the Value drop-down list box.

16. Now let's define the labels for each part of the graph. Choose the Category tab on the Graph Object property sheet.

17. In the Label edit box enter "Employee ID."

18. Select the Value tab on the Graph Object property sheet.

19. In the Label edit box enter "Number of contacts."

20. Select the Graph tab on the Graph Object property sheet.

21. In the Title edit box, type "Contacts per Employee."

22. Click OK when you have finished.

23. Run the report. The final report should look similar to Fig. 14.19.

At this point you can continue to modify the report and graph. As an exercise, add a title, date, and page number to the report. In addition to displaying the employee names, display the employee numbers in the report so that they match the graph. Sort the report by employee name and display the employees in the leftmost column.

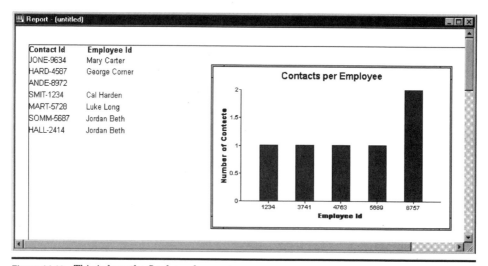

Figure 14.19   This is how the final graph report appears.

Summary

In this chapter you learned about each of the different attributes and the options available for them on each of the tabs of the Graph Object property sheet. You learned the parts of a graph, and the types of graphs InfoMaker creates, and the type of data they display. We created an embedded graph from the beginning, outlining step by step what you need to do to create your own graphs. You are now familiar with graphing and can take advantage of the many capabilities available in InfoMaker.

The Data Pipeline

What You Will Learn

Chapter 15 discusses in detail the Data Pipeline. You will learn what a pipeline is and how to transfer data from one table or database to another. You will learn about source and destination databases. By the end of this chapter, you will be able to transfer data to any database.

About Data Pipelines

The Data Pipeline in InfoMaker is a tool to transfer data between two tables in the same database, from one SQL Anywhere database to another, or from one database management system (DBMS) product to another. The Data Pipeline makes it easy to transfer data anywhere.

The Data Pipeline painter creates a structure that, when executed, transfers data from a defined source to a defined destination. When a pipeline is created, the source is the database from which data is copied, and it may consist of one or more tables. The data in the source table(s) remains unchanged. However, the destination, or where the data is copied, can have only one table. The data and the table attributes can be reproduced in the destination. Whether both the data and the table attributes (display formats, edit styles, and validation rules) are copied is specified when the pipeline is created. However, the extended attributes will not be replicated in the destination database if an attribute with the same name exists in the destination database.

Creating a New Pipeline

Before data is transferred, a pipeline must be created with the correct source and destination table(s) selected and the update options specified.

To create a data pipeline, do the following:

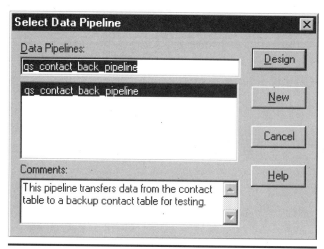

Figure 15.1 To create a new pipeline, choose New on the Select Data Pipeline dialog box.

1. Select the Data Pipeline painter button on the PowerBar or PowerPanel. The Select Data Pipeline dialog box displays, as shown in Fig. 15.1.

2. Press the New button. The New Data Pipeline dialog box displays, as shown in Fig. 15.2.

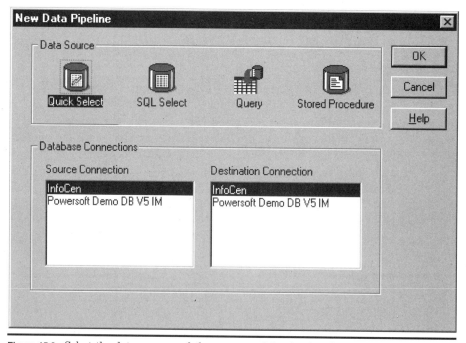

Figure 15.2 Select the data source and the source and destination databases in the New Data Pipeline dialog box.

3. Choose the data source. For more information on data sources, see Chap. 9, Data Sources.

4. Choose the source connection. For more information on choosing a source, see the section "Changing the Pipeline Source and Destination" in this chapter.

5. Choose the destination connection. For more information on choosing a destination, see the section "Changing the Pipeline Source and Destination" in this chapter.

6. When you have finished, choose OK. What happens next depends on the data source selected. For more information on data sources, see Chap. 9.

A new pipeline can also be created within the Data Pipeline painter. The current pipeline closes, and the new pipeline is defined.

To create a new pipeline within the Data Pipeline painter, do the following:

1. Choose the New button on the Data Pipeline painter bar, or choose File | New on the menu.

2. If any changes to the current pipeline have not been saved, InfoMaker verifies that you want to close the pipeline.

3. When the current pipeline has not been previously saved, InfoMaker opens the Save Data Pipeline dialog box, as shown in Fig. 15.3.

4. Enter the name of the pipeline to save it as and any comments related to the pipeline. Comments are useful when you return later to make modifications.

5. Then choose OK. The New Data Pipeline dialog box displays.

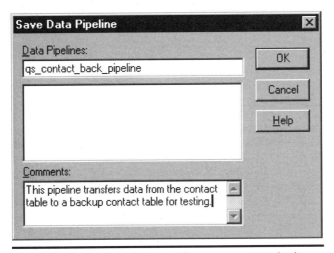

Figure 15.3 Save a data pipeline with a new name, or give it a name in the Save Data Pipeline dialog box.

6. If No is selected when InfoMaker verifies the save, any changes to the pipeline are discarded and the new pipeline is defined.

7. Choose Cancel when InfoMaker verifies a save, and the painter returns to the current pipeline without saving any changes.

Opening an Existing Pipeline

Once a pipeline is created, it can be opened at any time for viewing or for modifications. To edit an existing pipeline, do the following:

1. Open the Data Pipeline painter from either the PowerBar or PowerPanel. The Select Data Pipeline dialog box appears.

2. Press the Design button. The Data Pipeline painter workspace appears, as shown in Fig. 15.4.

While you are in the Data Pipeline painter, it is possible to also open an existing pipeline created earlier. To open a pipeline within the Data Pipeline painter, do the following:

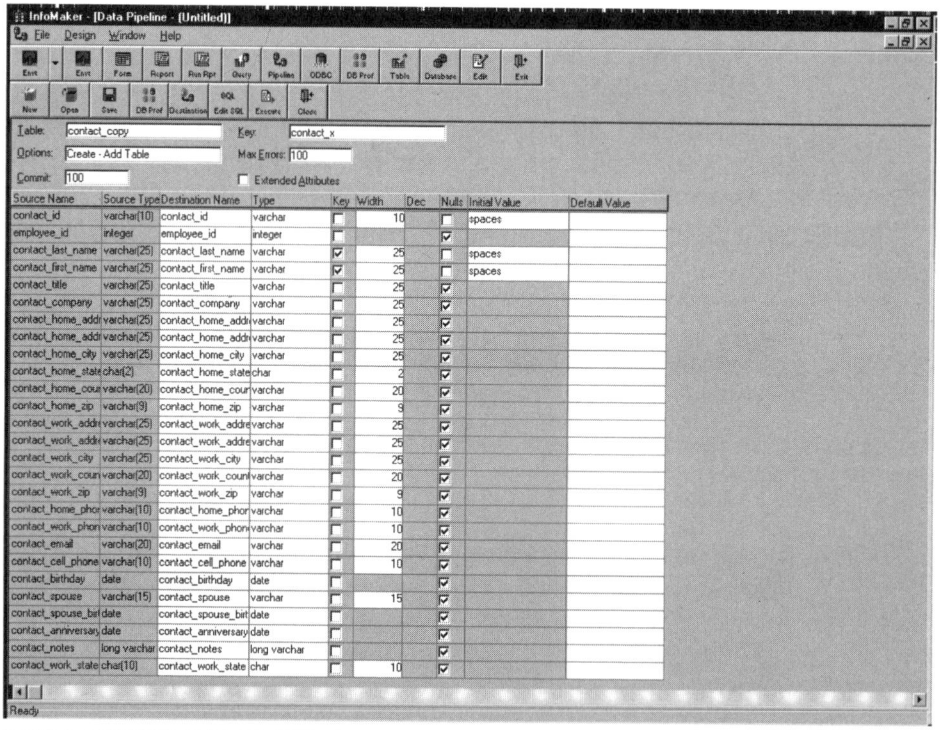

Figure 15.4 This is an example of the Data Pipeline painter.

1. Choose the Open button on the Data Pipeline painter bar, or choose File | Open on the menu. InfoMaker prompts to save any changes in the current pipeline.

2. Then the current pipeline is closed, and the Select Data Pipeline dialog box displays.

3. Choose the pipeline to open by clicking on it with the mouse.

4. Choose Design. The Data Pipeline painter opens with the pipeline definition.

Saving a Data Pipeline

When a pipeline is defined, it can be saved without exiting the Data Pipeline painter. To save a pipeline, do the following:

1. Choose the Save button on the Data Pipeline painter bar, or choose File | Save from the menu. The Save Data Pipeline dialog box appears.

2. Enter the name for the pipeline and any comments that describe it. If the pipeline has already been saved, InfoMaker will automatically save it to the existing name.

To save a pipeline with a different name, do the following:

1. Choose File | Save As... from the Pipeline menu. InfoMaker prompts for the new name of the pipeline.

2. Enter the name and any related comments for the new pipeline.

3. Choose OK when you have finished.

Deleting a Pipeline

Once a pipeline is no longer needed, it can be deleted. A pipeline can be deleted only from the Environment painter. For more information on deleting objects using the Environment painter, see Chap. 6, The Environment Painter.

Defining Database Profiles

In order to pipe data from one database to another, InfoMaker must have a database profile on file. A database profile is simply a way for InfoMaker to find a database. A profile may be changed or deleted, or a new one can be created.

To create, edit, or delete a database profile, choose the DB Prof button on the Pipeline painter bar. The Database Profiles dialog box displays, as shown in Fig. 15.5. For more information about database profiles, see Chap. 7, Working with Databases.

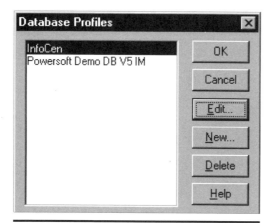

Figure 15.5 Create a new database profile, edit, or delete an existing profile from the Database Profiles dialog box.

Changing the Pipeline Source and Destination

Once a pipeline is created, the source and destination databases may be changed. The process of changing the source and the destination databases are very much alike.

To change either the source or destination database, do the following:

1. Choose File | Source Connect... from the Data Pipeline menu to modify the source; or choose File | Destination Connect from the menu or press the Destination button on the Data Pipeline painter bar to modify the destination. All the database profiles currently defined are displayed, with a check mark next to the current database.

2. Choose the database profile to modify in the Database Profiles dialog box.

For more information on defining a database profile, see Chap. 7.

Editing the Data Source

To change the columns available in the pipeline or to change the way data is selected, choose the Edit SQL button on the Data Pipeline painter bar or Design | Edit Data Source... on the Data Pipeline menu. Which painter opens to modify the data source depends on the data source selected for the pipeline.

For more information about modifying data sources, see Chap. 9, Data Sources.

Executing a Pipeline

Once a pipeline is defined, it must be executed to transfer the data. To execute a Pipeline, do the following: Choose the Execute button or Design | Execute from the painter menu. InfoMaker transfers the data from the defined database table(s) to the destination database table. There is no indication that the data is transferred. Depending on the size of the source table(s), the transfer occurs very quickly.

To verify that data is transferred, choose the Database button from the PowerBar and view the new table.

Closing the Data Pipeline Painter

When you are finished working with a pipeline, it can be closed and edited again at a later time.

To close the Data Pipeline painter, do the following:

1. Choose File | Close from the menu or select the Close button on the painter-bar.

2. If any changes have been made to the current pipeline, InfoMaker prompts to save them.

Transferring Blob Data Types

Binary large object, or blob, is a data type that contains large objects, such as a Microsoft Word document or a bitmap image. It is possible to pipe these types of objects from one database to another, but they can't be piped as other data types can. SQL Select statements cannot handle blob data types. To pipe blob data types, define the pipeline. Then once the pipeline is created, add the blob column(s) to the definition.

Supported data types vary from one DBMS to another. For instance, in SQL Anywhere, long binary and long varchar support blobs. However, in Oracle, the data types are raw and long raw. To find the supported data types for your database, refer to your DBMS documentation.

To transfer a blob data type, do the following:

1. Choose Design | Database Blob... from the pipeline menu. If the Database Blob... menu item is dimmed out, this means one of several things: (*a*) The pipeline definition doesn't have a unique key in the source table(s). (*b*) The pipeline operation is Refresh, Append, or Update, and the destination table doesn't have any blob columns. (*c*) All destination blob columns have been associated with source blob columns, and no further definition is necessary.

2. The Database Binary/Text Large Object dialog box displays, as shown in Fig. 15.6. It contains one property sheet, General.

3. The Database Binary/Text Large Object property sheet shows the Destination Column. InfoMaker pulls the first column it finds in the destination table that contains a long varchar or long binary data type. If this is the column to which the blob data is to be sent, leave it alone; otherwise, change the name to the column to transfer the blob data.

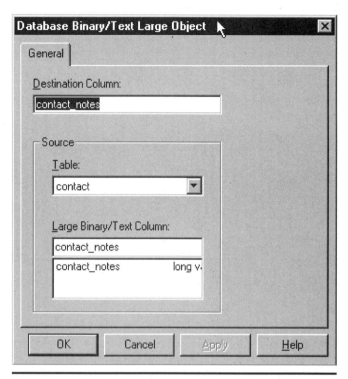

Figure 15.6 To define a blob data type to transfer in a pipeline,
use the Database Binary/Text Large Object dialog box.

4. The Source group contains the Table drop-down list box. InfoMaker displays
    all the tables in the source database that contain blob objects. Here, select
    the source table in which the data resides. In the Large Binary/Text
    Column, select the column from which to copy the data from the source
    table.

5. Choose OK.

**Changing the source or destination name of
a blob column**

Once a blob column is defined, you can change either the source or the destination in a pipeline definition. To change the source or destination name of a
blob column, do the following:

1. Right-click on the blob column in the Data Pipeline workspace to display the
    column's property sheet.

2. Select Properties... to display the Database Binary/Text Large Object dia-
    log box.

3. Make the necessary changes.

4. Choose OK. InfoMaker changes the blob column's definition.

Removing a blob column from a definition

Once a blob column is no longer needed, it can be removed from the pipeline definition. To clear a blob column from the pipeline definition, do the following:

1. Right-click on the blob column.

2. Choose Clear from the pop-up menu.

Defining Pipeline Attributes

The Data Pipeline painter workspace has several options to set transfer data. It is shown in Fig. 15.7.

At the top of the workspace is the area used to define the destination table and how the data is transferred. The main area of the Data Pipeline painter contains definitions for the source and destination columns involved in the pipeline. The source definitions cannot be changed, but the destination can.

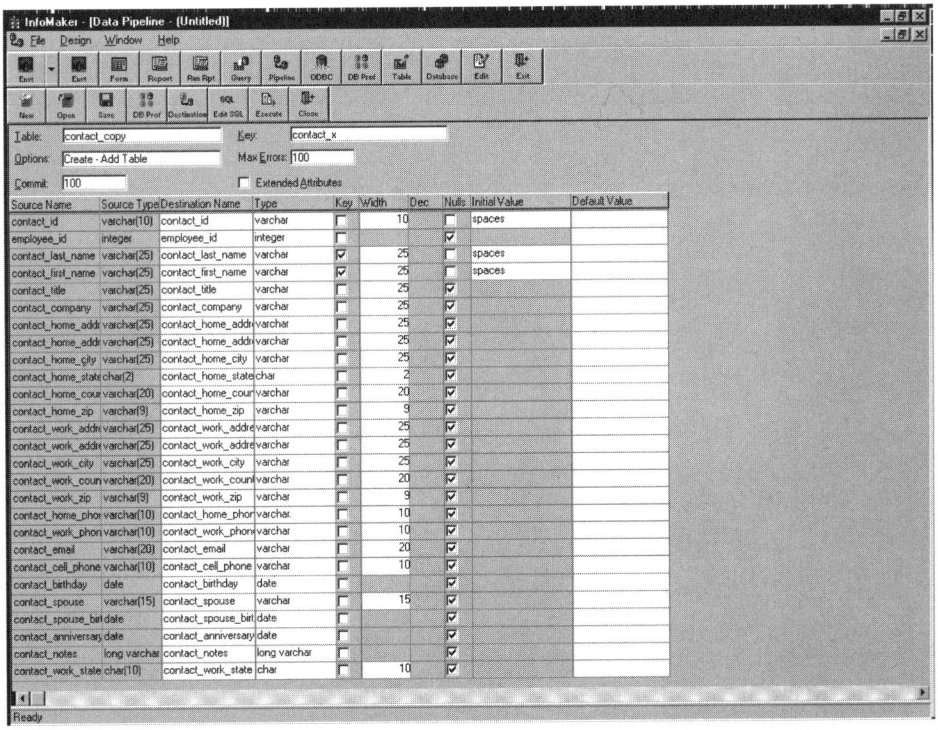

Figure 15.7 This is an example of the Data Pipeline painter workspace with the attributes to set at the top of the workspace and the source and destination definitions below.

Effectively, when a data pipeline is created, a table is created. The table is defined in the pipeline workspace.

Selecting the destination table

InfoMaker automatically enters a table name in the Table edit box. It is the name of the source table with _copy appended to it. For instance, to copy information from a table named contact, the destination table is automatically named contact_copy. Of course, the name can be changed.

Setting the pipeline operation

The Options drop-down list box contains several choices on how the pipeline creates the destination table.

Create—Add Table.   If Create—Add Table is selected, when the pipeline is executed, it creates an entirely new table. All the data selected in the source table is copied to the destination table. If the destination table already exists, the message shown in Fig. 15.8 displays. Another pipeline operation must be selected, or the name of the destination table must be changed.

Replace—Drop/Add Table.   Use the Replace—Drop/Add Table option to delete or drop the existing destination table and create a new table with the same name. If the table doesn't exist, InfoMaker creates it.

Refresh—Delete/Insert Rows.   The Refresh—Delete/Insert Rows option deletes all the data in an existing destination table. Rows selected in the source table(s) are copied to the destination.

Append—Insert Rows.   When the Append—Insert Rows option is selected, new rows added in the source table are appended to the destination table. All the existing rows are unchanged.

Update—Update/Insert Rows.   Use the Update—Update/Insert Rows option so that rows in the destination table that match the selection criteria of the rows

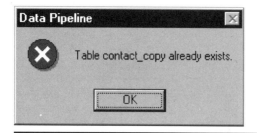

Figure 15.8 If the Pipeline option is set to Create and the destination table already exists, Info-Maker displays this error message.

selected in the source table are updated. The rows that don't meet the selection criteria are inserted into the destination table.

Setting commit value

When defining a data pipeline, you can specify how many rows in the source table(s) are transferred to the new table before actually being saved to the database. InfoMaker defaults to 100. This means 100 rows of data are transferred to the new table before being saved to the database.

Setting an error limit

There may be errors when data is transferred to another table. For some reason a row may be locked out by another user, or a network connection may go down. For whatever type of problem there may be, the Maximum Errors edit box sets a value that tells InfoMaker to stop the process after there are x errors.

Setting the key name

To set the name of the unique identifier for the new database table, type a name in the key column. By default, InfoMaker creates the key as the table name followed by _x.

Extended attributes

Certain options are available or not depending on the pipeline operation. For more information on what each of the columns contains in the Data Pipeline workspace, see Chap. 7, Working with Databases.

Putting It All Together

In this example, let's copy all our contact information to another table called contact_copy.

1. Select the Data Pipeline button on the PowerBar. The Select Pipeline dialog box displays.
2. Choose the New button. The New Data Pipeline window displays, as shown in Fig. 15.9. You'll notice that you can choose a data source of Quick Select, SQL Select, Query, or a Stored Procedure. For more information on data sources, see Chap. 9.
3. Choose the Quick Select data source.
4. Select InfoCen as both the source and destination databases.
5. Choose OK when you have finished. The Quick Select dialog box displays.
6. Choose the contact table in the Tables list. All the columns in the Contact list display in the Columns list.

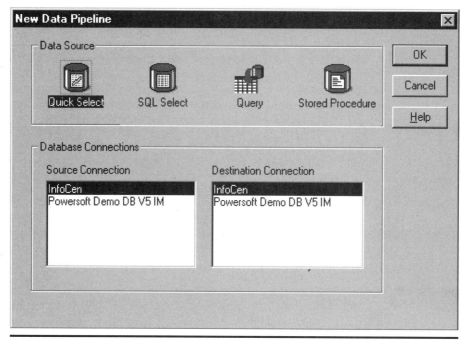

Figure 15.9 Select a source and destination database from the New Data Pipeline dialog box.

7. Click on the Add All button. This adds all the columns in the table to the data source.

8. Choose OK. The Data Pipeline painter displays.

9. We want to copy all the extended attributes defined for the Contacts table, as well as all the data, so we select the Extended Attributes check box on the workspace.

10. Select the Execute button on the Data Pipeline painter bar. The pipeline is executed, and a table called `contact_copy` is created.

Summary

In this chapter you learned what a data pipeline is and how to transfer data between different tables and databases. You learned all the attributes that can be set to customize the pipeline and change the source and destination databases. You can now transfer data to and from your applications.

16

Creating and
Distributing a
Complete Application

What You Will Learn

By the time you finish reading this chapter, you will thoroughly understand
what an application is and why it's a useful tool. You will know how to gather
forms and reports into one convenient package for easy access and distribution.
We'll talk about how to distribute an application to others either manually or
by building an installation routine. Finally, we'll go over the default functionality included in an InfoMaker application and how to use it.

The Application

Now that you know how to create a database containing information and can
build forms and reports to enter and extract that information from a database,
you can gather objects into what is called an *application*. An InfoMaker application is simply a way to gather many related reports and forms into one executable file that is distributed royalty-free to others. The application is also a
convenient way to gather related forms and reports into one place for your own
use. When we build an application, InfoMaker automatically includes the functionality needed to insert, update, and move through the rows in a database.
Look-up, or as it is called in InfoMaker, query, capability is also built in, so we
can view and change specific information in a database. Within an InfoMaker
application, menus and toolbar buttons are specified which access the many
form and report objects quickly and easily. And once an application is built, it
is run from an icon in Windows as any other software, such as Word or Paint.

The terms *application* and *executable* are used interchangeably. This is
because an application and an executable are basically the same. The only dif-

ference between them is that the executable version of the application can run
on its own, outside the InfoMaker environment. It is when an executable is created that application-level specific information is defined, such as the application icon, items on the toolbar, and the application name. If the application isn't
translated into an executable, or in other words, it remains a collection of form
and report objects in an InfoMaker .pbl file, then InfoMaker must be started
and the Form and Report painters are used to access each object individually.
Accessing objects in this manner requires that everyone using an application
have InfoMaker installed on his or her computer. Depending on the number of
stations on which the application runs, distributing an application in this way
can be quite expensive.

However, keep in mind, when you are building objects to include in an application, that the executable version of an application doesn't include data
pipelines and queries. Nor will you be able to import data into the application.
But data can be exported to another product such as Excel or Word for mail
merges or data manipulations.

Building a New Executable

Before a collection of forms and reports is accessed independently of InfoMaker,
an executable version of the application must be built. This is accomplished
within the Environment painter.

Before you create an executable file, all the forms and reports to be included
in the application must reside in the same library. Forms and reports must be
moved or copied to one library as needed by using the Environment painter, as
we discussed previously in Chap. 6, The Environment Painter.

When an executable file is built, InfoMaker creates an executable (.exe) file
and an initialization (.ini) file with the same application name.

To create an executable, do the following:

1. Choose the Environment button from InfoMaker's PowerBar or Power-
   Panel.

2. Select all the form and report objects to include in the executable from the
   Environment painter by using the mouse.

3. Click on the CreateExe button in the Environment painter bar, or choose
   Entry | Create Executable from the menu. The Create Executable wizard
   displays, as shown in Fig. 16.1.

4. Fill in the necessary information to create the executable by using the wizard. For more information on completing the first screen of the Create
   Executable wizard, see the section "Specifying Executable Options" in this
   chapter.

5. When you have finished, choose the Next button. The Executable Items dialog box appears, as shown in Fig. 16.2. For more information on the options
   available on the Executable Items dialog box, see the section "Setting the
   Application Toolbar and MicroHelp" in this chapter.

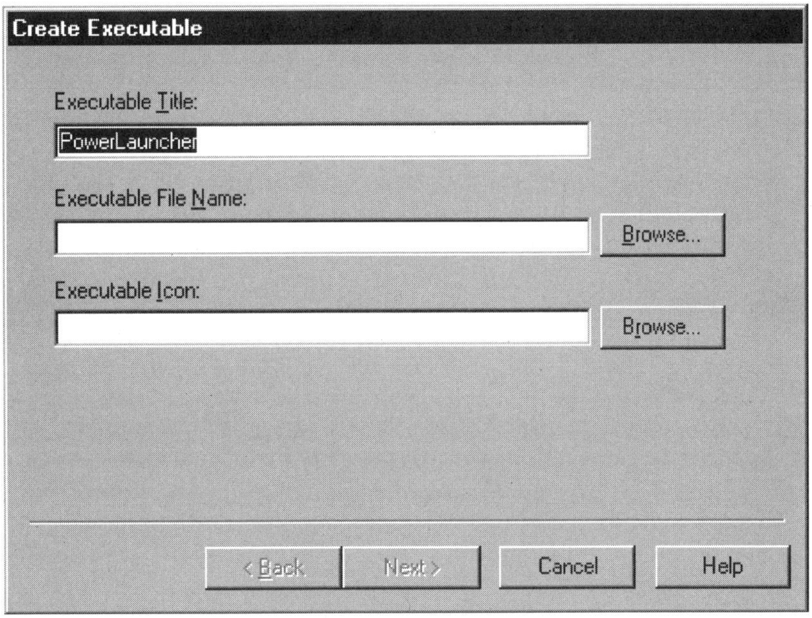

Figure 16.1 The Create Executable dialog box is accessed from the Environment painter.

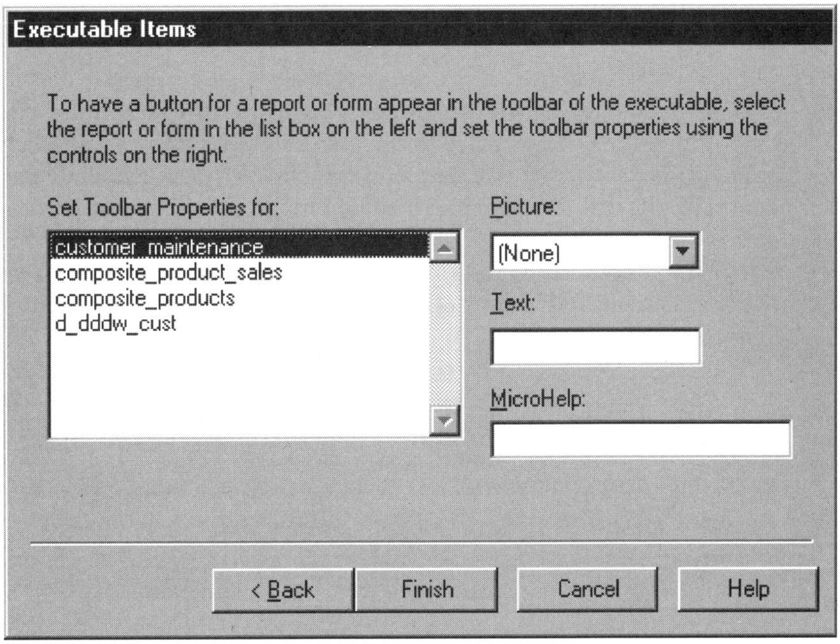

Figure 16.2 Define the toolbar for an executable by using the Executable Items dialog box.

6. Choose Finish when all options are completed. InfoMaker creates the executable and the initialization file in the specified directory.

Specifying Executable Options

When you build an executable, it is necessary to specify the information about an executable in order for InfoMaker to correctly build the application. The executable's title, filename, and location and the executable icon must be selected before the executable is built. Each of these options is discussed in the following sections.

Setting the executable title

In the Create Executable dialog box is an edit area named Executable Title. The title is the name given to an executable and either is viewed from the Windows 3.1 Program Manager or is available from the Programs menu in Windows 95/NT.

Setting the executable file name

To build the executable in a specific directory, specify the directory in the Executable File Name edit area in the Create Executable dialog box. If you don't know the directory in which you want to save the file, choose the Browse... button. Once the directory is set, give the file a name.

Set an icon for an executable

It is on the Create Executable dialog box that an icon is selected to display in the Windows 3.1 Program Manger or Windows 95 Programs menu to access the application. When selecting an icon on this dialog box, you are creating an icon for the application itself. Thus when an application is installed on another computer, the icon you've defined is selected by default. Of course, you or someone else can always change it, but this gives you a starting point. If you don't know the location or the name of the icon to use for an application, select the Browse... button.

Setting the Application Toolbar and MicroHelp

InfoMaker makes all the reports and forms in an application available from a menu by default. But if you want the reports and forms to display on the toolbar in your completed executable file and to have MicroHelp display at the bottom of the application workspace when the mouse passes over the toolbar, fill out the Text, MicroHelp, and Picture areas in the Executable Items dialog box. If there are many form or report objects in an application, put only popular objects on the toolbar. This provides a fast way to access these items and leaves the application work area uncluttered.

To add objects to the toolbar, do the following:

1. In the Executable Items dialog box, highlight the entry in the Set Toolbar Properties list.

2. In the Text box, type the name of the option to appear on the menu. This displays on the button in the application toolbar. For more information about menu text items, see the "Setting Menu Text" section in this chapter.

3. In the MicroHelp box, type the text to describe the option.

4. Then specify an icon for the item from the Picture drop-down list box. For more information on selecting icons, see the "Setting Toolbar Pictures" section in this chapter.

5. When changes are complete, choose Finish. The executable and application initialization file are created.

Setting menu text

To display reports and forms on the toolbar, enter the text in the Text area. A report called `ff_sql_emp_count_report` can be called Emp Cnt on the toolbar, for example. Keep the names of buttons to six or seven characters. If they're longer, the name for the button will be truncated.

Setting toolbar pictures

To place an object on the application toolbar, select an icon from the Picture drop-down list box. Select the picture by selecting it with the mouse, or using the cursor keys, go through the list of pictures available. Each time a picture is selected, a sample of the graphic appears to the right of the list box. To not have an item appear on the toolbar, select None.

Changing an Executable File

If an executable has already been created for an application, objects can be added and removed at any time. When the executable already exists, InfoMaker asks if you want to reuse the same parameters that were used when the executable was last created. In other words, use the executable name, menu items, and so on. If you do, choose Yes and you can modify the existing executable. Otherwise, choose No and you can create a completely new application.

Distributing an Application

There are two ways to distribute an application to others within an organization. The tools to implement both methods are bundled with InfoMaker. The first method is to use is the Deployment Kit. However, using the Deployment Kit involves a lot of manual file parameter setting and requires that you personally install the application. The second tool is InstallBuilder. InstallBuilder creates an installation routine and a set of distribution diskettes that you can distribute to others. InstallBuilder has a graphical interface, which makes it easier to distribute applications. We discuss both methods in the following sections.

The Deployment Kit

When you distribute an application, there are many files besides the actual application executable that must be installed, and each must be copied to the correct directory in order for an application to run. To facilitate this process, the Deployment Kit installs the deployment files and database interface files in the correct locations. The procedures for distributing an application differ depending on whether the person has InfoMaker installed on her or his system.

To install an application, do the following:

1. Create a Windows 3.1 directory or a Windows 95 folder in which to place the application.

2. Copy the executable and initialization file created in the Environment painter to the application directory.

3. Exit all programs.

4. Run the Setup program on the InfoMaker CD-ROM.

5. Select the Deployment Kit from the list of products.

6. If the machine already has InfoMaker installed, choose the custom installation and select the ODBC drivers only. None of the other options need to be installed.

7. Click on OK.

8. Select Finish when the installation is complete.

9. Ensure that users have access to the database that the application uses, and install the database files needed. The database files consist of the application .db and .log files. If the file is not available to the executable, a message displays indicating that the application cannot connect to the database.

10. Configure ODBC drivers and system path and registry files by using Microsoft's ODBC Administrator, if available, or Microsoft's ODBC API. Define the specific data sources accessed through each driver in the odbc.ini file. The odbc.ini file lists all the applications a person has access to and specifies the database driver, such as the SQL Anywhere engine, the user ID and password for the database, the parameters needed to start the database, the directory in which the database is located, the name of the database, and other database options.

   Modify the odbcinst.ini file with the ODBC driver for the database being used. For example, in SQL Anywhere:

For Windows 3.1:
[Sybase SQL Anywhere 5.0]

```
Setup = c:\sqlany50\win\wod50w.dll
Driver = c:\sqlany50\win\wod50w.dll
```

For Windows 95/NT:

```
Setup = c:\sqlany50\win\wod50t.dll
Driver = c:\sqlany50\win\wod50t.dll
```

Modify odbc.ini to allow the user to connect to a data source.
For Windows 3.1:
[ODBC Data Sources]

```
Products = Sybase SQL Anywhere 5.0
```

[Products]

```
Start = c:\sqlany50\win\dbeng50w.exe
Driver = c:\sqlany50\win\wod50w.dll
Database = c:\pb\myapp.db
```

For Windows 95:

```
Products        Start           c:\sqlany50\win32\dbeng5t0w.exe
                Driver          c:\sqlany50\win32\wod50w.dll
                Database file   c:\pb5\myapp.db
Sybase SQL      Setup           c:\sqlany50\win32\wod50t.dll
Anywhere        Driver          c:\sqlany50\win32\wod50t.dll
```

11. Edit the application initialization file, and remove your name and password from the lines that read UserId = yourId and DatabasePassword =.

12. Set the path in the computer's setup files so the application can find the various files.

13. Add the application icon to the Windows environment in either Program Manager or the Program menu.

InstallBuilder

InstallBuilder builds a set of diskettes, a CD-ROM, or installs an application to a network. It installs all the executables, resource files, data sources, and configuration files that users need to run an application. In addition, Install-Builder updates .ini files and the registry. Users install the application by using the Powersoft Setup program. All the information InstallBuilder needs to install an application is held in a configuration file. Each time a change is made to the application, the configuration file can be modified to update the installation process.

Creating a new configuration file.   All the parameters that define how an application is distributed are contained in a configuration file. This configuration file contains all the settings necessary to install an application.

To create a new configuration file, do the following:

1. Choose the New button on the InstallBuilder toolbar, or choose File | New from the menu. The New Config File Name dialog box appears.

2. Choose the directory and enter a filename.

3. Choose Save when you have finished.

4. The Installation Captions dialog box displays, as shown in Fig. 16.3.

5. Enter the caption to display when you install an application.

6. Select the icon to install.

7. Select the default billboard.

8. Select the colors for the installation routine.

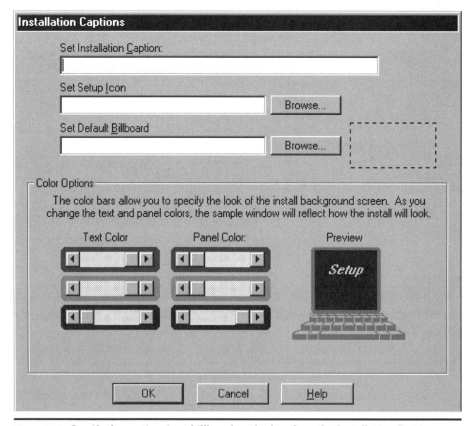

Figure 16.3   Specify the caption, icon, billboard, and colors from the Installation Captions dialog box.

InfoMaker files, SQL Anywhere files, and the application home directory are each set here. The Advanced button refers to reusable components only.

Viewing INI files.   To view the ODBC settings for a profile, choose the INI file button or Edit | ODBC Entries | From INI File from the menu. The ODBC Choice dialog box displays all the ODBC data sources defined for the system and its current entries.

Viewing registry files.   To view registry information for an application, choose the Registry button on the toolbar or select Edit | ODBC Entries | From Registry on the menu. The ODBC Choices from Registry dialog box displays. Select the registry file to view by clicking on it with the mouse. The entries display on the bottom portion of the dialog box, as shown in Fig. 16.7.

Generating a registry file.   In Windows 95/NT, you can maintain user and application information in the system registry from InstallBuilder. If an application includes objects used for OLE automation, InstallBuilder must update the system registry. InstallBuilder can create a globally unique identifier (GUID), a registration file (REG), and a type library (TLB) to update the system registry.
  To generate a registry file, do the following:

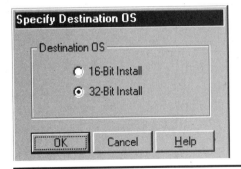

Figure 16.4   Select the destination operating system on which the install routine will run from the Specify Destination OS dialog box.

9. Choose OK when you have finished. The Specify Destination OS dialog box displays, as shown in Fig. 16.4.

10. Select the target operating system.

11. Choose OK. The InstallBuilder main workspace appears, as shown in Fig. 16.5.

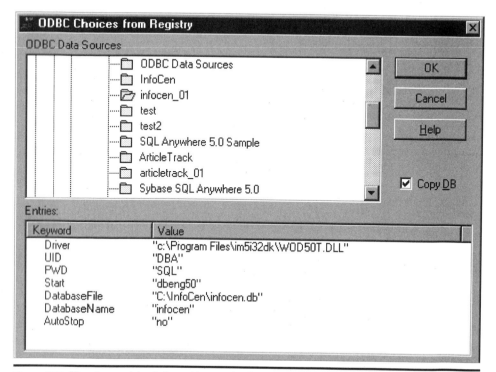

Figure 16.7   Viewing registry information on the ODBC Choices from Registry dialog box.

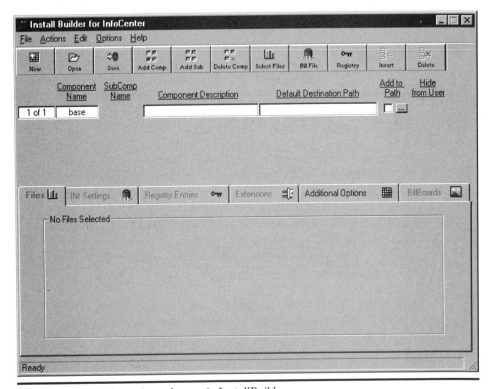

Figure 16.5   This is the main workspace in InstallBuilder.

Opening an existing configuration file.   Once a configuration file is created, anytime there is a change to the application setup, the configuration file can be modified.

To open an existing configuration file, do the following:

1. Choose the Open button on the InstallBuilder toolbar, or choose File | Open from the menu. The Select Configuration File dialog box displays.

2. Choose the file to open and select the Open button. The InstallBuilder workspace opens, and the configuration file can be modified.

Save configuration.   When changes have been made to the configuration file, the Save option is enabled. This allows you to save the configuration file for future changes.

To save a configuration file, do the following:

1. Choose the Save button on the toolbar, or select File | Save from the menu.

2. To give the existing file a different name, choose File | Save As from the menu.

Adding components.   When created, a configuration file is composed of a base component. A component contains files that make up a certain piece of an application. A configuration file has one base component with any number of other components or subcomponents. A base component usually consists of the actual application files.

To add a component, choose the Add Comp button on the InstallBuilder toolbar or select Edit | Add Component from the menu. A new line is added to the InstallBuilder workspace where additional parameters can be defined.

Adding subcomponents.   Subcomponents are located within a base component. An example of a subcomponent is one that contains the application's Help files.

To add a subcomponent to a configuration file, choose the Add Sub button on the InstallBuilder toolbar or select Edit | Add SubComponent from the menu. A new line is added to the workspace where additional parameters can be defined.

Delete component.   Once a particular component of a configuration file is no longer needed, it can be deleted from the workspace. To delete a component from the InstallBuilder workspace, choose the Delete Comp button on the toolbar or Edit | Delete Component.

Selecting files.   Once a component is defined, it is necessary to add files which will be installed with that particular component.

To select files for a component, do the following:

1. Select the component in which to add files from the InstallBuilder workspace.

2. Choose the Select files button or Edit | Select Fi 'Base Component' dialog box displays, as shown i

3. Select the files by clicking on them with the mou Remove buttons.

4. When you have finished, choose OK. The InstallB the files for the current component on the Files toolbox.

Setting file locations.   When you install an applicatio fy initialization files. InstallBuilder has the function during the install process. You can specify line-by-setup program to create and modify these files. The ages the location of InstallBuilder files. These setting Options | INI Settings menu item. The location

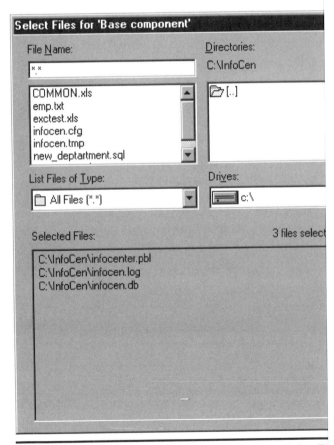

Figure 16.6 Select the files to add to a component in the Select Fi dialog box.

1. Select the Registry button on the InstallBuilder toolbar, or choose Actions | Generate Registry File... from the menu. The PowerBuilder Automation Object Registry File Generator appears.

2. Fill in the necessary information. For more information on completing this dialog box, refer to the on-line Help files.

3. Choose the Generate Registry File button to create the registry file.

4. Choose the Generate Type Library button to create the library.

Adding information.   The Insert button is enabled when in the INI setting, Registry Entries, and Billboard tabs. Click on this button to insert a line to add new information to the configuration file.

Deleting information.   The Delete button is enabled when in the INI setting, Registry Entries, and Billboard tabs. Click on this button to delete a line of information in the configuration file.

Defining reusable components.   Reusable components are those components that are used repeatedly, regardless of the installation routine. Reusable components normally are InfoMaker files, SQL Anywhere files, and so on. Reusable components are saved in the `instbldr.ini` file.

To define reusable components, do the following:

1. Select Actions | Define Reusable Components from the InstallBuilder menu. The InstallBuilder workspace fills with all the components currently defined.

2. Add and remove the components as needed.

3. On the INI file settings tab of the InstallBuilder toolbox, ensure the location for the file is set.

4. Choose the Compress button or the Actions | Compress option from the menu which saves the reusable component information in the `instbldr.ini` file.

Defining program groups.   When the setup runs, it is possible to have the installation routine create the program group and icon for the application.

To define a program group for an application, do the following:

1. Choose the Actions | Define Program Group... menu item.

2. Enter the title for the program group.

3. Click on the Add button, and enter the information needed for the application to start.

4. To create an Uninstall option, choose the Create Uninstall Icon check box.

5. When you have finished, choose Save.

Specifying a project object.   A project object specifies the executables and `dll` files to include in a component.

To specify a project for the current application, do the following:

1. Select the Actions | Read Project Object... menu item. The Select Project object displays.

2. Select the application project.

3. Choose OK when you are done.

Creating diskette images.   Diskette images are created after all components have been defined for an application. They are a compressed, local copy of an application's install files and support files for the Powersoft Setup program.

To create diskette images, do the following:

1. Select Actions | Create Diskette Images from the InstallBuilder menu. The Create Diskette Images dialog box displays.

2. Enter the directory of where to place the diskette images.

3. Choose the reusable component to add to the diskette images.

4. Choose the diskette size.

5. When you have finished, choose the Create button. InstallBuilder compresses the application files into compressed files the size of the disk specified.

Creating diskettes.   InstallBuilder can create installation diskettes which can be distributed to users. The diskettes are created after an image is generated.

To create a diskette set for the current application, do the following:

1. Select the Actions | Create Diskettes menu item. The Create Diskettes dialog box displays.

2. Specify the number of copies to create.

3. Select the drive.

4. Choose OK.

Setting captions.   Although a caption for an application is specified when the configuration file is created, there may be a time when you want to change it. This is accomplished from the Options | Set Captions... menu item.

Setting the operating system.   Each installation routine creates a setup program for a specific operating system. InstallBuilder can build installation routines for 16-bit Windows 3.1 applications or 32-bit Windows 95/NT applications. This option is available from the Options | Set Dest. OS menu item.

Specifying application paths.   In Windows 3.1 the directory is added to the directory path in `autoexec.bat`, and this path is used each time the application runs. To specify path information for Windows 3.1, select the Add to Path check box in the InstallBuilder workspace on the same line as the component. Install-Builder updates `autoexec.bat` when it installs the application.

In Windows 95/NT, each application has an entry in the registry file. When adding a component to the path, InstallBuilder allows you to specify executable files that require application paths.

To specify path information for Windows 95/NT:

1. Select the files for all components.
2. Check the Add to Path check box.
3. Click the ... button to the right of the Add to Path check box. The App Paths dialog box displays.
4. Specify the executable files which require an application path.
5. Click OK when you have finished.
6. Repeat for each component.

Setting a destination path.   Regardless of where users specify they want the application installed, the setup program should be able to install the files in that location without any problems. InstallBuilder includes what are called *symbolic variables*. These variables read the user's entry and install the application to those directories. Symbolic variables can be used wherever a directory path is specified. The symbolic variables defined in InstallBuilder are:

`@base`	path to the base component
`@system`	path to windows/system directory
`@windows`	path to windows directory
`@componentname`	path to specified component

Duplicate file handing.   If an application is reinstalled on the same machine for some reason, there's a chance your installation routine will have to handle the contingency of duplicate files. There are five options to choose from: Make Backup, Overwrite, Prompt, Backup and Prompt, and Skip, if exists. The Make Backup option specifies that if the setup encounters any duplicate files, the current files on disk are renamed and the new files are copied to the system to take their place. The Overwrite option has the setup program overwrite any duplicated files. The original is deleted. The Prompt option tells the setup program to prompt the user whenever it encounters a duplicate file and give the user a choice of either overwriting it or keeping it. The Backup and Prompt option has the setup prompt the user whenever it encounters a duplicate file and give the user a choice of backing up the original file or just overwriting it. The Skip, if exists option has the setup program leave any duplicated files on the system and doesn't copy new ones. These options are accessed from the Extensions tab in the InstallBuilder toolbox.

Additional options. Within InstallBuilder it is possible to specify descriptive text for each component, long directory path names (Win 95/NT), and installation defaults such as typical and compact installs. These types of options are available on the Additional options tab in the InstallBuilder toolbox.

Setting billboards. Billboards display during the setup program and are assigned to each component. Billboards add a level of professionalism to installation routines. The billboard displays at timed intervals during file copy. Billboards can be either bitmap files or bitmap resource IDs within a dll. You can set billboards for an application installation from the Billboards tab of the InstallBuilder workspace.

Using the Application

Once an application is compiled into an executable and is distributed, users get the chance to work with the new system. InfoMaker includes many default actions, including manipulating the database, viewing options on the menu, and so on. We'll look at some of the things you can do when the application runs in the following sections.

Opening objects in an application

Once an application is built, you can open forms and reports by using several methods. From the File menu you can select either Open Form... or Open Report.... When you choose one of these menu options, the Select Form or Select Report dialog box opens, displaying all the forms or reports in the application, as shown in Fig. 16.8. All you have to do is to click on an object, thereby highlighting it, and choose OK.

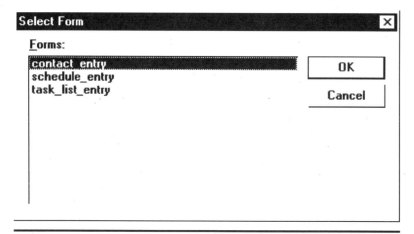

Figure 16.8   The Select Form dialog box displays all the forms in an application.

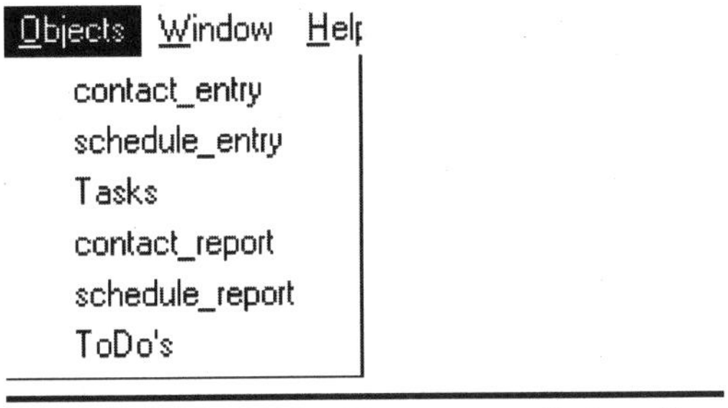

Objects Window Help
contact_entry
schedule_entry
Tasks
contact_report
schedule_report
ToDo's

Figure 16.9 This is the Objects menu listing all the form and report objects from an application.

Another way to access an object is by using InfoMaker's default Form or Report toolbar buttons. Clicking on one of these buttons displays either the Select Form or Select Report dialog box. Then you can select an object as described previously.

Yet another way to open an object is by selecting the Objects menu item. This lists all the forms and reports in the system, and you can select whichever one you choose, as shown in Fig. 16.9. If you've defined a toolbar button for a report or form, this title displays on the Objects menu instead of the object name. Unfortunately, InfoMaker only includes Help tips for those items we've defined as having toolbar items, so you must make your form and report names very descriptive.

Default window and Help menus

Another menu item InfoMaker creates by default when it builds the executable is a Window menu item with the usual Tile, Layer, Cascade, and Arrange Icons items. There is also a Help menu item. Clicking on Help reveals the About application name. When chosen, a nondescript message box displays with the application name. And finally, InfoMaker includes an Exit option on both the menu and the toolbar.

Database manipulation and navigation

InfoMaker also creates database manipulation and navigation buttons for forms and reports by default, as shown in Fig. 16.10. The database manipulation buttons include options to specify criteria to locate a specific record and to save, update, and delete records. In addition, the navigation buttons include those to go to the first record in the database, the next, prior, and last. This default functionality makes building useful applications easy and fast, without any programming.

Putting It All Together

Now that we've covered how to create an executable using InfoMaker, let's practice a bit.

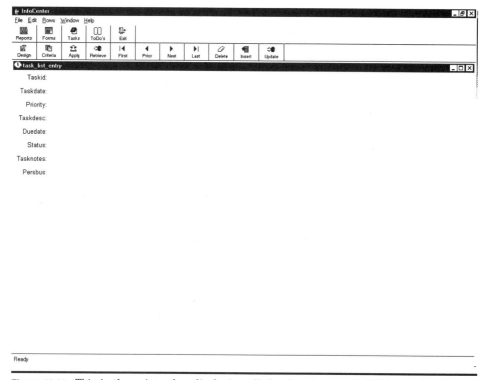

Figure 16.10 This is the painter bar displaying all the functionality InfoMaker builds by default into an application.

1. Choose the Environment button from InfoMaker's PowerBar or Power-Panel.

2. Make sure you have the application library, InfoCenter, open. If you don't, choose File | Open from the menu, and choose the `infocen.pbl` file. All the reports, forms, queries, and pipelines in the InfoCenter library we've built will display in the Environment painter window, as shown in Fig. 16.11.

3. Select all the form and report objects we've created in the InfoCenter application from the Environment painter, using the mouse. If all the objects you wish to add are listed in a group, click on the first object, then while holding the *shift* key, select another. All items between the two objects are highlighted. If you just want to select specific items that aren't necessarily listed together, click on the first one, and then while holding down the *Control* key, click on the others.

4. Once the objects that you want to include in the application are selected, click on the CreateExe button in the Environment painter bar or choose Create Executable from the Entry menu option. The Create Executable wizard displays.

5. In the Title box, type "InfoCenter." This sets the title of the application.

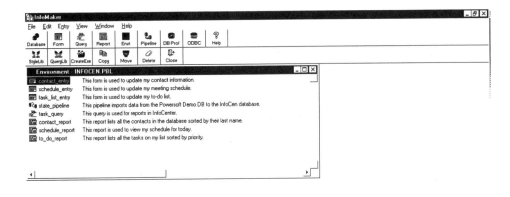

Figure 16.11 This is the Environment painter showing all the objects available in the InfoCenter.

6. In the Directories list box, select the directory in which to save the executable. In this case it's saved on the local machine in `c:\infocen`.

7. Give the actual executable file a name by typing `"infocen.exe"` in the File Name box.

8. Click the Next button. The Executable Items dialog box appears.

9. Highlight the item to add to the toolbar in the Set Toolbar Properties list.

10. Select an icon for the item by selecting an icon from the Picture drop-down list box.

11. In the Text box, enter the name to display on the toolbar.

12. In the MicroHelp area, enter a short description for the object.

13. Define another object for the toolbar.

14. Choose Finish.

Summary

Building an application allows you to bundle related forms and reports into a convenient package. There are advantages to creating an application whether it's for your own use or if you want to distribute it to others. For yourself, it's more convenient to run an application from an executable because you don't have to start InfoMaker, change libraries, and search through a long list of reports or forms to find the one you want to run. With an executable version of an application, all you have to do is start your application from an icon in Windows. If it's a report or form you use frequently, hopefully you've included it on the application toolbar for even faster access. And to distribute an application, others don't need to have InfoMaker installed on their computers. This makes distributing applications less expensive because purchasing numerous copies of InfoMaker isn't necessary. Last, InfoMaker includes default functionality in applications that can manipulate and traverse the database and can find specific information. All these features combined result in increased productivity for yourself and your coworkers.

InfoMaker and the PowerBuilder Connection

What You Will Learn

Chapter 17 discusses the connection between the InfoMaker and PowerBuilder environments. You will learn how and why these two products are so closely integrated and how the interoperability between the two environments enhances the power of both InfoMaker and PowerBuilder. We will discuss how to create forms in PowerBuilder and make them accessible to InfoMaker. By the end of this chapter, PowerBuilder developers will be able to support InfoMaker users in their organizations.

About Form Styles

InfoMaker includes several form styles: free-form, grid, master/detail one-to-many, and master/detail many-to-one. However, PowerBuilder developers in an organization can create custom form styles to add to InfoMaker. Using custom form styles, developers can enforce standards and provide extra functionality to InfoMaker users. With custom form styles, developers can add a company logo to all forms and add drag-and-drop functionality to InfoMaker forms.

Additionally, InfoMaker has a limited number of actions available to command buttons on a form. Using a custom form style, a PowerBuilder developer can create functions that InfoMaker users can access as actions in the InfoMaker environment. These actions could open another form or do any myriad number of other tasks.

Almost anything possible in a PowerBuilder window can be added to a custom form style and made accessible to InfoMaker form users. The interoperability between the two environments helps PowerBuilder developers by shifting some of the application development burden to InfoMaker users. And the connection between PowerBuilder and InfoMaker aids InfoMaker users by allowing them to build more sophisticated applications without any coding. It's a win-win type of partnership.

A form style consists of a window and a menu. The window contains one or more DataWindows and any type of control that can normally be placed on a form, such as radio buttons, check boxes, and pictures. Controls placed on a custom form can be moved in InfoMaker, but they cannot be deleted. Menus with specialized options are available when a custom form is executed. The form style determines how the data is presented, what menu and toolbar are available when running a form, and actions that users can attach to command buttons in a form.

Creating Form Styles in PowerBuilder

To create a custom form style in PowerBuilder, you must be an experienced PowerBuilder developer familiar with the InfoMaker environment. There are two possible ways to create a custom form style. One is to use the `imstyle.pbl` library, which comes with PowerBuilder, as a model. The `imstyle.pbl` library contains the windows and menus that are used for the form styles in InfoMaker. You can use these objects as a foundation upon which to build your custom forms. The other way is to create a form from scratch. We'll discuss both methods in the next sections.

When a custom form is added to the InfoMaker environment, it is displayed in the New Form dialog box when creating a new form, just as other form styles are, as shown in Fig. 17.1. These custom form styles are used in the same manner as any other form style.

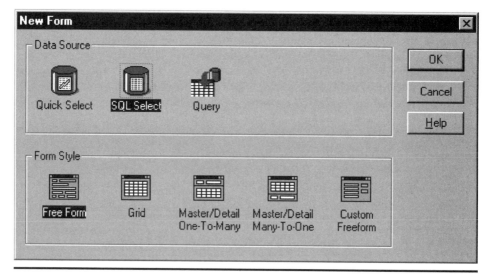

Figure 17.1 This is an example of the New Form dialog box in InfoMaker when a custom form style is defined in the environment.

Using an existing form as a model

If a form style you want to create is much like one of the existing form styles available in InfoMaker, it is much faster and easier to create a custom form style based on a form that already exists. Any necessary modifications can then be made to this base report. Follow these steps to create a PowerBuilder window, and use it as a custom form style in InfoMaker.

To copy a window and menu from an existing form style and modify it, do the following:

1. Create a directory and library for the new form style(s).

2. Open the Library painter in PowerBuilder.

3. Select the window and menu you want to copy, as shown in Fig. 17.2.

4. Choose Entry | Copy from the Library painter menu. The Select Library dialog box displays.

5. Go to the directory created in step 1, and choose the form style library file.

6. In the PowerBuilder Application painter, open the application by choosing Open from the application painter bar. The Select Application Library dialog box displays, as shown in Fig. 17.3.

7. Choose the library and select the Open button. The Select Application dialog box displays, as shown in Fig. 17.4.

8. InfoMaker pibble files are automatically named "default." Choose OK.

9. Add the form style library to the application path from the Application painter in PowerBuilder.

10. Then rename the objects. Using the Library painter, go to the directory where the window and menu models were copied.

11. Open the window.

12. Choose File | Save As...from the Window painter menu. The Save Window dialog box displays.

13. Name the window. Remember that all form style names must be unique.

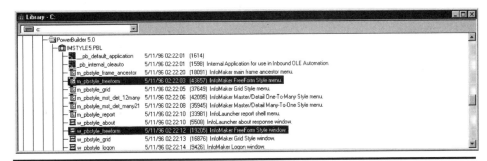

Figure 17.2 Selecting the window and menu to use as models in the PowerBuilder Environment painter.

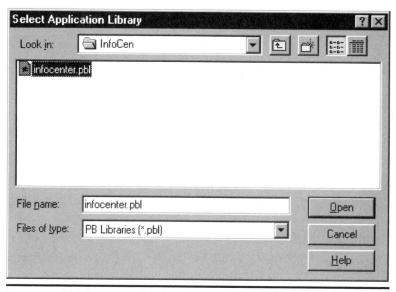

Figure 17.3   This is an example of the Select Application Library dialog box.

Figure 17.4   Selecting the application libraries in the Select Application dialog box.

14. Specify a comment for the new form. The comment must start with "Style:". This is an indication to InfoMaker that it is a form style. The text that follows "Style:" is what displays on the New Form dialog box when in InfoMaker.

15. Select the form style library in which to save the window.

16. Click on OK to save the window.

17. Rename the menu copied to the form style library. The menu doesn't need a comment, but it is helpful later when you want to know what it is.

18. Select the form style library in which to save the menu.

19. Choose OK to save the menu.

20. Add the style library to the InfoMaker search path.

Creating a new form style from scratch

If none of the existing form styles are close to what you need to create for InfoMaker users, create a new window in PowerBuilder and place one or more DataWindow controls on it.

To create a new form style from scratch, do the following:

1. Create a directory and library for the new form style(s).

2. Open the Window painter in PowerBuilder and create a new window.

3. Place a DataWindow control in the window.

4. Double-click on the DataWindow control. The DataWindow property sheet displays with the General tab on top.

5. Name the DataWindow control following these conventions:

```
dw_freeform
dw_grid
dw_master_12many
dw_detail_12many
dw_master_many21
dw_detail_many21
```

6. Change the properties for the control as desired.

7. Leave the DataWindow Object Name blank. This field associates the control with the DataWindow. InfoMaker users specify the data for the control when they create a new form using this style.

8. Make any changes you want to the form, such as creating actions for use in InfoMaker.

9. When you have finished, choose File | Save As...from the Window painter menu. The Save Window dialog box displays.

10. Name the window. Remember that all form style names must be unique.

11. Specify a comment for the new form. The comment must start with "Style:" This is an indication to InfoMaker that it is a form style. The text that follows "Style:" is what displays on the New Form dialog box when in InfoMaker.

12. Select the form style library in which to save the window.

13. Click on OK to save the window.

14. Create a custom menu and associate it with the window.

15. When you have finished, choose Save As.

16. The menu doesn't need a comment, but it is helpful later when you want to know what it is.

17. Select the form style library in which to save the menu.

18. Choose OK to save the menu.

19. In the PowerBuilder Application painter, open the application by choosing Open from the application painter bar. The Select Application Library dialog box displays.

20. Choose the library and select the Open button. The Select Application dialog box displays.

21. InfoMaker pibble files are automatically named "default." Choose OK.

22. Add the form style library to the application path from the Application painter in PowerBuilder.

23. Add the style library to the InfoMaker search path.

Creating InfoMaker Actions in PowerBuilder

Each public function defined in a PowerBuilder window is available as an action to InfoMaker users when using the custom form. Actions are defined in the form style. You will learn how to create these actions in this section.

To define an action, do the following:

1. Choose Declare | Window Functions from the menu in the PowerBuilder Window painter. The Special Function in Window dialog box displays.

2. Choose the New button. The New Function dialog box displays, as shown in Fig. 17.5.

3. Define the function. For instructions on how to create a PowerBuilder function, refer to the PowerBuilder documentation.

4. For any function which will be accessed as an action in InfoMaker, the function must be defined as having Public Access.

5. When you have finished, choose OK.

Using the Custom Form Style

Once the form style is created, it must be available to the InfoMaker application. For more information on adding a style library to the InfoMaker environment, see Chap. 6, The Environment Painter.

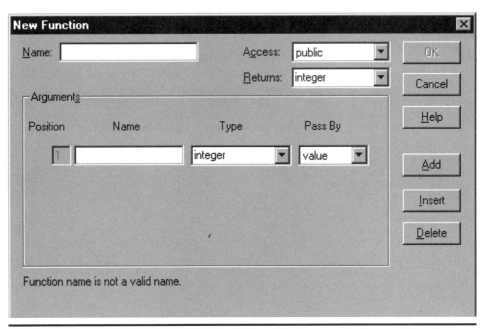

Figure 17.5 Define an action for an InfoMaker custom form style in the PowerBuilder New Function dialog box.

Distributing Style Libraries

Once a style library is created, to allow InfoMaker users to access the objects, the library must be placed in a directory on a network where all InfoMaker users can access them.

To distribute a style library, do the following:

1. Place the `.pbl` library containing the style library on the network in a directory where everyone has access.

2. Enter InfoMaker and ensure that all style libraries are listed in the style library path.

3. Exit InfoMaker and copy your `im.ini` file to the shared directory. All the libraries are located in the Application section of the `im.ini` file.

4. Each InfoMaker user must select the Options button from the InfoMaker PowerBar and enter the location of the shared `im.ini` file on the General property sheet.

5. Choose OK when you have finished.

Summary

In this chapter you learned how to create a style library. You learned how to create a form in PowerBuilder and distribute it to InfoMaker users across a network. You now have the ability to extend the power of InfoMaker users in an organization by building the custom forms they need by using PowerBuilder.

Getting Help

If you get into a situation where you need training or run into a problem, there are several sources of information. Whether you need training, an answer to a question, or resolution of a problem, help is as close as your telephone or your computer.

Powersoft Training

Powersoft offers training courses to help InfoMaker developers get up to speed quickly. The InfoMaker fundamentals course covers the creation of forms and reports. You'll also learn graphing techniques. It covers how to use each of the painters and shows you how to create executables. Another course available either in a classroom setting or on video is Reporting with InfoMaker. This course covers the creation of reports and graphs and data retrieval. For more information about these and other courses, as well as a list of authorized education partners near you, contact Powersoft at 1-888-769-7338.

CompuServe

If you have a question or want to talk to another InfoMaker developer, CompuServe has a forum dedicated to InfoMaker. To access this forum, type GO PSFORUM and select the InfoMaker section. This section is visited by both experienced and inexperienced InfoMaker developers to share their knowledge and ask questions. Powersoft also maintains a library on CompuServe where you can download the latest maintenance patches. The patches are available at GO PBFORUM.

The Internet

Powersoft maintains a web site at http:\\www.powersoft.com. You can find marketing and sales information, white papers, and file downloads here.

BBS

Powersoft's bulletin board service is available to download many types of files, including those from Powersoft's technical support. The number for the BBS is 508-287-1850. Set your modem for 8N1.

InfoBase CD

The InfoBase CD ships with PowerBuilder and is available from Powersoft. It includes Powersoft's Technical Support trouble calls and the complete library of fax-back documents. You may find that someone else has already reported a problem similar to yours and you can find a fix.

Data Express

Powersoft included DataExpress with InfoMaker, which is a wizard to walk you through the steps of filling out problem reports to fax or send via e-mail to Powersoft. The main window is shown in Fig. A.1. You can create a new problem report or edit an existing report. Each problem is categorized according to product category—InfoMaker in this case—the problem severity, how often it

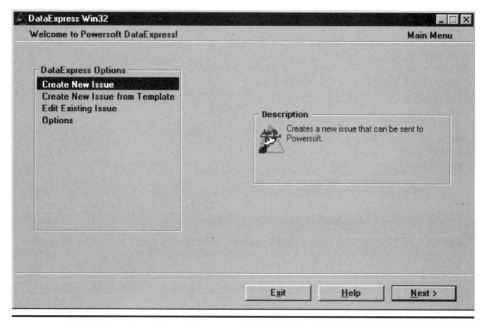

Figure A.1   This is the main window of DataExpress.

occurs, and if there is an abort module. The wizard then asks for environment information, such as what version of the database is running, the type of computer, and memory available. You can even attach whatever files you think technical support could use to try to fix your problem, such as initialization or configuration files. DataExpress makes it easy to report problems to Powersoft and gives the technicians the information they need to try to solve the problem quickly.

ABOUT THE AUTHOR

Jane Roseen (Warroad, MN) is Managing Editor of the webzine *The PowerBuilder and Java Journal* (http://www.pbmag.com) and edited the recent *Secrets of the PowerBuilder Masters*. She is a widely experienced developer of mainframe, PC, and client/server applications.

Index

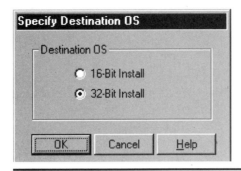

Figure 16.4   Select the destination operating system on which the install routine will run from the Specify Destination OS dialog box.

9. Choose OK when you have finished. The Specify Destination OS dialog box displays, as shown in Fig. 16.4.

10. Select the target operating system.

11. Choose OK. The InstallBuilder main workspace appears, as shown in Fig. 16.5.

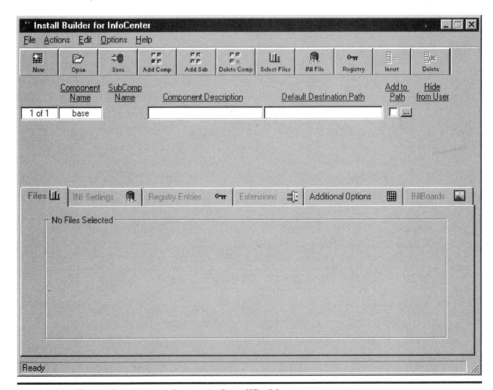

Figure 16.5   This is the main workspace in InstallBuilder.

Opening an existing configuration file.   Once a configuration file is created, any-time there is a change to the application setup, the configuration file can be modified.

To open an existing configuration file, do the following:

1. Choose the Open button on the InstallBuilder toolbar, or choose File | Open from the menu. The Select Configuration File dialog box displays.

2. Choose the file to open and select the Open button. The InstallBuilder work-space opens, and the configuration file can be modified.

Save configuration.   When changes have been made to the configuration file, the Save option is enabled. This allows you to save the configuration file for future changes.

To save a configuration file, do the following:

1. Choose the Save button on the toolbar, or select File | Save from the menu.

2. To give the existing file a different name, choose File | Save As from the menu.

Adding components.   When created, a configuration file is composed of a base component. A component contains files that make up a certain piece of an appli-cation. A configuration file has one base component with any number of other components or subcomponents. A base component usually consists of the actu-al application files.

To add a component, choose the Add Comp button on the InstallBuilder tool-bar or select Edit | Add Component from the menu. A new line is added to the InstallBuilder workspace where additional parameters can be defined.

Adding subcomponents.   Subcomponents are located within a base component. An example of a subcomponent is one that contains the application's Help files.

To add a subcomponent to a configuration file, choose the Add Sub button on the InstallBuilder toolbar or select Edit | Add SubComponent from the menu. A new line is added to the workspace where additional parameters can be defined.

Delete component.   Once a particular component of a configuration file is no longer needed, it can be deleted from the workspace. To delete a component from the InstallBuilder workspace, choose the Delete Comp button on the tool-bar or Edit | Delete Component.

Selecting files.   Once a component is defined, it is necessary to add files which will be installed with that particular component.

To select files for a component, do the following:

1. Select the component in which to add files from the InstallBuilder work-space.

2. Choose the Select files button or Edit | Select Files.... The Select Files for 'Base Component' dialog box displays, as shown in Fig. 16.6.

3. Select the files by clicking on them with the mouse or using the Select and Remove buttons.

4. When you have finished, choose OK. The InstallBuilder workspace displays the files for the current component on the Files tab of the InstallBuilder toolbox.

Setting file locations.   When you install an application, it is necessary to modify initialization files. InstallBuilder has the functionality to modify these files during the install process. You can specify line-by-line modifications for the setup program to create and modify these files. The `instbldr.ini` file manages the location of InstallBuilder files. These settings can be accessed from the Options | INI Settings menu item. The locations of InstallBuilder files,

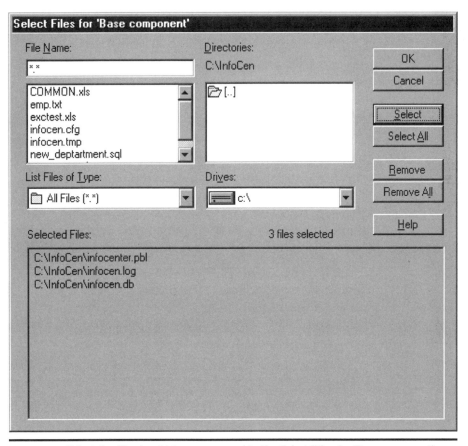

Figure 16.6 Select the files to add to a component in the Select Files for 'Base component' dialog box.

InfoMaker files, SQL Anywhere files, and the application home directory are each set here. The Advanced button refers to reusable components only.

Viewing INI files.   To view the ODBC settings for a profile, choose the INI file button or Edit | ODBC Entries | From INI File from the menu. The ODBC Choice dialog box displays all the ODBC data sources defined for the system and its current entries.

Viewing registry files.   To view registry information for an application, choose the Registry button on the toolbar or select Edit | ODBC Entries | From Registry on the menu. The ODBC Choices from Registry dialog box displays. Select the registry file to view by clicking on it with the mouse. The entries display on the bottom portion of the dialog box, as shown in Fig. 16.7.

Generating a registry file.   In Windows 95/NT, you can maintain user and application information in the system registry from InstallBuilder. If an application includes objects used for OLE automation, InstallBuilder must update the system registry. InstallBuilder can create a globally unique identifier (GUID), a registration file (REG), and a type library (TLB) to update the system registry.

To generate a registry file, do the following:

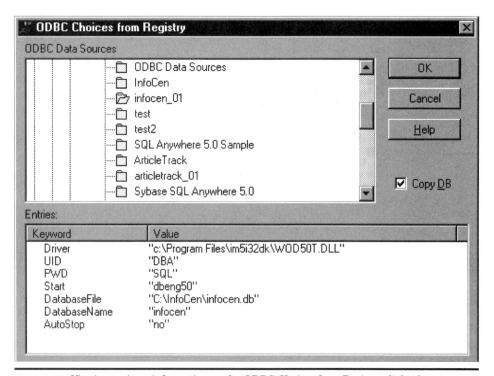

Figure 16.7   Viewing registry information on the ODBC Choices from Registry dialog box.